THE BATTLE FOR
SHAGGY RIDGE

PHILLIP BRADLEY

THE BATTLE FOR
SHAGGY RIDGE

ALLEN&UNWIN
SYDNEY·MELBOURNE·AUCKLAND·LONDON

Allen & Unwin
83 Alexander Street
Crows Nest NSW 2065
Australia
Phone: (61 2) 8425 0100
Email: info@allenandunwin.com
Web: www.allenandunwin.com

 A catalogue record for this
book is available from the
National Library of Australia

ISBN 978 1 76087 867 2

Maps by Keith Mitchell unless otherwise attributed
Set in 12.75/17.5 pt Adobe Garamond Pro by Midland Typesetters, Australia

Dedicated to NX101723 John Aloysius Bradley
2/27th Battalion

CONTENTS

LIST OF MAPS

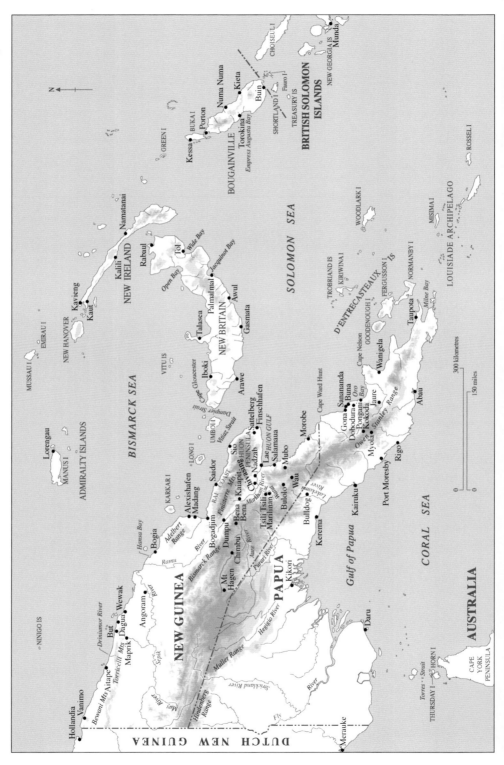

Map 1: Papua and New Guinea (Keith Mitchell)

Chapter 1

KAIAPIT

They marched by night. The orders from Major General Masutaro Nakai had been explicit because the extensive grasslands of the Ramu and Markham valleys offered little concealment from the many Allied aircraft that flew along the valley corridor by day. The advance party from the 78th Regiment, made up of some 370 men under the command of Major Tsuneo Yonekura, hid by day.[1]

The Japanese move was in response to an Allied offensive against Lae. On 4 September 1943 Australian forces had made an amphibious landing 20 kilometres east of Lae and the following day an American airborne regiment had landed at Nadzab, 40 kilometres north-west of Lae. It was the start of a series of Allied offensives called Operation Cartwheel which were designed to move through New Guinea, isolating the main Japanese base at Rabaul as well as those Japanese forces on the New Guinea mainland and Bougainville and establish forward bases for an attack on the Philippines in 1944. Within days Australian pioneers and engineers had developed the rough landing ground at Nadzab into an operational airfield into which an Australian infantry brigade had been flown. With Australian forces advancing on Lae from two directions, orders were issued for the Japanese evacuation of Lae across the Saruwaged Range to the north coast, and Lae fell to the Australians on 16 September.[2]

Prior to the landing at Lae the Japanese 78th Regiment had been based on the coast at Bogadjim near Madang; they were helping to build a road from there up into the Finisterre Range at Yokopi. Yonekura's III/78th Battalion was responsible for building that section of the road leading south from the coast up the Mindjim River valley. Three of the infantry companies were each given a sector to build while the fourth company hauled river gravel using straw baskets. Short on rations, weakened by malaria and lacking modern road-making equipment, Yonekura's men, many of whom were now in the advance party heading to Kaiapit, had worked tirelessly. On 11 August the 78th Regiment commander Colonel Matsujiro Matsumoto ordered that an 'advance to the bank of the Ramu River must be made quickly' and by 26 August five companies under Major General Nakai had taken over road construction operations further forward from Yokopi towards Kankiryo.[3]

On the evening of 5 September, in the wake of the capture of Nadzab airfield, orders were issued to Yonekura to 'quickly complete preparation to move out' and his detachment left the supply base at Yokopi on 12 September to advance to Kaiapit in the Markham Valley. Orders were for the detachment to strengthen the defences at Kaiapit and then prepare to attack the

Allied base at Nadzab with each man to carry maximum ammunition and rations for ten days.[4] On 6 September Yonekura
reduced the rations to seven days and ordered his men to also
carry 80 anti-tank mines.[5] Each man was given 10 kilograms of
rice, salt, powdered miso soup, soy sauce and five bags of biscuits.
'We also carried 120 rounds each for our rifles and two grenades,'
Sergeant Kenji Ueda said. 'It was understood that if necessary we
would use one of those grenades to commit suicide.'[6]

After leaving Yokopi, Yonekura's advance party camped by
the Surinam River on 14 September then moved via Wampun and
Bumbum to reach Ragitsaria on 17 September, always marching

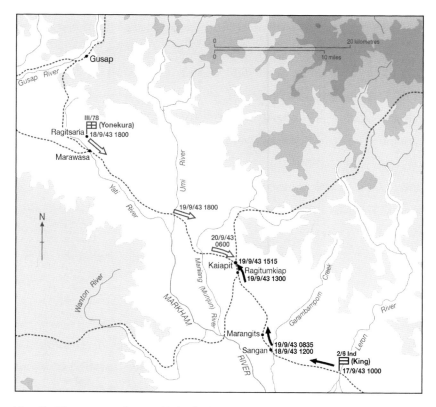

Map 2: The approaches to Kaiapit, 17–20 September 1943 (Keith Mitchell)

by night and hiding by day.[7] At this stage Yonekura had been informed that enemy troops had reached Sangan, 14 kilometres south-east of Kaiapit, and 'It is believed that the attack on Kaiapit is progressing.' Yonekura was now ordered to take command of about 100 men from the 80th Regiment already in the Marawasa–Kaiapit area and immediately advance to Kaiapit and attack any enemy troops there. 'English and American blood will soon flow freely,' Sergeant Isamu Yamashita wrote. 'Made battle preparations . . . All useless gear will be left behind here.'[8] Kaiapit was only 30 kilometres down the valley from Ragitsaria but the best speed the detachment had made so far was 15 kilometres a night and there was a major river obstacle between the two locations. This was the Umi River which tumbled out of the northern ranges to join with the headwaters of the Markham River in the valley. Yonekura reached the river bank as dawn broke on 19 September but his men would have to wait until dusk to begin the crossing. On the next night they crossed the river but it took considerable time and it would be a hard march to reach Kaiapit before dawn on 20 September. So far during the march Sergeant Hideo Kadota's company had lost about one-third of its strength and with rations at half rate the men were further weakened.[9] Tsuneo Yonekura was down to less than 300 men when he reached Ragitsaria before picking up about 60 men from the 80th Regiment at Marawasa.

•

On 14 September Captain John Chalk, the Australian commander of a company of the Papuan Infantry Battalion, travelled on a raft down the Markham River to Nadzab to meet with 7th Division headquarters. With orders to move further up the Markham

Valley, two Papuan Infantry Battalion [PIB] platoons crossed the Leron River on 17 September and moved west to Sangan. Japanese troops had been at Kaiapit since 9 September and some had moved to Sangan but they withdrew once it was reported that the PIB troops were moving into the area. About 40 Japanese troops remained in and around Kaiapit.[10]

While any Japanese move to Kaiapit was limited to ground movement across the daunting Finisterre Range and then along the open kunai-grass plains of the Ramu and Markham valleys, an Australian force could be flown directly from Port Moresby to a staging area within a day's march of Kaiapit. At 6.00 pm on 18 September, while Yonekura's advance force was at Ragitsaria, 30 kilometres north-west of Kaiapit, a fresh and fully equipped Australian independent company was concentrating at Sangan, only 14 kilometres south-east of Kaiapit and preparing to move to Kaiapit on the following day. The Australians were a day ahead of the Japanese and were able to move by day without any fear of air attack. How a fully equipped Australian independent company had managed to be in that position was the result of one of the boldest moves of the war in New Guinea.

An Australian independent company was a compact hard-hitting force of commandos comprising three fighting platoons plus attached signals, medical, intelligence, engineer and transport sections. Each platoon was akin to a scaled-down version of an infantry company with each of the three sections acting like an infantry platoon and further divided into two subsections. An eight-man subsection was equipped with a Bren machine gun, five Australian-designed Owen sub-machine guns and two rifles, one of which was also used with a grenade discharger. With eighteen subsections in the company, that meant eighteen Bren guns and

90 Owen guns could be brought to bear in a firefight. A captain commanded each platoon while a lieutenant commanded each section, allowing considerable autonomy.

Captain Gordon King commanded the 2/6th Independent Company. The 24-year-old King had been second-in-command during the earlier Kokoda campaign under the First World War veteran Major Harry Harcourt and was put in charge soon thereafter. The unit had had four weeks of uninterrupted training in northern Queensland before being shipped to Port Moresby on 1 August. 'Div left us alone,' King recalled, 'supplied everything we needed, tons of ammunition, trained all our specialist force, trained our cooks, [intelligence] personnel, the whole thing'. The men were specifically trained in firing weapons from the hip and picking up targets, all part of King's creed of fighting on your feet. The company was earmarked for the advance north-west from Nadzab into the Markham Valley once the capture of Lae was complete. On 3 September, the day before the Lae operation began, King was informed of his mission to spearhead the subsequent advance into the Markham Valley and detailed planning for operations began. The company was also put on immediate notice for air movement. 'A lot of us had flown to and fro in aeroplanes,' King remarked. 'As an operational thing we had done it before because in the first campaign we were in the first airborne operation to Wanigela.'[11]

•

Aware that the fall of Lae was imminent, Major General George Vasey, the 7th Division commander, wrote to the New Guinea Force commander Lieutenant General Edmund Herring on

12 September saying, 'I think we should now get on with the development of a strip at Kaiapit, so that as much as possible of the division can be landed there.'[12]

After Lae had fallen on 16 September, Vasey wrote, 'the very quick fall of Lae has occasioned some lengthy if not quick thinking'.[13] The Markham Valley 'was made to order for quick airdrome construction' and that would be Vasey's next objective. As the Fifth US Army Air Force commander, Lieutenant General George Kenney later wrote, 'Vasey not only believed that the airforce could perform miracles but that the 7th Australian Division and the Fifth Air Force working together could do anything.'[14] The first airfield site that the Americans wanted was at Kaiapit and Vasey's job was to secure it.

On 14 September King's company moved to the marshalling area at Ward's Strip in Port Moresby to fly to Nadzab. 'Men in great spirit at prospects of going over the top,' Lieutenant Maurie Davies wrote.[15] The men were to be disappointed as weather conditions and enemy air activity caused the flight to be called off on that day and the following two. 'For three days we went to the airport and couldn't get off,' King remembered. The original plan had been for the company to be flown to Nadzab and then walk up the Markham Valley, crossing two major rivers on the way, the Erap and Leron.[16] However, the three-day delay had led to a change of plan.

Vasey knew that the further up the Markham Valley he could land King's company, the sooner he could capture Kaiapit. One of Kenney's top airmen, Colonel David 'Photo' Hutchison, had flown Vasey over the Leron River in a Piper Cub and they had decided it might be possible to land transports on the extensive floodplain on the western side of the river. This would mean there would be no major rivers for the independent company to cross on the way to Kaiapit. Natives had burned some of the ground cover off and fighter planes had then dropped incendiaries to complete the job.

At 8.00 am on 17 September the thirteen C-47 aircraft carrying the nineteen officers and 207 other ranks of King's company had finally left Port Moresby and headed north. As the larrikin private Larry Dulhunty wrote, 'suddenly the two-up games, bare knuckle fights and dealing in moonshine was brought to an abrupt end'.[17]

The American airborne engineer Lieutenant Everette Frazier had landed on the rough burned-off kunai beside the Leron before the C-47s arrived. His Stinson L-5 Sentinel had managed it despite a strong cross-wind: 'Picking a wide place at one end and still heading into the wind, I wished the L-5 to a stop just short of the river bank.'[18]

At 10.15 am Major Frank Church landed the first C-47 transport plane, which had King aboard. 'As they reached me,' Frazier said, 'I would guide them off to one side, getting them out of the way of the next to land.'[19] King was able to watch the others fly in. 'I saw the two, the one that belly landed and the one where the tyre blew out and it spun around in a cloud of dust,' he said.[20] Corporal Bill Klotz recalled, 'Our Yank pilot advised we would not land if the first planes met enemy opposition. He was surprised when some 40 fully armed commandos said we didn't think he had the right idea.' As the plane landed, 'each man was ordered to lie flat on the floor with hands crossed firmly behind his head. We were participating in a crash landing.'[21]

Private Fred Ashford was in the fourth plane down, bouncing back off the ground three times before the pilot got down. The men were sitting along the sides of the plane with all the gear stacked up in the middle and although the gear went everywhere there were no major injuries. Ashford then watched as one plane blew a tyre and spun around while another circled with only one wheel down, which collapsed on landing and the plane bellied in. The crew from the two damaged aircraft quickly jumped onto other aircraft for the return trip.[22] 'The rest of the planes came from all directions,' Corporal Wally Hagan noted. 'It was funny to see the American crew scramble out and run like hell to the other planes.'[23] Despite the two damaged aircraft, the landing 'spoke highly for the skill of a bunch of courageous and dedicated American pilots,' Larry Dulhunty observed.[24]

A PIB patrol had come up from Chivasing to act as a screen out to the west of the landing area. 'As we flew over and around there was the PIB waving to us,' King saw. 'They were at least halfway between Leron and Sangan.'[25] Once King's men were down they established a perimeter and patrols were sent out, but the PIB soldiers confirmed there were no enemy troops in or around Sangan. At 5.07 pm Colonel Hutchison landed his Sentinel to inspect the two damaged transports and to tell King to wait for Vasey to fly in the next morning.

•

At 7.54 the next morning, 18 September, fifteen officers and 176 men headed for Sangan, carrying their heavy loads. Wally Hagan had over 50 kilograms to carry including a 2-inch mortar.[26] Captain King stayed behind to meet with General Vasey who flew in and confirmed his orders. 'Go to Kaiapit as quickly as possible,' he told King. 'Destroy any enemy resistance there, occupy Kaiapit and prepare a landing strip.' Vasey then added,

'I want you to move as quickly as you can but I do not want you to take any unnecessary risks.'[27]

Meanwhile, following an urgent request to confirm if enemy troops were in Kaiapit, Lieutenant Ted Maxwell's 6 Section had left Sangan with two native guides at 1.45 pm.[28] The men walked through the night until 3.00 am when they had a three-hour rest before reaching the foothills overlooking Kaiapit. Maxwell saw no evidence of enemy troops in Kaiapit but natives were seen to be moving about freely. At 1.00 pm he moved his section closer to the village but his men were spotted coming up over a ridge.[29] Private Alex Mackay was a Bren gunner in Maxwell's section and watched as an enemy patrol with some native guides came up the other side of the ridge. To Mackay the men in the enemy patrol 'were sitting ducks' but Maxwell ordered his men back down into a dry gully. Mackay was the last one to get into cover after the sling on his Bren gun slipped down between his legs and tripped him up, but the enemy patrol stayed on top of the ridge and didn't chase them.[30] 'In retrospect Maxwell's patrol was ill-conceived and poorly executed,' said King.[31] Maxwell's section withdrew and returned to Sangan at 8.00 pm on 19 September, by which time most of the company had moved to Kaiapit.

King gave his final briefing for the move from Sangan to Kaiapit at 5.30 pm on 18 September. Lieutenant Eric Moorhead's 25-man engineering section and John Chalk's PIB company would remain at Sangan to form a firm base while the company went forward.[32] Warrant Officer Peter Ryan from the Australian New Guinea Administrative Unit [ANGAU] had flown up the valley from Nadzab that same day. 'Good luck buddy,' the pilot said as he dropped Ryan off. 'The 6th Company men were huddled under ground sheets and one-man tents dotted all over the kunai,' Ryan wrote. He organised 30 native carriers to help bring the considerable stores still at Leron to Sangan and that night went back and forth ensuring the job was done. 'We made several furtive trips by torchlight, and had all the cargo in Sangan before dawn.' This included the bulky but vital Number 11 radio set. Ryan's effort took its toll, bringing on a bout of malaria, and soon thereafter he was evacuated.[33]

•

King made sure his men had a good night's sleep before an early start for the move to Kaiapit. 'We tried to get as much of our walking done in the cool of the day . . . The idea was to tackle Kaiapit in the afternoon, leave ourselves time to clean it up and form a perimeter that night.'[34] The company left Sangan at 8.35 am but walking through 2-metre-high kunai grass was a hot, slow and tiring business. Knowing he had to keep his men fresh for battle, King halted for a 10-minute rest every hour.

King soon found he had a problem with the new AWA 208 radio sets that he and each of his platoon leaders carried but which had only been issued just before the flight across to the Markham Valley. 'We didn't even have a chance to try them out in Moresby before we left,' King said. The sets were meant to have a range of about 15 kilometres but, as King noted, 'I couldn't even communicate over 500 metres. Hopeless.' As a result, 'the company communication system was at best unsatisfactory and at worst, useless'.[35]

The company reached Ragitumkiap at 2.45 pm and stopped there for a rest before the battle. 'The guys were pretty weary,' recalled King. 'We had a good half hour's rest . . . everyone settled down.' The company then moved to the edge of the kunai about

1100 metres from the coconut groves that signalled the first of the three Kaiapit villages. Here the men dumped their packs and spread out into their attack formation. 'Once you take your pack off you feel as though you can fly,' King remarked. Besides their weapons, the men carried all the ammunition and rations that would see them through to the next day. King's Owen gunners had filled their pouches with loaded magazines and tucked spare rounds into their trousers. Each man also carried a full 50-round bandolier of .303 ammunition for the Bren guns.[36]

King had access to very good maps and recent aerial photographs, and the operation had been planned in detail back in Port Moresby. The Japanese 'based themselves in the big coconut plantation which contained the three villages,' King had noted. Although he couldn't be certain, King surmised 'that the enemy positions in this complex would most likely be on the southern end' so the first attack would go in at that point. King was confident in his plan. 'Every soldier, right down to the last man, knew exactly what we were planning to do and . . . what his platoon and section and sub section's part in it was and what his own part was,' while 'Gordon Blainey was probably the best soldier of any rank I ever served with'. Captain Gordon Blainey's A Platoon would move on a wide front to find the enemy positions and deal with them while Captain Derrick Watson's C Platoon would be in immediate reserve, ready to support Blainey on either flank. King positioned himself between the two platoons and considered the advantages his men had: 'We had the cover, we were on the move and they were trying to peer at us from out of their little slits and things.' If not on the ground the enemy riflemen were 'up in coconut trees, waving around, trying to see through the coconut fronds and trying to get a shot'.[37]

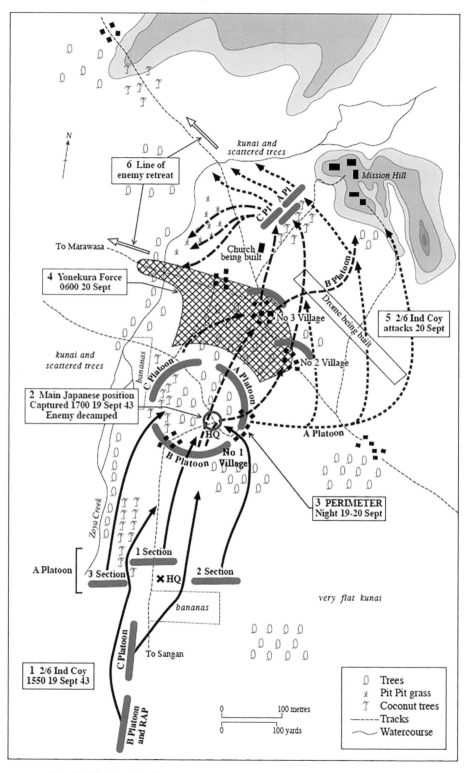

N

6 Line of enemy retreat

kunai and
scattered trees

Mission Hill

To Marawasa

C Plt
A Plt

B Platoon

Drome being built

Church
being built

4 Yonekura Force
0600 20 Sept

5 2/6 Ind Coy
attacks 20 Sept

No 3 Village

kunai and
scattered trees

bananas

C Platoon

A Platoon

No 2 Village

2 Main Japanese position
Captured 1700 19 Sept 43
Enemy decamped

HQ

No 1
Village

A Platoon

B Platoon

3 PERIMETER
Night 19-20 Sept

Zoya Creek

1 Section

A Platoon

3 Section

✗ HQ

2 Section

very flat kunai

bananas

1 2/6 Ind Coy
1550 19 Sept 43

C Platoon

To Sangan

B Platoon
and RAP

	Trees
𝑥	Pit Pit grass
⟰	Coconut trees
-----	Tracks
∿	Watercourse

0   100 metres

0   100 yards

Map 3: The battle of Kaiapit, 19–20 September 1943 (Keith Mitchell)

Blainey deployed 1 Section astride the track into the village, 2 Section to the right and 3 Section on the left of the track.[38] It was a raised track with head-high kunai grass on either side and King had told the men 'for chrissake don't anybody walk on that bloody track'.[39] Wally Hagan was with Blainey moving through the kunai with his mate Private Tom Gimblett in the kunai on the other side of the track. It was very hot without any breeze in the kunai and Gimblett was exhausted. 'I can't walk any further,' he told Hagan and moved up onto the causeway track. 'Don't go up there,' Hagan told him, but it was too late. A machine gun opened fire and 'he was killed stone dead'. It was 3.50 pm and the first shots of the battle for Kaiapit had been fired.[40]

Gimblett was not the only casualty as a ricochet caught King through the knee. 'I had my orderly and I just pulled out my field dressing and he helped me slap it on,' King said. 'It only took about a minute or two.'[41] The response was quick with Hagan and Sergeant Fred McKittrick firing a salvo of 2-inch mortar bombs at the likely machine-gun position in a clump of pandanus palms about 300 metres away. 'In the meantime, the rest of the company, yelling and screaming and shooting, had sailed into the village,' Hagan observed.[42]

Private Charlie Banks was out on the right flank with 2 Section, with two joined rifle slings across his shoulder enabling him to pivot his Bren gun on his hip and sweep the arc to his front. He could also support 1 Section's attack by firing across their front, enfilading any defenders. '1 Section's flank blokes were in vision from us,' Banks said. 'That was their last man and that was our first man. Flankers could see one another.' Banks kept moving towards the village laying down fire across the hut area where he could see the legs of one of the defenders moving behind a hut. 'That's where we cut the legs off him with a Bren gun.' The section had also had its losses after the commander Lieutenant Bert Westendorf was shot dead by a sniper firing from one of the coconut trees.[43]

Captain King moved into the village behind the attacking sections. 'I was probably again where I should not have been, but I walked out into a sort of a bit of shrubbery into a clear space under the coconuts and there was Blue Burrows busy dealing with a couple of Japs in their foxholes.' 'Look out sir, get out of my bloody way,' Corporal Burrows yelled as he rolled grenades into the enemy dugouts. King noted how the Japanese bunkers were slightly elevated but thought they had a limited field of fire and view: 'We could see them probably better than they could see us.' King's men were adept at picking up the muzzle blast and bringing neutralising fire to bear. 'If bullets are bouncing off through their slits they're not going to be too good at firing back at you,' King thought.[44]

Once A Platoon had captured the first village, the men of C Platoon chased off any remaining defenders, most of whom fought as individuals as they retreated and were soon killed. Very few got away and a patrol was also sent up onto Mission Hill to clear that area.[45] About 25 Japanese had been killed defending Kaiapit. 'You could never leave a wounded Japanese on the ground behind you because they would fight to the last,' King recalled, and 'we put the dead enemy troops into their own foxholes to get them out of the way'.[46] The defenders had been from the Takano Platoon, part of Captain Teruyuki Morisada's 5 Company, II/80th Battalion. Tasked with patrolling the Markham and Ramu valleys, many of Morisada's men, and Morisada himself, were not in Kaiapit at the time of the attack.[47]

Three Australians had been killed and seven wounded in the attack. Private 'Snowy' Boxall would die from his wounds that night.

In one of the huts the Australians found three natives with their hands bound behind their backs, their arms roped to their bodies and each tied to one of the three poles which supported the roof. When Sergeant Reg Thompson and Private Ken Bridge saw them, two were still alive and all had fresh bayonet wounds to the stomach and chest. Bridge couldn't stop to help them as his section was still in contact and by the time the intelligence officer, Lieutenant Maurie Davies, arrived they were all dead.[48] The incident certainly hardened the attitude of the commandos to their enemy.

With no radio communications, King decided to send a patrol back with the news that Kaiapit had fallen but then Lieutenant Doug Stuart arrived with three PIB soldiers and they returned to Sangan with the news that night. By 9.30 pm General Vasey knew that King's company had captured Kaiapit.[49] Stuart also reported to Captain Chalk that the 2/6th were in a tight spot and required the PIB to establish a firm base at Ragitumkiap, about half an hour to the rear of Kaiapit, by dawn.[50] The PIB made it and had a line of native carriers with them carrying the Number 11 radio set and a much-needed ammunition reserve. 'I don't think that Chalk could have got them and he certainly couldn't have got his carrier line any closer to Kaiapit than that no matter what he did,' King observed. 'In the circumstances their support and the loyalty they gave us and the risks that they took for us was little short of remarkable.'[51]

•

By the time darkness fell at about 6.00 pm, the company had formed a defensive perimeter around Kaiapit 1 village. This was ground considered vital to the Japanese, 'so that was where we formed our perimeter,' said King.[52] The men of A Platoon's 2 Section had become isolated and didn't join the perimeter until the following morning. 'We stayed in the background that evening on our own,' Charlie Banks recalled.[53] 'As the night dragged on, tropical rain fell in typical short heavy showers,' Larry Dulhunty wrote, and 'Between the showers we were attacked by swarms of various sized mosquitoes.' Hundreds of fireflies hovered, 'giving the tropical jungle an atmosphere of fairyland like beauty,' Dulhunty continued, 'a beauty that was in sharp contrast to the groans of wounded men and the periodical outbursts of howling New Guinea native dogs'.[54]

Private Jim Clews's foxhole was barely a scrape in the ground that offered no protection and he couldn't see much out in front where there was a lot of jungle-like undergrowth.[55] King knew it was pretty tense for the men on the perimeter and despite his best efforts they were jumpy. 'So there were occasional bangs going off all night, much as everyone was trying to stop people from doing it.'[56]

Despite the howling dogs and the odd angry shot, the night was fairly peaceful. However, at 7.30 pm a native approached the perimeter from the north, calling out 'Look, I'm coming in.' A candle was lit and as it 'illuminated the Australian uniform, the messenger . . . gave a cry of alarm and bolted'. The fleeing native then 'stumbled over two soldiers guarding their footage at the protective perimeter' who fired their Owen guns. The messenger was 'hurled in a somersault by the impact of the heavy 9 mm bullets'. A message stick with a note written in Japanese was recovered from his body that stated 'We believe there are friendly troops in Kaiapit. If so, how many and what units.' Although untranslated at the time, 'the message stick thing obviously meant something,' King observed. 'That was a wake-up signal to me that somebody was coming who hadn't been there before.'[57]

About an hour after the messenger was killed a small party of Japanese soldiers with their rifles slung over their shoulders walked up to the perimeter 'calling out passwords' and 'shouting to their mates, as they supposed'. The journalist Bill Marien wrote that 'The Japs were suddenly alarmed at the quietness of their old camping village and crouched and unslung their rifles.'[58] A Bren gun covered the track and 'their answer was a burst of fire from the nearest automatic weapons,' Larry Dulhunty recalled. Ten enemy soldiers were killed.[59]

•

Major Tsuneo Yonekura's men were tired after a hard night of marching across unknown country. As stated on the note that was sent by native messenger that night, Yonekura believed there were friendly troops in Kaiapit but, because the messenger had not returned, he would have had reservations. The noise of the battle may have been heard on the previous afternoon but Yonekura would not have known the result. One of his men, Masayuki Iwasaki, wrote that the Kaiapit garrison was fighting desperately and noted that the advance party was to be ready to support them at once.[60] What would have made Yonekura confident was that he had most of his force with him, around 350 men and at least one Juki heavy machine gun. However, Yonekura's overriding concern was that dawn was starting to break and he had to hurry and get his men under cover in Kaiapit before any Allied aircraft appeared overhead.

Just before dawn at 5.30 am King held a briefing with his three platoon commanders and told them that only scattered resistance was expected that morning. As planned, Watson's C Platoon was to depart the perimeter at 6.15 am and move clockwise via the mission and airstrip and return to the perimeter from the south. Watson's job was to clear this area and then continue with clearing patrols further out. 'Everything was so planned all you had to do was a conference just to confirm that nothing had changed really,' King noted.[61]

The Japanese reached the perimeter before Watson's platoon moved out and Yonekura would have been quite entitled to think his men had walked into a small ambush. 'They were more surprised than we were,' King said. 'They were just walking down the track until they struck us . . . we couldn't see what they were doing, but they were all milling around, bunching up and firing off rounds.'[62] It was just on dawn when this firing broke out in front of Watson's platoon on the north side of the perimeter. 'What it seemed at the time [was] that they had come upon us unexpectedly and there was a hell of a lot of firing but not much else was happening.' Despite all the firing, none of King's men was hit. 'They must have let off thousands and thousands of rounds mostly above our heads,' King noted, adding that 'our guys fired back to an extent but I don't think they wasted too much ammunition on them'. The Japanese were in shrubby ground in the coconut plantation, moving down the same track that the native messenger had used earlier. King's men had shot some of the leading group and the rest were bunching up behind. 'You can imagine,' King observed, 'say there were even 300, the distance they're spread out along the track. They'd be back half a mile . . . they'd all be coming forward and congregating.'[63]

King wanted Watson's men on their feet and advancing rather than sitting back waiting for whatever force was out in front. Watson also wanted to move right away and get on with his job. King's mind was racing as he held Watson up for a few minutes, thinking that 'the more they concentrated them, the more we could knock off in the one hit'. His second concern was that he had positioned a section of PIB troops on Watson's left flank and they had disappeared during the night to join up with the rest of their unit at Ragitumkiap. King needed security on that flank when Watson's men advanced, so he brought B Platoon forward to cover that gap.[64]

It was light enough now for King to clearly see Watson who was about 80 metres away. 'He was standing up there, looking back to me, waiting.' When King raised his arm and then dropped it, Watson blew a whistle 'and off they went and killed over a hundred Japanese in the first hundred yards'. The tired and strung-out Japanese were desperately trying to form up as Yonekura called the officers together but this command group was killed in the withering opening salvos from the Australian automatics. 'In 10 minutes they destroyed any possibility of offensive action by the Japanese,' King remembered, and 'used up all their ammunition in the process.'[65]

Private John Tozer was with Lieutenant Bob Scott's 7 Section on the right of the line. Tozer was hit in the chest while the man alongside him was shot through the neck and died almost immediately. 'The bullet was fired by a rifleman less than ten yards away and I was knocked right off my feet landing on my backside,' Tozer related. 'It was like being belted in the middle of my chest with a sledgehammer . . . I was rather surprised to find myself alive.' Despite his close call, Tozer thought that the Japanese 'were bluffed by our ferocity and the firepower that we could maintain'. The retreating Japanese troops 'were prepared to die and contested grimly at every clear space or track where they had a field of fire'.[66] Scott's section had done the most damage but had also taken the most casualties including Scott who was badly wounded in the chest. Watson was lucky when he was hit by a grenade blast, a shard cut his trousers but was deflected by a notebook and mirror in his pocket. An enemy round also broke the swivel off his rifle.[67] Private Lorie Vawdon was an Owen gunner with 9 Section and could see that 7 Section had 'copped the brunt of it'. One of the Bren gunners who had been hit in the wrist thrust his gun into Vawdon's arms, telling him 'Here, take this,' knowing that the gun must be kept in action.[68]

Jim Clews was with 8 Section, the men advancing in a line abreast. The commandos were firing as they went and also trying to conserve ammunition but it proved difficult to keep the line straight once resistance was struck. As the section advanced the men could hear the Japanese setting up a Juki heavy machine gun but the commandos got in first and knocked out the crew with grenades. Clews had gone about 20 metres when he saw the fallen Japanese crew around the Juki but he didn't realise that a couple of them were not dead. Clews then heard his mate Corporal John Haine call out a warning just before Clews was shot below the knee by one of the wounded gun crew. The bullet went clean through but his leg crumpled underneath him. Clews was taken back and left in a hut with another wounded man and a signaller to guard them.[69] The medical section was up there behind C Platoon and all the headquarters company people were acting as stretcher bearers bringing the wounded men back on groundsheets.[70]

The Australians knew that they had made a considerable dent in the enemy force but the extent wasn't yet apparent. Watson came part way back to meet King and told him his platoon was now held up and needed ammunition. He was particularly concerned about his right flank and thought that if A Platoon came round on that flank 'they could clean the thing up'.[71] Meanwhile the dead and wounded were stripped of ammunition. As John Tozer noted, 'the .303 rounds had to be passed on to the Bren guns in the sections out front keeping the pressure on'.[72] The commando who took Clews back after he was wounded had then taken his gun and ammunition for others to use.[73]

•

Captain Gordon Blainey's A Platoon was given the job to secure Mission Hill and then come up on C Platoon's right flank.[74] At 6.45 am the sections moved out through number 2 village to the east. After Wally Hagan's section was held up by a sniper positioned on the side of the hill, Fred McKittrick asked Hagan 'Do you think we can do a double?' They then set up the 2-inch mortar and dropped a bomb right on the sniper's position, duplicating their success of the previous day. Lieutenant Sam Southwood's 1 Section was soon on top of Mission Hill, the dominant position at Kaiapit.[75]

Charlie Banks's section, now led by Bill Klotz, moved out and cleared around the base of Mission Hill to the gully that led to the top of the hill. Banks 'heard the shooting start and we moved to where the sound was and brought our section up into line with that area'. Banks still had four full magazines on him plus the one on his Bren gun, while his number two, Private Frank Girdwood, had another four. From the top of the hill they could see Japanese soldiers moving in the distance and Banks opened up as they ran through the kunai. But it was Private Wally Roach and another commando, both of whom had sniper's rifles, who did the deadliest work.[76] Roach shot one soldier on the run at about 270 metres and another crouching in the kunai at about 350 metres. 'We could see every move the Japs made when they broke into the kunai,' Sam Southwood said. 'We could pinpoint every Jap for our men, and it was slaughter from that point, very much like quail shooting.'[77]

The men on Mission Hill 'had a grandstand view of the latter part of the fighting', one man saying 'It was almost like Flemington on Cup Day' as the watchers 'called the score of Japanese being hunted through the grass by their comrades below'. 'The Japanese in one open area lay in the kunai with their manes of grass attached to their backs,' the journalist Harry Williams later wrote. 'From above they would have been practically invisible but our men have learned to look for these artificial hummocks.'[78] Meanwhile Lieutenant Reg Hallion, the 3 Section commander, was killed as he led his section against an enemy light machine-gun position in a gully at the base of the hill. His men left a dozen dead Japanese in their wake.

Lieutenant Bob Balderstone's 9 Section and Lieutenant Jack Elsworthy's 8 Section from C Platoon continued to harry the retreating Japanese. 'There was just the one enemy sort of machine-gun post about 70 metres across open ground and another copse or village,' King observed. 'Balderstone supported by Elsworthy's section went across there and cleared them out.'[79]

Balderstone had joined the company with two other officers, Bert Westendorf and Reg Hallion, but he would be the only one of the three to survive Kaiapit. 'We charged across a fairly open area of ground with occasional coconut trees,' he wrote, 'The adrenaline was certainly pumping.' Two men from the section were killed while Balderstone was wounded when a bullet grazed his right arm. This heightened his determination to close with the enemy and, as ammunition was also getting short, the action needed to take place quickly.[80]

•

Meanwhile King still held Captain Geoff Fielding's B Platoon in reserve, protecting the regimental aid post and the wounded men held there. The platoon also had the job of protecting the left flank of the Australian position until the ammunition reserve was brought forward and all the wounded had been evacuated back to the PIB position at Ragitumkiap. 'I didn't release the reserve until I was quite certain the day was won and all that was left was mopping up,' King said.[81]

It was 7.30 am when Fielding sent one of his two available sections out through number 2 village. The men advanced through a coconut plantation where there were no huts, just enemy dugouts, and as the commandos went past they would toss in a grenade. Private Tom Strika was leading the men along the track when he spotted an enemy soldier. He turned around and called out 'Here the bastards are!' and it was then that he was shot in the back. 'Who the fuck hit me?!' he yelled before a first-aid man moved in and cut Tom's shirt off to apply sulpha powder and a dressing.[82] 'They would have cleared up

35 or 40 Japanese without loss which was not a bad effort,' noted King.[83]

Larry Dulhunty was with B Platoon and 'as yet hadn't fired a shot in the latest outburst of fighting'. When he finally moved out with the platoon on the right flank, he saw that the initial C Platoon attack had split the enemy force in two and 'we had the attackers on the run and I think we all realised that our only chance of survival was to keep them that way'. At the end 'approximately two hundred of the enemy were scattered dead through the clusters of jungle, around the thatched huts of the Kaiapit village, along the edge of the grass covered airstrip and between the overgrown graves of the native cemetery'.[84]

By this stage A and C Platoon had joined up and King decided to take his company headquarters, 'about three of us', onto Mission Hill. As they came out of the village into the kunai, King heard Fred McKittrick call out from up on Mission Hill: 'Sir, you've got three Japanese coming towards you.' There was a rifle leaning against a hut which King picked up and he and Private Charlie Enderby opened fire and killed one of the Japanese while the other dropped into the kunai to crawl away. 'The kunai was waving frantically where he was crawling through and all of a sudden it stopped after I shot so I probably got him,' King said. 'I didn't wait to see.' He then hobbled up the hill to watch as Bob Balderstone raised his rifle over his head signalling all was clear.[85] By 10.00 am there were only dead or dying enemy left on the battlefield. The fight for Kaiapit was over.

Private Herbert Harris was working with the medical section when he came across a wounded enemy soldier and tried to save him. 'He was with this wounded guy, [and I thought] oh well, I'll save this guy's life,' King recalled. 'I know the boss wants prisoners and this might do the trick.' Inevitably the enemy soldier had a grenade on him, which he detonated when Harris tried to help. King went to see the mortally wounded Harris before he died and found him to be very angry about what had happened. Harris told King, 'You're responsible for my condition, Sir, I was trying to follow your orders and this is what's happened to me.'[86]

With Kaiapit secure, King's first priority was to bring all the reserve ammunition forward and get everybody resupplied. The next task was to get the wounded up onto the hill and then he had the cooks prepare a meal. He also sent the men back, one subsection at a time, to collect their packs. The Australian dead were also buried. 'I would say by mid-, by late morning, early afternoon, we were all settled in on Mission Hill.' While his men rested and resupplied, King gave the PIB the responsibility of local protection. A standing patrol of one PIB platoon was down in the village while smaller patrols moved further afield. Everything was in place by late morning.[87]

•

The Japanese had already started clearing the Kaiapit airstrip so 'there was enough of it cleared for Lieutenant Frazier's light plane to land'. 'We had that strip, the first strip, pretty well right, that's where Frazier landed about midday,' added King. The original strip had been 1000 feet long and the Japanese had added 500 feet to that. 'That left at least 1000 feet to be cleared to accommodate C-47 transports,' Frazier wrote.[88] The airstrip also had a hill at one end so Frazier decided to also have a new strip cut closer to Mission Hill with clearer approaches but it would not be ready until 26 September so the original one still needed to be cleared.

'Frazier was there, he organised it all,' King recalled. To prepare the airstrip for use the kunai grass had to be cut along its length. King allocated some of his own men plus some PIB men and carriers to help with the work. Maxwell's 'lost' section had finally turned up so they were immediately sent to help prepare the strip together with the PIB platoon and the carriers.[89] 'We continued the tedious task of clearing the disused airstrip,' Larry Dulhunty wrote. 'This job was tackled, with small shovels we had brought from Port Moresby and some better ones that had been taken from the enemy.'[90] Just before dusk, Frazier dictated a message to be sent to Nadzab: 'Damned strip ready, for God's sake come in'.[91]

At dusk Lieutenant Fred Lucas took a PIB patrol into one of the villages where a group of enemy troops moving through the grass skirting the village wounded a native Bren gunner, Lance Corporal Fiope, and took his weapon. Lucas heard the gunfire, raced to the spot and opened fire with his Owen gun, forcing the Japanese to drop the Bren gun. That night, as another group of enemy soldiers approached, Lucas and Private Hau heard them. 'Down, Taubada, down,' Hau whispered to Lucas as the enemy opened fire, wounding Hau.[92]

Next morning, 21 September, Lieutenant Frazier paced out 3000 feet along the airstrip from the creek at one end and placed canvas landing T-sheets indicating the touchdown point.[93] Colonel David Hutchison landed an empty C-47 to test the landing before he sent in the loaded aircraft. Hutchison was able to take most of the wounded and a lot of the intelligence information back to 7th Division.[94] A US Army interpreter was flown in on one of the first aircraft to assess the importance of the captured documents and at 2.30 pm General Vasey arrived and more captured documents were flown out. They indicated that the occupation of Kaiapit had frustrated a large-scale enemy operation in the area.[95]

The remnants of John Tozer's section were given the job of meeting Vasey and escorting him up onto Mission Hill. 'It was quite a thrill for us escorting him up,' Tozer wrote, 'he was flanked by a bedraggled group of weary and hungry soldiers who held their heads high as they picked their way through the carnage and up Mission Hill'.[96] Vasey was shocked at the number of Japanese bodies scattered everywhere. 'My God, my God, my God,' he exclaimed.[97] King was sitting under a tree up on the hill when Vasey 'suddenly appeared and I struggled to my feet'. Vasey told him, 'No no, sit down, don't worry.' King stayed standing as he and Vasey 'chatted for a while'.[98] At 5.45 pm the first company from the 2/16th Battalion flew into Kaiapit and the rest of the battalion followed the next morning.

The day after he had visited Kaiapit, Vasey wrote to General Herring: 'We are absolutely full of beans here, and my confidence in these troops of mine has gone up even further since the action. It was an extraordinarily fine effort on their part. They went straight for the Jap, who couldn't take it.'[99] King knew what had counted: 'I think the success of the whole thing was that we maintained our objective all the time and we never lost the initiative'.[100]

Major General Ennis Whitehead, the forward 5th USAAF commander, also came to Kaiapit to see King to express not only his own thanks but those of General Douglas MacArthur and Lieutenant General Kenney for seizing such a key forward airfield. He then asked King 'What can I do for you?' and offered a plane load of whatever he wanted.[101] The offer was not that exciting for the men as they were told there was no beer available and the plane load ended up mostly soft drink, chocolate, cigarettes and reading matter.[102]

Geoff Fielding, who had been a bank officer in Perth before the war, got the job of searching and burying the dead and King 'knew that it would be done meticulously'. Each one was searched by Lieutenant Davies' intelligence section before burial and all papers were collected and documented. King's men buried 217 dead enemy troops but were still finding them and burying them when told to stop. 'We knew there were a lot more,' he said.[103] Tom Strika later met some 2/16th Battalion men who had flown in two days after the battle. 'You rotten bastards,' they said, 'we don't mind you killing them, just bury them when you do.'[104] The men of the 2/27th Battalion reckoned they buried 100 bodies on 24 September and the 2/14th Battalion was also involved. 'I remember sighting one hole with the dead in it and if there was two bodies in it there must have been 22,' Private Alf Edwards recalled. 'There was dead Nips in the kunai grass, oh dear oh dear.'[105] Abandoned blood-stained packs indicated other wounded men who had escaped.[106]

Captain Teruyuki Morisada later talked of 'the sudden encounter . . . with an enemy who had superior fire power [and] disrupted communication' and that 'The outcome became certain when the enemy took the key point which was a hill with a church on it', Mission Hill. He also confirmed that Yonekura's headquarters 'was annihilated in the disorder'.[107] Isamu Yamashita's diary was found on his body. The last entry on the day before he died read, 'The final day of fighting the Americans and the British has come for me.'[108]

Hideo Kadota, who was captured five days after the battle, told how tired the men were as they approached Kaiapit and how 'very frightened' they were at what lay ahead. They did not know the country and they were unsure of just how close they were to the village when they clashed with the Australians. Kadota had been acting as a runner between company headquarters and the two forward platoons during the battle. The third platoon had been delayed and was straggling behind. On returning to headquarters from the forward platoons, he found everyone gone and considered that the officers had deserted and run away. So he did the same.[109]

•

Lance Sergeant Norm Stuckey was an official photographer from the Military History Section of the Australian Army. Stuckey had left Australia on 8 September with the imprimatur of the Commander-in-Chief of the Australian Army, General Sir Thomas Blamey, who urged that 'the widest use be made of photographers in New Guinea' and that they be provided with 'all facilities to successfully carry out their duties'. The photos and film that the photographers produced would provide a historical record but it was also recognised that, as long as security was not compromised, the Department of Public Relations and the Department of Information could make use of the material.[110]

The former *Melbourne Herald* staff photographer arrived at 7th Division headquarters at Nadzab on 17 September. By 21 September Stuckey had made some good contacts among the staff and was able to jump onto one of the first flights into Kaiapit the following day. He was on the ground before the war correspondents and the Department of Public Relations people. He had arrived just two days after the battle and dead enemy bodies still lay on the ground. Stuckey held 'a stock of about 20 film packs', each one of twelve exposures and his first exposed negatives reached Nadzab the next day. After processing, his senior officer noted that Stuckey had taken 'many excellent shots of better quality than we have been accustomed to get from New Guinea'.[111]

•

The *Argus* war correspondent Merv Weston titled his despatch 'Bayonets routed Japs at Kaiapit', while the ABC's Bill Marien wrote about how 'the boys are turning on a bayonet blue'. Private Cliff Russell told Weston that 'The Japs fought like hell until we went at them with bayonets.'[112] The Japanese had indeed fought like hell, but, although it made a good headline, it was not bayonets that routed them. Some men may have used them but it was rare. As John Tozer observed, 'The Japs just didn't know how few we were but they did know that we could throw a lot of hot lead around, hard, fast and with accuracy.'[113] Larry Dulhunty backed that up, writing that 'except for a few machine guns, the Japanese were armed only with five shot rifles and that fighting them with our Owen guns for which we carried readily loaded, quickly interchangeable magazines was practically legalised murder'.[114] Gordon King put it very simply: 'You find that they say that Derrick Watson said to fix bayonets, well that's a lot of bullshit.' There were actually only four rifles per section to fix bayonets to. 'When you talk about bayonet charges you don't kill 100 people in 100 yards with bayonets do you? It's bullets,' King added.[115]

When King was recovering from his leg wound back at Nadzab, General Vasey invited him around for morning tea. 'We were lucky, we were very lucky,' Vasey told him. He then looked at King and could see he did not agree so asked 'What's wrong?' 'Well, if you're inferring what we did was luck,' King replied, 'I don't agree with you sir, because I think we weren't lucky, we were just bloody good.' Vasey laughed and said, 'Yes, well, I take your point' but explained that what he was saying was that he was lucky. Vasey not only had his people in the right place at the right time but he had the right people there. 'We just had to,' King stressed, 'we had to win'.[116]

Chapter 2

TO THE END
OF THE EARTH

Following reverses in Papua and the Solomon Islands in early 1943, the Japanese high command switched its emphasis in the South Pacific to defending New Guinea. The 51st Division had been sent to Rabaul in late 1942 and then transferred across to the New Guinea mainland but had taken considerable losses from Allied airpower in doing so. In early 1943 the 20th and 41st Divisions were shipped to Wewak and Hansa Bay on the New Guinea north-west coast as the convoy route was out of range of Allied airpower. These troops had come a long way south from Korea and Japan to reach the shores of New Guinea to reinforce Lieutenant General Hatazo Adachi's 18th Army. The soldiers that the Australians had encountered at Kaiapit and those that now defended the Ramu Valley and the Finisterre Range to the north were from Lieutenant General Shigemasa Aoki's 20th Division. This division, comprising the 78th, 79th and 80th Infantry

Regiments plus the 26th Field Artillery Regiment and 20th Engineer Regiment, had been based in Korea until ordered south in January 1943.

A typical infantry company in the 78th Regiment was made up of about 30 per cent *Geneki Hei*, that is, men with two to three years' service, 35 per cent *Shoshu Hei* or reservists and 10 per cent *Shigen Hei*, Korean volunteers.[1] Private Masao Takayama had been one of a biannual intake of 1800 Koreans who volunteered for service with the Japanese army in June 1941 at which time he adopted his Japanese name. According to Takayama, who had been posted to the 78th Regiment in December 1942, Korean volunteers received the same treatment and pay as their Japanese counterparts.[2]

The first convoy carrying 20th Division troops left Fusan in Korea in early January 1943 and after a stop in Japan sailed south for Palau. Second Lieutenant Yoshinori Matsuda, who served with Colonel Sadahiko Miyake's 80th Infantry Regiment, embarked on *Hakozaki Maru* on 6 January 1943. 'The holds were converted into men's quarters and seemed very uncomfortable and cramped,' he wrote.[3] On the early morning of 15 January a medical officer with the division stood on the deck of his transport looking out over the ocean when he saw the wake of a torpedo approach the ship. The torpedo struck 'directly amidships before I could utter a word. We thought this was the end but it did not explode.' Three other torpedos went underneath the ship but at midday the vessel safely anchored off Palau. On the next day the lucky ship headed south and helped rescue some men from the *Yasakuni Maru* which had been torpedoed, although not sunk. On 21 January the convoy reached New Guinea. 'It is said that Wewak New Guinea is an unexplored land,' the medical officer wrote.[4]

Yoshinori Matsuda also disembarked at Wewak on 21 January and he began airfield construction three days later. 'Because the tools are not strong enough, it is regrettable to see the pick handles and axe blades being damaged day by day,' he reflected. 'Having stripped to work yesterday and today, my body is burned red, and my legs have become swollen as though I had beri-beri.' In March, Matsuda headed down to Madang where the unit carried out bridge work. 'We ate hard bread, dipping it in coconut juice. Recently we are being bothered by skin irritations. Perhaps it is due to eating too many coconuts.'[5]

The airfield construction was a dangerous task with regular attacks by USAAF bombers. The first attacks came on 30 January with many casualties and other attacks followed by night with the transports also targeted while unloading. On 25 March flares were dropped 'so that Wewak was lit up like day' and 'spouts of flame shot high into the sky'. During a B-25 attack on 9 April, 'They were flying so low it seemed as if they were scraping the top of the coconut trees.'[6]

On 20 January 1943 Kobayashi, an officer with the 80th Regiment, was on the way south to Palau in a later convoy. 'The lofty moon casts her pure light on the waters of the Pacific and I dream of home,' he wrote. Three days later, as his transport reached Palau, 'The sub chasers began to lay down a smoke-screen and our patrol plane began to bomb something.' Then shouts of 'torpedo, torpedo' rang out and 'we spotted the wake of a torpedo as it sped towards us'. The ship turned to starboard and the torpedo passed underneath the bows. 'We all missed a sticky end by about 5 metres,' Kobayashi reflected. On 26 January he disembarked, writing 'we have at last this very morning planted our resolute steps on the soil of the South Sea island of Palau'.

He didn't leave Palau until 5 March and landed at Hansa Bay a week later. A trek down the coast to Madang followed.[7]

Kenji Ueda went south with the 78th Regiment, kept busy by frequent anti-aircraft and anti-submarine drills. 'I noticed a lot of the drills seemed to be not so much for defending the ship from attack,' he wrote, 'but more like a drill to abandon the ship if it sank'. He remembered passing the equator: 'There was no wind, and all of us went up on deck and stayed there. We didn't see any enemy, and for a while we forgot that we were sailing to a battlefield.' He then experienced his first tropical shower in the South Seas. 'We took all our clothes off and washed ourselves. A thousand men, stark naked on the deck, laughing, shouting to each other, happy.' On 9 March Ueda's transport reached Hansa Bay. 'The shallow water in the bay was so blue and calm and clear and there were hundreds of palm trees along the beach. It was like a painting and I was entranced.'[8]

The I/78th Battalion preceded the II/78th and III/78th to New Guinea.[9] When one of the convoys arrived on 29 May a medical officer on shore who couldn't sleep went to the shore-line at midnight as the convoy arrived. 'One by one the big black forms of the transports came into the Hansa Bay . . . Four ships of 10,000-ton class anchored in the bay and unloaded . . . The freight was all piled up like mountains.'[10]

•

The Japanese had been taking steps to build a new supply route to Lae since the demise of direct sea transport in March 1943 following the Battle of the Bismarck Sea. One option was to build a 300-kilometre road from Madang to Lae so that supplies

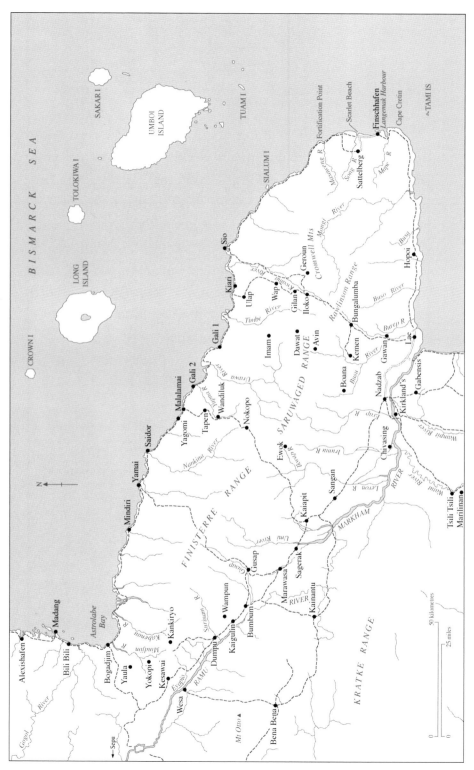

Map 4: The Huon Peninsula (Keith Mitchell)

could be unloaded on the north coast and transported overland to Lae. To build such a road was a daunting task as the imposing Finisterre Range lies between Madang and the Ramu Valley. On 20 April the 20th Division began work on the road with little more than hand tools, initially working on the sector from Madang down the coast to Bogadjim and then inland along the Mindjim River valley to the base of the Finisterre Range. Three bridges were required on the coastal section, and many more along the Mindjim River valley, but this was relatively straightforward compared to pushing the road up into the mountains. On 9 July, First Lieutenant Torahiko Koga, a company commander with the 20th Engineer Regiment, wrote that 'the beginning of the work consisted of a steep incline traverse and many ravines, which did not permit the work to progress as desired'.[11] Lieutenant General Kane Yoshihara, who was the Chief of Staff of General Adachi's 18th Army, later noted that 'it was a fine road crossing the left bank mountain stream and cutting off the right bank precipice, going from this side of the Bogadjim Valley to the other side'.[12]

The 80th Regiment officer Kobayashi was in Madang on 27 March when the aide de camp to the Japanese Emperor visited to inspect the progress of the road and give the emperor's encouragement to the soldiers working to build it. Kobayashi was very enthused with all things military and believed his work would contribute to the Japanese conquest of the world, reciting a military academy song he was fond of: 'We will drag the very crocodiles out of the Ganges, where it flows at the foot of the Himalayas . . . Our grandchildren shall raise a monument to us in a Chicago purged of gangsters.' But Kobayashi could do nothing about the reality of American airpower over the region. 'Since our landing the enemy has had control of the air,' he wrote on

26 May. His men were 'exasperated to the pitch of cold fury by this and were thirsting for vengeance', but the air attacks continued. On 3 August 'We were the target of a mammoth raid. We were boiling over with rage and resentment but there was nothing we could do about it. In a previous raid on 20 July the division lost 114 officers and men.'[13]

'We called it National Road Number One,' Kenji Ueda said. 'It was a bit of a joke as, from what we had seen New Guinea didn't have any roads, so we claimed to be building the very first one.' As Ueda put it, 'We took shovels instead of rifles, dug holes, cut away the sides of hills, all under a harsh strong sun.' The men did the work but they didn't like it. 'In effect we were not soldiers, just construction workers.' Despite the air attacks the work progressed but after June there were daily rainstorms and 'Each day we were soaked,' Ueda wrote, 'and had to look for banana leaves to cover ourselves.' By this stage the men were only working by night to avoid the daily air attacks. 'During the day we set mosquito nets and fourteen men from my same section would put their heads under one net and sleep,' but the mosquitoes 'bit our legs and most of us got malaria very quickly'.[14]

After his initial positive impression, General Yoshihara soon realised that 'the efforts of officers and men had become fruitless'. The bombardments continued but it was the intense rainfall that continually washed away the roadwork that was now the greater problem. 'Supplies and carriers suddenly dwindled to about one third of before, and there was a grave shortage of food.'[15] 'We are now living in tents in the mountains and helping engineers to construct roads,' one of the soldiers wrote on 30 March. By mid-April he was sick: 'Food is scarce, rice is scarce, nothing in the canteen. Even the hospital patients go off into the mountains to try to get supplementary food.' On 2 July the 20th Division commander General Aoki died from the effects of malaria. 'Our most highly esteemed and main pillar,' Torahiko Koga wrote of Aoki. 'It was indeed a thunderbolt from a clear sky.' On 7 July Lieutenant General Shigeru Katagiri took over command of the division.[16]

The section of road from Yaula to Yokopi was just a narrow track on which the Japanese used horse transport and from Yokopi to the Finisterre divide at Kankiryo it was foot traffic only. Private Tsutomu Eigashira took six days to travel from the coast near Bogadjim up the road to Kankiryo, pulling a handcart most of the way. Kankirei or 'summit of joy' as the Japanese knew it, was so named because, in June 1943 when the troops of the 20th Division had reached the top of the mountain range and were looking down into the Ramu Valley, they cheered with joy (*kanki*).[17]

General Adachi suspended road building once the Australians landed at Lae on 4 September 1943. The remaining two battalions of the 80th Regiment were sent to defend Finschhafen and the 79th Regiment now followed while the 78th Regiment remained in the Finisterres.

•

With road construction suspended, a supply track from Kankiryo into the Ramu Valley was to be established comprising fourteen key points. This would enable the main Japanese force to follow Major Yonekura's advance force to Kaiapit. Kankiryo was key point 1 and the track reached the Ramu Valley at key point 7 near the Surinam River. It then continued along the Ramu Valley to key point 14 at Marawasa where there was a Japanese outpost.

From Marawasa it was another 28 kilometres to Kaiapit. In order to support the advance of the 78th Regiment to Kaiapit the fourteen key points all needed to be manned and each day those soldiers manning them were to walk for half a day back to the previous key point and bring a load forward to theirs. There were 1485 troops allocated to hold key points 1 to 13, with 151 troops at key point 1 progressively decreasing to 84 at key point 13 at Ragitsaria. Assuming there were 151 loads at Kankiryo each day and allowing for consumption by the key point troops, this meant that 84 loads would arrive daily at Ragitsaria. Of these 84 loads it was considered that 50 would be food and 34 ammunition, enough to support about 1500 men forward of Marawasa. However, the Japanese plan was not to maintain a supply line of this magnitude indefinitely but, after about one week's supply had been gathered at Marawasa, to use the supply-line troops as part of the main Nakai force advancing towards Kaiapit and Nadzab. This would mean that when Nakai advanced with his main force he would have most of the I/78th and II/78th Battalion plus the I/26th Field Artillery Battalion under his command.[18] With the defeat of the advance force at Kaiapit the supply line would never come to fruition.

Weakened by a bad dose of malaria, Kenji Ueda had fallen well behind Major Yonekura's advance force as it headed for Kaiapit. He joined five other stragglers and, after four days of walking through the Finisterre foothills, the six men reached the Ramu Valley near the Surinam River. Here they came across their regimental commander, Colonel Matsujiro Matsumoto, who was coming back from the front lines on his horse. Matsumoto told Ueda's group that Australian commandos were operating behind them, attacking the supply line, so the force must pull back into the Finisterre Range. Ueda wondered why Matsumoto had come back alone and later found out that the colonel had had an argument with General Nakai about what to do next. Matsumoto, who was lower in rank but had more experience than Nakai, didn't want to serve under him so had been sent to deal with the Australian commandos. Ueda's small party turned around and started walking back the way they had come. 'The rain was so heavy that, for several days, it was like walking in a flood,' he said.[19] Matsumoto had left the Kankiryo area on 17 September heading for Marawasa, and two days later had reached the Ramu Valley. Referring to the track from Kankiryo to the Ramu Valley, Matsumoto observed that 'Although the road is well concealed from the sky it is not good to march on because it has steep hills.'[20]

On 23 September a new order was issued to Nakai Force to hold the Kankiryo area 'to fiercely meet and check the movement of the advancing enemy'.[21] Lieutenant Kumao Ishikawa was the commander of the battalion gun platoon in Captain Shoichi Kagawa's II/78th Battalion. Ishikawa's unit normally had about twenty horses to transport the guns and ammunition, 'but here in the battlefield of New Guinea there was not a single horse [allocated to his unit]'. Ishikawa's 57 men therefore had to carry the guns and ammunition in addition to their own gear. Armed with only ten rifles, 'if we encountered an enemy in the jungle, we would have been annihilated in no time,' Ishikawa believed. Kagawa's battalion established a line of defence in the Finisterres south of Kankiryo, looking to receive any survivors from Yonekura's advance force. When a weary group of men approached his position, Ishikawa asked the leading officer, 'Which unit?' 'The 9th company of the 3rd Battalion,' the officer replied. They were the survivors of Kaiapit. 'The faces of the men who followed him were in mud, utterly exhausted, with no word uttered, passing by,' Ishikawa wrote.[22] On 8 October the final remnants of Yonekura's force reached Kankiryo. Only about 100 of Yonekura's men returned and most of them would have been stragglers who never reached Kaiapit.[23]

•

The movement of Japanese troops into New Guinea seriously disrupted the lives of the resident population. Australian operatives based in the occupied areas instructed the local natives to go bush and, although many had done so, in many cases this was not an option. For the coastal natives their life revolved around access to the ocean so most stayed put and thus came under the direct influence of the Japanese. 'Their attitude is one of acquiescence in the present situation,' an Australian officer observed during a mid-1943 patrol. The villagers were unconvinced by the Australian patrols because the Japanese had armies on the spot 'while all we have to show is isolated white men being hunted through the bush,' the officer added.[24] Considering the number of native labourers working on the Japanese road across the Finisterres, it was clear that there was a limit to Australian influence. 'I have come to understand the natives clearly,' a Japanese soldier wrote in June. 'It seems that the white people did not consider the natives as human beings.'[25]

General Yoshihara had told the troops in New Guinea that 'kindness is the paramount factor, and it is necessary to refrain from unjust cruelty and treatment' of the native population and to 'avoid using them as slaves'. On the north coast the Japanese garrison commander was responsible for engaging labour via the village chiefs and each native labourer was paid.[26] Kindness and process was well and good but the reality was not so clear cut once the fighting started. At the end of October 1943 a local native from near Shaggy Ridge told the Australians that the Japanese had come and killed his son so he had taken to the bush.[27] Corporal Norm Maxwell was on a patrol in mid-January 1944 that came across a Finisterre village where the natives would not talk. 'You couldn't blame them for their attitude,' Maxwell wrote, 'They were like meat in the sandwich with Japs on one side and us on the other. If they had favoured one side the other side would have done them over.'[28]

The Australians certainly had better support from the Markham–Ramu natives than the Japanese. As General Vasey observed on 22 January 1944, 'At the present time 18 Bde has got 1045 natives and it needs them all.'[29]

•

With the victory at Kaiapit, General Vasey had the chance to let his 7th Division off the leash. His outline plan was to fly one of his brigades from Nadzab to Kaiapit and then move part of it to Marawasa. A second brigade would then fly to Marawasa and advance to Dumpu where airfields would then be constructed to fly in his third brigade plus divisional troops.[30] After the diffi-culties of the Kokoda campaign, Vasey was upbeat. 'There is no struggling for days & weeks through mountain tracks with short & poor rations,' he wrote to his wife, Jess, 'Mostly everyone is on the flat & <u>every</u> one is well fed & clothed.'[31] However, for the moment Vasey was handicapped by the intelligence that had been found in the captured documents at Kaiapit. There was still an expectation that some of the Japanese troops that had withdrawn from Lae may be moving through the foothills towards Kaiapit but of greater concern was the expectation that the main part of General Nakai's force was still heading his way. Vasey had to ensure that the Kaiapit area was well defended but he was also constrained by his own mindset. The bold risk he had taken in capturing and holding Kaiapit with a single independent company, when all his inclination as a divisional commander would have been to use a battalion or even a brigade for the task, was now clearly on his mind. He also had little confidence in his superior, the temporary New Guinea Force commander Lieutenant General Iven Mackay. 'Iven the terrible is again over here running the show,' he wrote to Jess.[32]

Late on 21 September the first company from the 2/16th Battalion landed at Kaiapit after a 20-minute flight from Nadzab. The rest of the battalion flew in the next day. Private 'Tich' Pearce was told to get off the plane ready to shoot but the only enemy soldiers they saw were dead. 'It stunk, and the Jap dead were staring at you as if still alive,' he said.[33] 'There were dead Japs everywhere,' Private Allan Cook added, 'even standing life-like behind coconut palms.'[34]

On 23 September the 2/27th Battalion flew directly from Port Moresby to Kaiapit. Some 2/14th Battalion elements also flew in from Nadzab that day and the rest of the battalion was on the ground by 25 September, completing the concentration of Brigadier Ivan Dougherty's 21st Brigade. Despite having his first brigade flown to Kaiapit, Vasey had his issues with access to air transport. 'I'm having my troubles,' he wrote to Jess. 'Working with Allies and another branch of the service is not easy.'[35] A brigade from 9th Division had landed at Finschhafen on 22 September and considerable air and logistics support was required to support that operation. At a meeting in Port Moresby on 23 September, General Kenney had said that he could not move Vasey's third brigade into the Markham Valley for at least a month other than in an emergency.[36] He was having enough trouble getting the 25th Brigade from Nadzab up to Kaiapit. Although two transport squadrons were available, there were major restrictions on landing at Kaiapit during daylight hours.[37]

On 25 September Vasey visited Dougherty at Kaiapit. Both men flew over the ground between Kaiapit and the Umi River and Vasey said it would make a good killing area when the expected enemy advance came. Dougherty agreed but felt the Japanese were not coming and he wanted to get his brigade moving. 'Let go the leg rope,' he told Vasey.[38] 'I'm bloody well leg roped and so are you by [General Herring] and even higher command,' Vasey replied.[39] In the following days it became apparent there would be no enemy attack on Kaiapit. 'I had a royal reception prepared for him but the little swine hasn't played his part & has sneaked off,' Vasey wrote. 'As far as I can see the Jap is running fast & it is difficult to foretell where he will stop on this island, if at all. I should not be surprised to see him right out of NG before Xmas.'[40]

•

Lieutenant Colonel Jack Bishop was the 35-year-old commander of the 2/27th Battalion. After serving pre-war with the militia, Bishop had been appointed as the intelligence officer to the 17th Brigade in 1940 and soon rose to be the unit's brigade major in the Middle East. For his fine work he was awarded an MBE in 1941 and when he returned to Australia in June 1942 he was appointed as a senior instructor at Duntroon military college in Canberra. Brigadier Dougherty had personally asked for Bishop to command the 2/27th and, over the objection of General Blamey who wanted Bishop on his staff, a delighted Bishop was given that command in March 1943, although only for the one campaign.[41] At the end of the Papuan campaign the 21st Brigade 'was 217 strong and not one man of this 217 was in any way fit'.[42] Like the other two battalions of the brigade, the 2/27th had to be rebuilt and retrained and that was Bishop's initial task. 'It is good to be back with the troops,' he wrote after his appointment. After being shipped from Townsville to Port Moresby in August, the battalion was flown across to Kaiapit on 23 September by 'a transport squadron which seems to land on any old piece of country that is bare of trees. They land, park and take off in much the same way as cabs awaiting their turn on a taxi rank.'[43]

On 25 September Bishop wrote from Kaiapit that 'There are only two types of hills in this man's country: steep hills and bloody steep hills.'[44] Two days later the first units of the 25th Brigade began to fly in to take over the defence of Kaiapit, allowing the 21st Brigade to finally advance. As Vasey had promised Dougherty, 'when 25 Brigade does come up . . . I remove your leash'.[45] On the afternoon of 28 September the 2/27th Battalion left Kaiapit. 'The game was on,' the war diary noted, 'and from then on the game was played very fast.'[46] The objective was to advance north-west up the Markham and Ramu valleys, securing the vital flat ground in the valley for the construction of advanced airfields to further the range of Allied airpower. With the 2/6th Independent Company and a PIB company guarding the right flank, the battalion moved up to the Umi River and crossed it on 29 September. The men of Captain Charlie Sims's A Company 'rested till dawn and proceeded to wade across stream with full equipment, helped by rope spanning river'.[47]

Dougherty's brigade advanced up the valley, keeping the Ramu River on its left flank and staying away from the foothills on the northern side. 'By keeping to the south side and leaving the whole of the very barren valley between me and the Jap,' Vasey wrote, 'I was able to by-pass him for about 50 miles before we turned north into the hills in the Dumpu area.'[48] Out ahead of 21st Brigade, patrols from the 2/7th Independent Company checked for any enemy presence and were able to confirm that the valley was clear.

On 30 September Bishop's battalion crossed the Markham–Ramu divide near the Gusap River. It had been a long day as the men had to go further than the planned staging point after a supposed waterhole there had dried out. When General Vasey's light plane landed he noted that the troops were footsore and weary but because the area around Gusap was ideal for airfields he wanted to find a suitable location that day. 'Righto, Reddin, come on. We've got to find a suitable place for an airstrip,' he told Captain Jack Reddin, the 2/27th intelligence officer. 'We were absolutely dead beat,' Reddin said but, accompanied by a few engineers, he and Vasey headed out across the kunai grass. 'He strode along with his great long legs at a great pace,' noted Reddin. 'Well, Reddin, isn't this great,' Vasey told him, 'No more mountains now. Lovely open, flat going.' 'Yes, sir' was all an exhausted Reddin could reply. Having selected a suitable location, the next day each of the four infantry companies was given an area to clear and the men got to work using machetes and bayonets to cut down the kunai grass. It took four hours to prepare a 900-metre airstrip and the first supply plane landed at 2.45 pm that afternoon.[49]

Sergeant Clive Edwards was with the battalion as it approached the Gusap River. On 2 October 'we bathed in the Ramu and even washed our clothes'. He also noted that the hard march was a struggle for one of his comrades, whose feet were in a pretty bad way—he was 'keeping up by a miracle of guts'.[50] Edwards' company had the job of digging cuttings into the side of the Gusap River to facilitate the building of a small bridge.

•

After being wounded at Kaiapit, Captain King rejoined his men on 6 October as his unit, now renamed the 2/6th Commando Squadron, approached the Surinam River. On the night of 6 October Corporal Joe Brammer was catching up on some much-needed sleep in a place where you always slept with the expectation that you could come face to face with death at any time from enemy troops close by in the foothills. Alert to any unusual sounds or sights in the darkness, Brammer suddenly woke to the glow of lights seemingly just outside the perimeter and immediately fired in that direction. He was actually firing at the headlights of a jeep making its way along the valley. Not everyone had seen the lights, but everyone heard Brammer's rifle fire and another commando woke in fright and raced out of the perimeter, the movement drawing another shot from Brammer. The startled commando then turned back and suddenly encountered another man, Trooper Reggie Belling, who had also woken ready to engage the enemy with his rifle. Belling was shot dead at point-blank range by the tragically disoriented commando, who was then tackled by Trooper Don Ford; in the tussle, Ford's Owen gun accidentally discharged. More shooting ensued and two more men were wounded, one of them Lieutenant Charlie Campbell, raked down the leg by the Owen gun. The other man who was wounded was the still-disoriented commando, who had been shot through the right side.[51]

That was the version recorded in the war diary but Fred Ashford, who was right in the middle of it, remembered it differently. There was one cardinal rule when on perimeter defence, Ashford said: 'In our perimeters nobody stood up . . . that was a dead giveaway.' If you wanted to go anywhere, you crawled. Apparently the piquet went to wake his replacement but he stood up to do it. When the sleeping commando woke up with a start and saw this figure standing over him, 'that's when it all started'. 'It is a strange one,' King said. 'It wasn't till the morning that we sorted out that it was not enemy fire.' With the strain on the men in the front line so intense it would not be the last friendly-fire incident in the campaign. When King reported the details of the incident to Brigadier Dougherty, King was told to let the matter rest.[52]

•

In the mountain ranges south of the Ramu Valley, two Australian independent companies had operated throughout most of 1943. On 27 September the 2/2nd Independent Company commander, Major Geoff Laidlaw, signalled Captain David Dexter that a reconnaissance of Kesawai in the Ramu Valley was required and he 'should take advantage of all favourable chances to harass' the enemy while doing so. At 8.00 am on 28 September Dexter led a patrol out from near Wesa comprising Lieutenant Doug Fullarton's section plus two native policemen and five native carriers. The party reached the Ramu River at 3.30 pm that afternoon. Here Dexter left three of the commandos, a native policeman and the carriers on the south bank of the river to hold the crossing point. A route for the advance and the rendezvous point was also worked out before nightfall.[53]

At 9.30 pm Dexter took his ambush party across the eight streams of the Ramu River. The last crossing was the most difficult but was made with the help of a wire rope that was swum across and anchored on the opposite bank. Having crossed the river, the party then set off for Kesawai following an 87-degree compass bearing until the men had reached the rainforest of the northern foothills around 1.30 am on 29 September. The men rested until 6.30 am and then proceeded to a point west of Kesawai to set the ambush. At 7.40 am Corporal Joe Poynton, Trooper Arthur Birch and the native policeman Tokua headed towards Kesawai until they were spotted and fired on. 'They went to rouse the throng,' was how Dexter later put it. Once sighted, the three men hurried back to the ambush site, leaving their footprints along the muddy track and hoping that their ruse would draw out the Japanese.[54]

Dexter's men had set up in a semicircle centred on the track with all his men aiming their weapons at a bend in the track about 100 metres away. Fullarton was at the apex of the semicircle with his Bren gun aimed directly down the track to Kesawai. At 9.50 am they could hear men approaching from the direction of Kesawai. Two native trackers appeared first, followed by small groups of two or three Japanese soldiers, all following the footprints left by the Australians. By the time the first Japanese were within 30 metres of the ambush, some 60 men had rounded the bend and it was then that the commandos opened fire. The Japanese fell 'like corn before the reaper'. Dexter estimated they had suffered about 45 casualties in the ambush: 'We cut them to pieces.' More troops moved up from Kesawai including machine guns and snipers and they traded fire with the Australians, killing Lance Corporal Cyril Doyle and wounding Dexter. 'I felt a searing across my melon head . . . and then I copped a couple in both legs and one arm,' as Dexter later described it.[55]

Soon thereafter the Australians broke contact and withdrew south to the agreed rendezvous, with Dexter carried most of the way. 'I thank the Lord for men like those,' Dexter wrote. The patrol then headed for the Ramu River, reaching the north bank in only 45 minutes. As Dexter's party crossed the river in broad daylight, the Japanese searched for their ambushers in the foothills of the Finisterre Range way to the north. On the south bank of the river Dexter was put on a stretcher and Kaipa, a Kesawai villager, chewed leaves and applied the mixture with lime to the wound on Dexter's forehead to stop the bleeding. He also helped carry Dexter back up to the camp behind Wesa, which was reached at 7.30 pm. When asked in later years if he still remembered Kesawai, Dexter pointed to the white scar on his forehead and replied 'Kesawai is indelibly marked on my mind, body and soul.'[56]

On 4 October the 2/2nd made another attack near Kesawai during which Lieutenant Val Nagle was killed. Eight enemy troops were also killed and on the following day the Japanese withdrew from Kesawai into the foothills of the Finisterre Range—in French, the 'end of the earth'.

Chapter 3

'HOP IN FOR YOUR BLOODY CHOP'

'The morning mist has lifted and it gives promise of a hot and windless day, so I suppose I shall be a few pounds lighter when day is done,' Jack Bishop wrote on 4 October.[1] On the next day his battalion crossed the Surinam River following the 2/16th Battalion which had already reached Dumpu and begun work on preparing an airfield. 'This was the day the battalion had been waiting for,' Jack Reddin noted, 'We were now to take over the Vanguard.'[2] Late on 5 October the battalion bypassed Dumpu and led the 7th Division out of the Ramu Valley into the foothills of the Finisterre Range to the north. 'Here we are on the fringe of those mountains which have been rearing their forbidding crests to the North during the whole march,' Clive Edwards wrote. 'Although we could see the Japs withdrawing from a couple of hilltops, all we did was trudge wearily over the plain with our loads dragging more heavily with each step.' The men were so tired that when given positions for the night, 'we just flopped down where we were without erecting a shelter—let it rain!'[3]

Kumbarum was a small native village beside the Uria River hemmed in by two towering foothills. Lieutenant Bob Johns' 7 Platoon was given the task of capturing the hill on the south side, later named Three Pimples Hill. When his lead section reached a native hut up on the hill, one of the men sprang back and exclaimed, 'There's a Jap in there!' Johns went forward as his men 'fired a few rounds into the shack to see what would happen' and watched as 'this fellow came hurling out the door without arms [weapons] or anything'. None of Johns' men had previously seen a Japanese soldier with his hands up so Johns went forward and ripped the pockets off the prisoner's uniform 'because we heard stories that the Japanese put a grenade without the safety catch on in their pockets'. 'My platoon only ever took one prisoner,' Johns said. 'We had the ability to shoot him if we wanted to but we didn't.' There had been a directive from head-quarters stating that a prisoner may provide useful information and Johns had that in his mind. 'He was lucky because some other time we might have shot him as he came out of the hut.'[4]

Johns' men had captured a twenty-year-old Korean private, Masao Takayama from 4 Company of the I/78th Battalion. The battalion had moved to Dumpu at the end of September and Takayama's company had been engaged further east at Wampun on 4 October but Takayama was one of six men from his company who were ill and had been left behind when the company had gone forward. After hearing the rifle fire from Wampun on the previous day the group had decided to return to Kankiryo but Takayama had become separated from the others. He had then found the deserted native hut on Three Pimples Hill and decided to rest there. He gave some interesting insights into life in New Guinea, considered the worst of the fighting fronts as sickness and hunger prevailed. Malaria was rampant among those units in the Finisterres with some 40 per cent stricken with the disease. 'Even dying was unpleasant in New Guinea,' Takayama observed. Nonetheless in the Japanese Army orders simply had to be carried out and difficulties and hardships endured. Takayama used the phrase '*Shikata Ga Nai*'—it can't be helped.[5]

Meanwhile an officer and eight men from 15 Platoon, part of Captain Gordon King's C Company, captured King's Hill, which towered above Kumbarum on the northern side. There was a small Japanese detachment there but when engaged they ran off from their observation post and the rest of the platoon climbed the hill on the next day.[6] From the top of the hill the broad southern shoulder of the massive feature that would soon become known as Shaggy Ridge was visible to the north.

Shaggy Ridge, known as Byobuzan or Byobu Yama to the Japanese, would become the linchpin of the Japanese defences in the Finisterre Range, but as the first Australian troops moved into the foothills the Japanese were more concerned with holding positions closer to the Ramu Valley, particularly those covering the key points on the supply route. Once the Australians had crossed the Surinam River on 5 October, the 78th Regiment had withdrawn into the mountains to secure the key points in the area of Gurumbu village. From 7 to 11 October General Adachi was at Kankiryo, stressing the importance of holding the area to prevent any Australian advance on Madang which would cut off the majority of his army in New Guinea.[7]

•

On 5 October Corporal Ron Box and nine men from 15 Platoon had patrolled 1400 metres up the Uria River, which ran between Three Pimples Hill and King's Hill. With precipitous river banks and many potential ambush positions, Box concluded that the river gorge was not suitable for moving a large body of troops. However, deep, distinctive enemy split-toed sandal imprints and footprints were seen going upstream, indicating it was being used as an enemy supply route.[8]

Jack Bishop was keen to move his men further into the mountains to maintain a forward defence and Captain Guy Fawcett's D Company would be the first company committed. This was a result of circumstances a year earlier when D Company had been the only company not committed to the fighting during the battle at Brigade Hill on the Kokoda Track.[9] After commanding the Bren gun carrier platoon in Syria, Fawcett had returned to Australia and been allocated to the School of Infantry as an instructor, missing the Kokoda campaign before taking over D Company for the current campaign.

On 6 October Bishop told Fawcett to have his company draw two days of rations, march into the foothills, cut the enemy line of communication, form an operating base and capture a few prisoners. When Fawcett returned to his company his three platoon commanders were waiting for him. Lieutenant Rex Trenerry had 16 Platoon, Lieutenant Gordon Macdonald 17 Platoon, and Lieutenant Gordon Robilliard 18 Platoon. 'What's the form, skipper?' they asked him. After Fawcett explained the orders, one of them piped up with his tongue firmly in cheek, 'We'll all be killed.'[10]

'Soon after lunch an order that Don Coy [D Company] would proceed into the hills on a fighting patrol at 1700 today had me going like a mad snake getting hard rations, tea, sugar, and rice issued,' Clive Edwards wrote. The company would move up the Uria River but then cut across a ridge to the north to follow the Faria River deeper into the Finisterres. Accompanied by a local guide, Fawcett's men soon found themselves zigzagging through a maze of cliff faces following the course of the Uria River upstream. The men waded in the river for long periods as they made their way forward hemmed in by the gorge and had only progressed about 900 metres before the company established its defensive position for the night. The men were crammed into a position only 150 metres long on a shelf above the Uria River with scouts out on the high ground above. 'Here we are right on the bank of a rapid stream which effectively drowns the noise of any approach and we are completely hemmed in by steep hills but, to our rear, enemy patrols can easily gain positions from which to fire down at us,' Clive Edwards wrote.[11]

Bishop was also determined to find the Japanese supply track further up the Uria River from where Fawcett planned to go. As Bob Johns remembered it, Bishop 'wanted to send a fighting force in there to ambush them on their own freeway'. On 7 October Johns led out his platoon on a fighting patrol with three signallers and seven native carriers attached. 'I was sent up the Uria Valley to find a Japanese track that air photographs had shown was there,' Johns noted.[12] The platoon left Kumbarum at 11.15 am and headed up river into the gorge. 'The course of the river twisted like a snake,' Johns wrote. Rounding one of the steep curves in the narrow river valley, they came across three unsuspecting Japanese soldiers with their rifles slung across their shoulders, also moving up the river. Johns' batman, Private Ron Barnes, wanted to open fire but Johns, unsure if there were more enemy troops on the hills above, stopped him. At 4.30 pm the patrol reached a fork in the river and fired at two other enemy soldiers who escaped up the right-hand fork. Johns decided not to follow them but to continue up the main river branch until 5.00 pm when the patrol stopped and set up camp for the night under the precipitous west bank. No bridge had been found as it actually never existed. Johns' patrol had laid out a phone line as they went but at 7.00 pm the line went dead.[13]

On the next morning Johns sent out two section patrols, one back down the river and up the bypassed fork and the second further up the main river to the left. The second section found no enemy but the first section was ambushed at the river fork by ten to twenty enemy troops on high ground and two men were wounded before the section was able to break contact. Some native carriers 'were carrying our sig wire and things and they were in the ambush and they behaved like trained soldiers and knew exactly what to do,' Johns observed. 'They disappeared into the scrub.' Johns' route back down the river was now blocked so he moved the patrol further upstream and then up onto the high ground west of the river and then back down again to the Uria River on the other side of the ambush position. Here the patrol came across a commando section that had been ambushed at the same place as Johns' section had been, at the river fork. 'As I got to the track,' Johns said, 'they were coming back from there, saying that they'd lost their platoon commander.' Johns had his men assist with the casualties and then followed the broken commando patrol back to Kumbarum 'where they told me that the battalion had been moved out and had gone further up the Ramu Valley to another position, and that I was to join them'.[14]

•

The commando patrol that Johns had come across had been led by the 2/6th's Lieutenant Jim Graham and had moved up the Uria gorge earlier that afternoon to contact Johns after the phone line had gone down. Graham had done his officer training with Bob Balderstone and the two Melbourne boys were good mates. As Graham had led his section out, Balderstone told him, 'See you later Jim.' 'Yep,' Graham replied. Later that afternoon Balderstone would go out and return with his mate's body.[15]

Graham's mission had worried the 2/6th's commander Gordon King from the start. It had been allocated by 21st Brigade headquarters and King had been assured that the gorge was clear because Johns had been through on the previous day. 'It was a bit of a foul up, the whole thing,' King said. He thought the brigade major, Major Stan Owens, had 'got it a bit wrong . . . he didn't give us the correct information'.[16]

At 4.50 pm the lead scout, Trooper George Mudford, fired at a Japanese soldier about 60 metres away who was cutting the phone line to Johns. Graham then sent Joe Brammer and three men up a steep bank on the right to provide cover, but as Graham stood up the commandos came under fire from a kunai spur about 60 metres away. Graham was killed and Mudford wounded by the first burst of fire before Trooper Cyril Eddy was killed as he crossed the creek. The rest of the patrol took cover under the creek bank and returned fire.[17]

It was then decided to pull back. Brammer returned to the creek bed and covered the withdrawal with his Bren gun before confirming that Graham and Eddy were dead and securing their personal effects. Then as the men withdrew Trooper Cyril Tyter was shot in the leg, fracturing the bone and rendering him immobile. Brammer got to him and part carried and part floated him downstream with the help of Trooper Bernie Little. Once safely out of range, Tyter's leg was dressed and splinted. Johns' patrol then arrived and a bush stretcher was made up for Tyter. At 5.55 pm an exhausted Don Ford arrived back at Kumbarum to report the ambush, and a patrol under Bob Balderstone was also sent out to help. At 9.30 pm all the patrols returned to Kumbarum.[18]

•

On 9 October General Vasey visited Brigadier Dougherty and repeated his order that Dougherty's three battalions were to remain in their positions and, with the help of active patrolling, maintain control over the area from Dumpu to Gusap. Securing the airfield sites in the Ramu Valley was Vasey's main task and he accepted that the division could be in that role for some time.[19] This confirmed what had already been made clear to Vasey on 22 September: his division's role was the defence of the Markham Valley and the airfields therein and he was not to advance towards Bogadjim without orders from army headquarters.[20]

Meanwhile, on the morning of 7 October, at about the same time as Bob Johns' platoon was heading off up the Uria River, Captain Fawcett's company left the Uria River gorge. 'Eventually the Jap track which we were following led us to the left up a steep climb and over a ridge to another river, the Faria,' Clive Edwards wrote. Corporal Josh Sullivan's section was soon in action, shooting up an enemy patrol moving into the area and causing its members to flee, leaving three dead behind. The path the Australians were now following along the Faria River was covered with the split-toed mark of Japanese rubber sandals and towards evening enemy troops were sighted on the top of a high hill on the right. Fawcett, a first-class rifleman, took a shot at them before ordering Rex Trennery's platoon up onto the position. 'Go up that feature, Buff, and see if there's anybody there,' he told Corporal Bruce 'Buff' Deering, one of Trenerry's men. The men from the platoon made their way up through the thick scrub, only to find nothing on top. 'The poor cows must have thought that a division was coming, the row we made,' Clive Edwards wrote. Fawcett then decided to bivouac for the night in the creek bed rather than on the high ground so Trennery's men had to slide back down the hill, now christened Buff's Knoll. As always in the late afternoon it began to rain but despite the risk the men got some fires going for a brew of tea and a hot meal.[21]

At about 1.00 the next morning, 8 October, a Japanese patrol of ten to twenty men moving down the Faria River clashed with Fawcett's company in the river valley. For most of the men it was their first time in action and confusion and fright abounded in the darkness. 'A few of the Nips were coming down and we had two or three casualties before we'd even hit a Nip,' Corporal Les Thredgold observed. Thredgold was an old hand in the battalion, having served in the Middle East before an arduous time cut off on the Kokoda Track and then fighting for his life at Gona. When Corporal Ted Lawson heard the gunfire he went to wake one of the sleeping men; however, as the young soldier woke in fright to the sound of gunfire, he only saw the dark outline of a soldier above him and instinctively fired a burst from his Owen gun into Lawson. Then, as he realised what he had done, the distraught soldier ran blindly through the company position in search of help, whereupon another soldier shot the running figure. The young man would die of his wounds that night but Lawson would pull through. Les Thredgold just took cover behind a stack of rocks with his Bren gun for hours, waiting for an enemy breakthrough that never came. 'Some of the boys got a little bit excited,' he later reflected.[22]

The men dreaded the coming daylight as they knew how exposed they were down in the river valley if enemy troops had reached the higher ground during the night. At 7.00 am a patrol was sent up Buff's Knoll to provide protection but as the day broke the only enemy to be seen were five dead ones lying in the creek only an arm's length away from the company positions. Among them was a Japanese major. Guy Fawcett had been trying to contact battalion headquarters since the first attack but the signal wire had been cut. Once reconnected, Fawcett told Bishop that he was surrounded and needed help. 'Hang on, I'll bring the crowd up,' Bishop replied. While Fawcett waited for the rest of the battalion, he moved his company onto a plateau overlooking the Faria River which would bear his Christian name, Guy's Post. Having taken an easier route, the rest of the 2/27th Battalion crowd had already gathered there.[23]

'The next day the colonel decided to push on,' said Fawcett, 'and blow me down, put me out as leading company again.'[24] The day had already got off to a bad start when a shot was heard just before dawn causing the company to stand to, expecting an enemy attack. Private Col Hickman had shot himself through the leg when trying to free his rifle from some vegetation. 'Half the goats are completely trigger happy,' a frustrated Clive Edwards wrote.[25]

Private Edgar 'Skeeter' Zander was only 16 when he had joined D Company, prompting Guy Fawcett to ask him, 'What, are they going to take them out of the pram next?'[26] Zander was in Trennery's platoon, two sections of which headed back up the Faria River that morning as the battalion's advance guard. Soon thereafter, at 8.50 am, three shots rang out from the two scouts furthest upstream. Zander and Lance Corporal 'Rocky' Chellew had been sent out as scouts to cover the track about 50 metres in front and when they heard noises in the undergrowth their first thought was that it could be wild pigs. However, it was an enemy patrol moving through the scrub rather than along the track. The two men 'simultaneously saw they were Japs,' Zander recalled. When six Japanese soldiers with their rifles slung over their shoulders emerged from the scrub the two Australians didn't hesitate and fired their rifles from the hip at near point-blank range, killing at least three of them, one an officer who had been carrying a sword. The others, one of whom had been wounded, took off back into the scrub.[27] Like the rest of Fawcett's company, Chellew and Zander had been trained to fire from the hip by Fawcett, shooting rolling jam tins using a finger aligned along the rifle to point at the target while using the other hand to fire and reload the rifle.[28]

'Straight after, all hell broke loose,' Zander recalled. The main enemy force, which was not far behind their careless scouts, unleashed a torrent of fire over the top of where their comrades had fallen, perhaps expecting to catch the Australians searching the bodies. However, Chellew and Zander had kept under cover and now pulled back to the rest of the platoon. Trenerry then sent out another patrol which reported that there were about twenty enemy soldiers coming down the river and decided to have his men lie in wait for them. The Japanese infantry crept forward through the scrub along the river and a burst of light machine-gun fire from the left bank killed Private Les 'Acker' Brown as he crossed the river. Zander saw Brown lying against a large rock and Trennery said he was dead. Clive Edwards fired into some scrub that had moved from the machine-gun blast and thought he had got his man while Private Dave Blacker found it hard to get the Bren gun into a good firing position until Private Pat Myers lay down underneath and held the bipod steady. The enemy hit back by lobbing over a few grenades from a grenade discharger, the blast from one wounding Sergeant George Beveridge in the back. Orders then came up from battalion headquarters to withdraw and take up a position to guard the creek junction, about 200 metres further back down the river.[29]

Clive Edwards passed the message to Trenerry and then went back to look at the new position. A sniper had a couple of shots at him as he crossed the creek but missed both times, although a third shot just clipped the top of the rock he sheltered behind. For the rest of the way back he managed to keep out of enemy fire by crawling and bending double.[30] The rest of the platoon followed him back to hold the creek junction while the battalion moved up the creek to the east. Trennery's platoon then tagged on to the end and followed, climbing to the top of a seemingly never-ending hill to take up positions just as the afternoon rain arrived. The position would later be named Beveridge's Post after the wounded sergeant. With his main objective to find the Japanese supply track through to the Ramu Valley, Bishop had realised it was better to be on the high ground than moving along the narrow Faria Valley.[31] He couldn't send the battalion too far as he had to base his headquarters within a day's reach of his supply base at Dumpu. Bishop could send out patrols from the battalion's forward position to find and cut the Japanese supply route while Fawcett's company would remain in the Faria River valley to hold the supply line back to Guy's Post.[32]

•

Lieutenant Gordon Macdonald's 17 Platoon had led the battalion east up the gully from the Faria River to higher ground and Bishop's headquarters went up behind, followed by Lieutenant Tom Cook's pioneer platoon. When Macdonald's men reached the top of the ridge, they were about to have lunch when they noticed an enemy patrol on a wide track north of what would become known as Trevor's Ridge. Macdonald moved his men up to a saddle where the track crossed Trevor's Ridge with the intention of setting an ambush, but as his men approached they heard talking and the rattle of mess tins from the saddle area. A party of fifteen Japanese with no sentries posted had gathered and were about to have their own lunch so at 2.35 pm Macdonald ordered an attack with the simple command, 'Here they are boys! Hop in for your bloody chop.' Led in by the Bren and Owen gunners firing from the hip, Macdonald's platoon attacked and surprised the enemy patrol.[33] 'They were taking their equipment off so he allowed them to take it off and then just about wiped them out,' Tom Cook said.[34]

Corporal Jack Daniel was in charge of the leading section and was wounded by a grenade during the attack, one of five Australians wounded in the action. His wounds would prove fatal and he would die as he was being carried out to Guy's Post the next day. Daniel had been at the forefront of the attack, accounting for five of the enemy dead, and Corporal Frank Lundie later wrote of his mate as 'This golden-haired boy of the blazing gun.'[35] Padre Harry Norman lay next to another wounded man holding a .45 pistol to protect him. Following Macdonald's attack another party of fourteen Japanese was spotted moving towards the newly captured position and Josh Sullivan's section was ordered to intercept them. Firing from the hip with his Owen gun, Sullivan had his right elbow hit so he shifted the gun to his left elbow and continued to fire and direct his men. At least three enemy soldiers were killed and Sullivan was awarded the Military Medal for his gallantry.[36] Two months later at the army hospital in Port Moresby, Jack Bishop went to present the medal to the young corporal; however, Sullivan was not in his bed, he was down the end of the ward playing poker with some mates. The nursing sister told Sullivan 'Your CO is here and has something important to give you.' Not looking up from his cards, Sullivan replied, 'Ask him to wait a moment, please, I'm holding a good hand.'[37]

The Australians had captured what would later come to be known as Johns' Knoll, overlooking the Japanese supply track through key point number 3, some 12 kilometres from Kankiryo. As Merv Weston wrote, 'Before the enemy realised what was happening, our force was on the ridge overlooking his track.'[38] There were at least eight enemy soldiers killed in the action and others wounded while twenty rifles and three light machine guns were captured.[39] As Frank Lundie moved among the dead, touching each with his boot, he found one body that did not feel right so he pulled a leg over to make sure and the Japanese soldier promptly sat up, flung up his hands and called out in a beseeching tone, 'No shoot, no shoot!'[40] The prisoner was Private Kinjiro Wada from the II/78th Battalion, 'suffering with jabbering malaria' and too weak to withdraw. He later confirmed that the Australians were indeed on the Japanese supply line.[41]

Further back Corporal Brian Castle was posted up on the higher ground east of the Faria River with a section from Lieutenant Wally Macpherson's 8 Platoon, which was holding Beveridge's Post, the high ground south of the gully that Macdonald's platoon had taken to the east. Castle watched as two Japanese soldiers came down the opposite side of the Faria River valley to get water and as they made their way back Castle asked a young Bren gunner, 'How do you feel about it?' The Bren gunner was unsure of his ability to hit the target, so Castle told him 'Give it here then' and proceeded to pick off both soldiers from across the valley.[42]

Up on Johns' Knoll, Jack Reddin heard a rifle shot as he made his way back through the jungle to battalion headquarters. He then met a platoon patrol and one of them asked if he'd heard the shot. 'It was a Japanese rifle,' Reddin told them. 'Trevor's out there,' the concerned patrol leader told him, referring to Lieutenant Trevor Martin, the 13 Platoon commander who had gone forward to try to contact B Company. Martin had been ambushed and killed. Reddin then saw a Japanese soldier about 20 metres away in the jungle and 'shot him before he even lifted his rifle'. Before the body hit the ground the patrol leader had also shot him with an Owen gun burst.[43] The ridge that ran from Beveridge's Post on the Faria River and ended at Johns' Knoll was named Trevor's Ridge after the fallen lieutenant.

•

Just after dawn the next day, 10 October, 'Tojo startled the early morning air with his usual heathen chorus presaging an attack'. The noise went on for about 4 minutes, giving the Australians time to get 'well and truly ready for the attack', which came in along the supply track. Of the six 'noisy intruders' that unsuccessfully attacked 13 Platoon, two were killed and one wounded.[44]

By now the 2/27th had brought forward a 3-inch mortar and a Vickers heavy machine gun to provide fire support but at 1.40 pm the Japanese trumped them both and opened up on Trevor's Ridge with two mountain guns at approximately 1400 metres range. These guns were 75 mm models that had been broken down and carried up from the coast. The first shot passed over the ridge and exploded about 2 kilometres away but the Japanese observers then lowered their aim and began to impact the Australian positions. About an hour later one of the two Australian light 25-pounders, which had been brought up the valley all the way from Kaiapit, opened fire on the suspected gun position. The signal line had only reached the front line that morning and the gun was directed by Bombardier Ewart Leggo, the forward observer working with Fawcett's company. Despite the 7000-metre range, this counter fire had the desired effect and there was no more Japanese artillery fire that day.[45]

On 10 October a section from Lieutenant Wally Macpherson's 8 Platoon had the job of recovering the body of one of their own, Acker Brown, who had been killed along the Faria River the previous day. It was a very personal mission for Corporal Lindsay Daw to bring back the body of the mate he had been at school with and with whom he had played football back in Adelaide before joining up.[46] After the body was recovered the stretcher party headed back but came under machine-gun fire at 'point blank range from a small feature east of the river'. Private Henry Fittock was wounded by a grenade as he scrambled for cover among the rocks before the rest of the section under Daw came back up the river to help. But they also ran into the enemy fire and Daw was hit. One of the stretcher bearers, Private Tom Chapman, crawled out and dragged Daw into the river and then floated him downstream to some shelter, but Daw's wound would prove fatal.[47]

The section was now pinned down in the river and at the mercy of the enemy ambushers and Corporal Merv McPhee was also wounded. However, Private Jack Simmons, the newest member of 8 Platoon, scrambled up the steep west bank of the river and, dodging enemy fire, scaled the cliff face out of the gorge. He then crawled further along to reach a point that overlooked the enemy ambush position below him on the opposite cliff face. He shot two of the ambush party and sent the remainder ducking for cover, thereby saving the trapped men in the gorge who were able to recover their casualties and withdraw. Simmons also withdrew but soon returned with a patrol to ensure the ambush position was cleared. The enemy ambush party fled, leaving four dead behind. Jack Simmons would be awarded the Military Medal for his brave action.[48]

The following day the Japanese again shelled Trevor's Ridge, firing about 40 rounds. A new radio set had come up to Ewart Leggo at the forward observation post that morning but the second shell from the Japanese gun put it out of action and wounded the operator, Gunner Lister Boyd. Without a radio Leggo shouted his orders about 30 metres back to Jack Reddin who stood up in plain sight for 10 minutes with shells lobbing so he could relay the instructions. One man lying nearby told Reddin, 'I wish I had your guts.' Reddin was relaying the fire orders back to Jack Bishop who had access to the number 11 radio set to call brigade headquarters. The fire orders were then passed on to the guns but unfortunately the short 25-pounder didn't quite have the range to reach the enemy mountain gun.[49]

Jack Bishop was operating the radio as one of the enemy shells had killed his two radio operators. Before the mountain gun had opened up, Skeeter Zander was discussing the depth of foxholes with Private Gordon Berrett, one of the signallers, who was in the adjacent foxhole. He told Berrett that his foxhole was not very deep but Berrett had replied, 'She'll be right.'[50] A shell then struck the edge of the foxhole and Berrett was killed along with another signaller, Lance Corporal Bill Wright. Private Bill 'Snow' Hannan, who was nearby was wounded but he managed to find shelter in another foxhole despite it being already occupied by Clive Edwards. 'I could feel him bleeding all over me and tried to get him to move so that I could tie him up but he insisted that he was OK,' Edwards wrote. 'Poor chap was evacuated but was killed by a direct hit on the way out.' That evening the men shifted their positions to the reverse side of the hill in defilade [under cover] from the shelling. As Captain Bill 'Bluey' Whyte observed, at this stage men were casual about the mountain gun and this led to casualties.[51]

Chapter 4

'DO OR DIE'

The 2/14th Battalion was a Victorian unit but most of the re-inforcements following the costly Papuan campaign were from interstate and at times their incorporation into the battalion came with considerable angst. New South Welshman Private Bernard 'Slim' Davidson gave as good as he got, telling his company commander that 'the only fucking good thing to ever come out of fucking Victoria, mate, was Tommy Pryor here, Peter Owens here and the Pacific fucking Highway'. Pryor simply told his mate, 'son, you will never ever make the diplomatic corps' and Davidson transferred to a New South Wales battalion.[1] Another interstate reinforcement, Private Tim Moriarty, remembered seeing parcels of personal belongings from those men killed in action under a tent fly. 'You blokes will get your parcels one day,' one of the veterans told Tim and his mates.[2] But the reinforcements were badly needed. 'We were only bloody kids,' Alf Edwards recalled. 'What was left of the battalion after Kokoda and through there, you'd be lucky if you could rake up 200 out of the whole battalion.'[3]

Lieutenant Nolan 'Noel' Pallier, 24 years old, was the newly appointed commander of 9 Platoon and he was also from New South Wales. To Pallier, being responsible for the life or death of thirty-odd soldiers was the role of a more mature man: 'They put you in charge of men's lives. In fact we were asked to do what they should never have asked for us to do.' But New Guinea was a young man's war and the sheer physical effort of carrying heavy loads over difficult terrain in a tropical climate soon sapped that youth. 'When we went into that campaign, I think we had 68-and-a-half pounds [30 kg] on our backs with our equipment and what we were carrying,' Pallier added.[4]

Sergeant Lindsay 'Teddy' Bear was Pallier's platoon sergeant and a veteran of all the earlier campaigns but despite that he still looked young. 'He had a boyish way,' Pallier remarked, and 'he enjoyed everything'.[5] The platoon had a very proud heritage and Teddy Bear was an important part of that, having been at the forefront of the fighting during the Kokoda campaign. 'Well, my Bren gun at Isurava was so hot I couldn't even pick it up,' he told his son-in-law. 'I burned my knuckles changing the barrel . . . there was no water . . . we were dehydrated, couldn't even piss on the barrel so we just kept changing it.' Bear was badly wounded during that battle, shot in the foot, knee, thigh and shoulder. At that stage he couldn't stand up so handed the Bren to his number two, Private Bruce Kingsbury. 'Righto Bruce, it's over to you.' Holding the Bren gun by the handle and balancing it across his hip Kingsbury advanced with the red-hot gun and cut down the Japanese attack before he was killed. Bruce Kingsbury was posthumously awarded the Victoria Cross.[6]

Some of the new platoon members didn't take the past history all that seriously. Private 'Lofty' Back had been a shearer out in the bush pre-war and was never short of a word. When a captain from the 2/14th talked of the battalion history in Syria, on the Kokoda Track and at Gona, he ended up by asking 'Any questions?' Lofty piped up, 'I'd like to say, lucky to get in, due for a win.'[7] The battalion commander, Lieutenant Colonel Ralph Honner, was also from out of state, having served with the West Australian 2/11th Battalion in the Middle East before being appointed to the command of another Victorian unit, the 39th Battalion in 1942. During the fighting along the Kokoda Track and then at Gona, Honner had shown himself to be the outstanding commander at any level during that campaign. On his appointment to the 2/14th on 9 July 1943, 'The battalion welcomed him as an old friend,' Bill Russell wrote.[8]

The 2/14th had been the last of the three battalions of the 21st Brigade to reach Kaiapit, flying in on 24 and 25 September. But from there, progress was on foot. 'That was a glorified walk,' Alf Edwards said, 'that's why they call it the two bar one four walking outfit I think'.[9] 'It was hot as hell,' Sergeant James Milbourne added, 'but better than forcing our way through the jungle.' The advance along the valley stretched back nearly 2 kilometres. 'It was a hectic march,' Milbourne wrote. 'About 20 miles a day loaded with about 70 pounds of gear.'[10] 'It's like a big flat valley with mountains, the Bismarck out to one side and the Finisterres on the other,' Noel Pallier observed.[11] By 4 October the battalion was closing in on Dumpu with the expectation of the first contact with the Japanese growing. As the battalion moved into the native village of Wampun it deployed for an attack but the village was clear. 'Nippon's birds of passage had flown well before their abandoned roost was reached,' noted Ralph Honner.[12]

Honner was a fast mover, an athletic type who had been a sprint champion before the war.[13] In the Ramu Valley, Honner and his adjutant, Captain Stan Bisset, who had been an Australian representative rugby player, had been ordered to have their bedrolls carried by native carriers so they were fresh throughout the day. After a punishing day of marching up the valley, the men were exhausted and very thirsty by the time they reached Wampun.[14] The native carriers carried no water and they also needed a supply to cook their rice for dinner but no water had been found that day.[15] Honner was still feeling fit so, taking Private Bill Bennett with him, he went to check out a creek further west. Tim Moriarty watched as Honner walked past along the track, picking berries and eating them, thinking 'He's a cool customer.'[16] Honner only intended to catch up with A Company but was unaware that the company had turned north off the main track. As Honner later recalled, 'the company, not encountering the river where expected had turned off the track to the right to find it'.[17]

Now joined by Sergeant Tom Pryor, Honner spotted troops around a small banana plantation about a kilometre to the west but he saw 'no detectable reaction to the group's continuing noisy approach as it advanced along the almost straight path, only two to three yards wide and walled in by kunai grass growing four to five feet high'.[18] Then Honner's group came under fire and Honner was shot in the thigh and hip while Pryor was hit in the chest and face. Unable to walk, Honner ordered Pryor to go back and get help and then dragged himself about 100 metres into the kunai grass.

Bill Bennet found Honner and refused to leave him and the two men hid in tall kunai grass 'midway between our approach track and our kunai-trampled withdrawal route' as two Japanese searchers passed either side of them. 'I could hear them only, and I must have been invisible to them,' Honner noted. 'Their swish through the grass and their excited chatter heralded their coming and proclaimed their passing. The searchers came back—again so close [before] the clamour died down through a distant haze to silence.'[19]

Meanwhile Pryor had reached Captain Gerry O'Day who sent Lieutenant Alan Avery's 16 Platoon out to rescue Honner. Avery called out Honner's name as he moved through the kunai and soon got the reply he was seeking. 'Here, over here,' Honner called out. He was smothered with black ants when Avery reached him. 'I'll get you out now sir,' Avery told him. 'Oh no Mister Avery, wait a minute, we are going to put an attack in on this position,' Honner replied. Avery persisted, telling Honner 'I'm sorry sir, my orders are to bring you out.' But Honner had the final say. 'Mister Avery, I think my orders are a bit above Captain O'Day's. Get your walkie-talkie going and get them to send up the rest of the company.'[20] Honner also ordered another company to move forward on the enemy's left flank.

Tim Moriarty was with 17 Platoon advancing on the village with the sound of bullets whipping through the kunai grass ringing in their ears. Moriarty was hit in the arm but he put a field dressing on it and kept going. As the defenders fled, a machine gun set up on the right mowed them down. Private Noel 'Bert' Bailey was one of the four men wounded during the attack and he would die of his wounds on the following day.[21] The defenders were from 2 Company of the I/78th Battalion. Sergeant Zenhichi Inoue had about 23 men in his platoon but as the Australians approached they fled. Inoue stayed to fight but was wounded and later captured. First Lieutenant Taniguchi's 2 Company had

26 men killed in the attack including the commander. Inoue was captured the next day.[22] After the war Gerry O'Day met up with Ralph Honner in Ireland who told him, 'It was a decision I took but a mistake.' Nonetheless the men got their water in the end.[23]

•

On the morning of 7 October Noel Pallier took 9 Platoon into the foothills on the north side of the Ramu Valley to locate Japanese observation posts and supply lines east of the Surinam River. After 10 kilometres Pallier sent two men from each section out to get water. When Alf Edwards saw some movement he called over his section leader Corporal 'Bluey' Whitechurch and said, 'Look, I definitely have seen movement up there at the top of that hill.' The platoon was out in the open and Pallier thought that before they went further up the river into the hills they should stop for a meal. He knew any enemy observers could see his men, so spread them out before sending two men from each section down to the river to fill the water bottles. 'So we came down alongside the river and lo and behold, bang, bang, bang,' said Edwards. 'The bastards were up there alright.' The enemy riflemen had opened up from much higher ground at about 300 metres range. Lofty Back also spotted them and called out, 'There they are, the bastards' as a bullet nicked his head. The men grabbed their equipment and ran for the cover of the river bank as bullets ricocheted off the rocks.[24]

'Then Georgie got shot,' Pallier recalled. Although Private 'George' Pottinger had been hit in the chest, Pallier thought 'he didn't look as if there was anything wrong' and wondered why he had dropped his gun. 'Georgie, why did you leave your Bren gun up there?' Pallier asked him. Pottinger didn't reply, he just fell against

Pallier with blood seeping through his shirt. There was a 'hell of a hole out the back and on the front you would swear they shot him through the heart'. Corporal Bill Pafrey came up and bandaged Pottinger before they constructed a makeshift stretcher to carry him back over 3 kilometres before a man was sent to hail one of the jeeps going up the valley. The jeep took him to the casualty clearing station but George Pottinger would die nine days later.[25]

Meanwhile Noel Pallier went back to get the Bren gun. He lined his men up and gave them orders to fire over his head as he crawled forward about 200 metres with bullets cracking above him. Then as he grabbed the gun he realised someone was behind him. 'This was Teddy Bear. He didn't get told to do it, I told him not to do it,' said Pallier. 'He reckoned if Noel got hit he was going to pick me up. The two leaders of the platoon doing silly things.' Bear picked up the Bren magazines and the two men ran back to cover.[26]

•

By 10 October the 2/14th Battalion had moved to Kumbarum to take over from the 2/27th, now forward along the Faria River. Noel Pallier's platoon was sent up King's Hill, a tough climb for men with about 30 kilograms on their backs. Alan Avery's platoon was about a kilometre further up the Uria River at the northern base of Three Pimples Hill protecting the supply line to Guy's Post. Just after dawn on 11 October Avery saw troops digging in on the skyline at the end of the narrow connecting ridge back to King's Hill. He initially thought they were men from the 2/27th who had fallen back but then noticed that they were frantically digging with entrenching tools, which were not a standard Australian army item.

'The Japs carried a good little trenching tool, shovel thing that would fold down,' Noel Pallier noted, 'something they had on us.'[27] At 8.00 am Avery made his report and a Vickers gun down in the valley opened fire up onto the suspect position at about 700 metres range, only for enemy counter-fire to kill Corporal Jack Barnard. At 9.15 am the Japanese also opened fire down onto Avery's position, wounding two of his men.[28]

Major Bill Landale had arrived from Port Moresby on 6 October to take over command of the battalion after Ralph Honner had been evacuated. Having received Avery's report Landale notified Noel Pallier of the situation. Pallier looked through his field glasses and saw the distinct Japanese helmet shape bobbing up and down as the men dug in at the other end of the ridge. Landale then told him to send a patrol out to confirm they were enemy troops. Pallier told Landale he would do it 'on one condition'. 'What's that?' Landale asked. 'That I'm one of them,' Pallier replied. 'Why?' asked Landale. 'Because it's suicide,' Pallier countered. 'Christ, don't do that,' Landale urged.[29]

Up on King's Hill, the men 'were sitting around in the glaring hot sun, talking and smoking after breakfast' when Pallier told them the 'unbelievable news' that Japanese troops were digging in at the other end of the ridge. Earlier that morning some men had moved part of the way along the ridge looking for wood without being fired on. At this stage Pallier didn't want the Japanese alerted but when they opened fire he had his men exchange shots to hamper their digging in.[30] 'Up where the 27th was, she was pretty angry up that way,' Alf Edwards observed, 'but then that batch of Nips snuck in overnight . . . Pallier got the bloody shock of his life next morning.'[31]

•

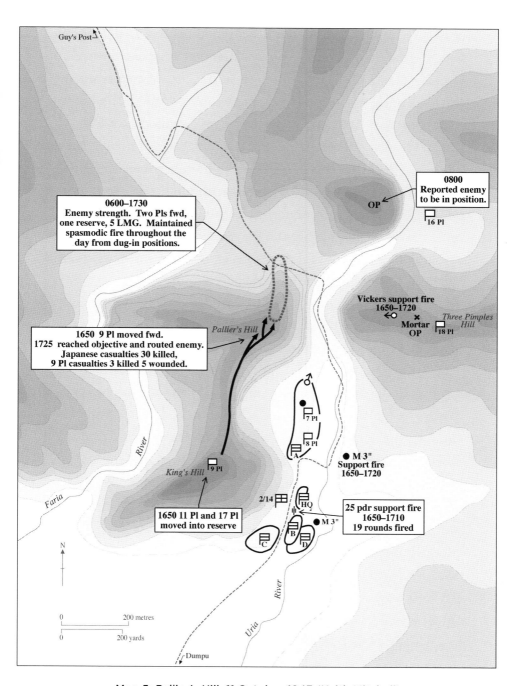

Map 5: Pallier's Hill, 11 October 1943 (Keith Mitchell)

Soon after Avery's report, Stan Bisset set off up Three Pimples Hill with a signaller and a walkie-talkie to observe the Japanese position. Looking across the gorge, Bisset could see at least twenty enemy troops digging in and they had cut the supply line to the 2/27th Battalion. At 11.00 am Lieutenant Tom Simmons' 18 Platoon plus a Vickers gun section under Sergeant Doug Chrisp headed up to join Bisset on Three Pimples Hill. It was a tough job getting the Vickers gun up but at 2.00 pm the section began digging two positions for the gun, one for initial support and the second to bring fire onto enemy troops on the reverse slope as they retreated. By 3.00 pm the gun was in position and a mortar observation post had been established under Sergeant Don McEwan.[32]

Brigadier Ivan Dougherty was concerned at developments. When Landale had phoned him to say some blokes were digging in about 400 metres in front, Dougherty's reply was simple: 'Kill 'em!'[33] Dougherty was also aware that an urgent supply train through to the 2/27th Battalion had been fired on and the native carriers had taken to the bush. Jack Bishop had been on the line stressing the importance of getting that supply train through. Dougherty sent his brigade major Stan Owens to the 2/14th headquarters to find out what was being organised to restore the situation and to stress the need for prompt action.[34] Knowing what was at stake Dougherty also called Major Mert Lee, the second in command of the 2/16th Battalion. Lee was a highly decorated veteran who had Dougherty's confidence and at 1.00 pm Dougherty told Lee to immediately take over command of the 2/14th.[35] Dougherty later told the official historian that Landale was a very fine fellow but had no grip.[36]

Noel Pallier had no idea of the changes happening down in the valley. The first he knew of it was when Mert Lee called on the phone line. 'I think he questioned me at about three or four o'clock when he took over,' Pallier recalled. Lee told Pallier to capture the position before dark or else they would never get the Japanese off the position. 'I was told to do or die,' said Pallier, 'that was in his words'. In Lee, Pallier thought he had 'a fearless type of man giving orders . . . he had an MC and I think he had a bar to it. He was a pretty formidable soldier . . . a very determined man.' Lee stressed that the job had to be done that day, telling Pallier that otherwise 'they'll put a battalion of God knows how many' on the feature, 'and we'll never get 'em off'.[37] 'Next bloody minute Pallier got the word that 9 Platoon was to go and take that hill, that ridge,' Alf Edwards remembered.[38]

•

Mert Lee had also confirmed with Stan Bisset that his plan would be put into effect. Two platoons under Gerry O'Day were sent up King's Hill to relieve Pallier's platoon, which would make the attack along the top of the connecting ridge. O'Day climbed up King's Hill with Lance Corporal Dick Doyle, swapping the lead as they went, each pushing the other up the steep slope, like climbing a flat-topped pyramid. O'Day arrived around 4.45 pm, just about too late. 'I went to meet him,' said Pallier, 'but I knew the first round of artillery was coming in. So as soon as that went, that was it'. Pallier just said, 'I'm on the way, boss' and returned to his men, lined up to go.[39] The wily old bushman Private Bill Kerr turned to Alf Edwards and said, 'OK mate, here we go.' Alf was scared; it was his baptism of fire.[40] All the men shook hands with their mates and wished each other luck. Lofty Back and Private Johnny Cobble had both worked in outback Queensland before the war and as the men shook hands Lofty told his mate, 'See you at the Winton races.' Both men would be dead before dusk.[41]

For Pallier there were three attack options—left, right or along the crest. On the left of the ridge it was not possible to give artillery support and the Vickers gun across on Three Pimples Hill would be unable to see them. Along the top the men would be open to fire from the higher enemy position and on the right it looked impossibly steep. Despite this, Pallier decided to take the option on the right—the platoon would advance in single file just below the crest of the ridge.[42]

He had already given his three section commanders their orders and they had their men ready to go. Corporal Ted 'Hi Ho' Silver's 7 Section would lead the advance and thus would be on the right flank for the final attack on the knoll. Pallier's headquarters group, which included Teddy Bear, would follow and take up a central position for the attack. Bluey Whitechurch's 9 Section would advance behind Pallier's group and deploy on the left for the final attack while Corporal Bill Pafrey's 8 Section would bring up the rear and be the reserve section for the attack.[43]

Hi Ho Silver was a tall balding man, looked up to by the men but also a tough bloke who could get wild with a bit of drink. 'I don't know whether I struck a finer leader or braver man than Hi Ho,' Pallier later said. He had deliberately put Silver's section in front and listened as Silver briefed his section. Silver turned to Private Johnny Twine and said, 'Now, Johnny, you stop by my right hand with that Owen gun.' Next he turned to Private Billy Howarth, saying, 'Now you keep on my left arm with that Owen gun, Billy.' Then, 'and don't you bloody well move from there'. Pallier felt that 'the way he said it you knew he meant it'.[44]

Bluey Whitechurch was of average height and whatever hair he had was reddish, hence the nickname.[45] His men had a hasty meal, checked their weapons and ammunition and filled their water bottles from some muddy pools on top of the hill. His section 'formed up with that frightening sensation of danger which now threatened our lives at any moment'. The boom of the artillery, the whine of a shell and the resounding crash as it burst 'echoing and re-echoing over the hills and valleys' signalled that it was time to go.[46]

At 4.50 pm the platoon moved down along the side of the hill through a bit of a washed-out gutter in single file, the men no more than a couple of metres apart. 'That, for me, was the worst part of the whole show,' Private Hugh Norton remarked. 'Just sitting there exposed waiting for the chaps in front to get clear so we could move on.'[47] 'We were down far enough to get as much cover as we could,' Pallier said. 'We couldn't get too far, it got too steep. Hi Ho blazed the trail really,' he added. 'It was his heel marks that we all just about followed . . . You had to climb while digging in your heel. You had a feeling we might get done over before we got far along the ridge,' Pallier recalled. As they progressed along the ridge, however, Pallier began to feel more confident: 'We knew we had a chance.'[48]

•

One of the main reasons that Pallier's men were able to advance unhindered was a single artillery piece down in the valley firing over open sights up onto the Japanese end of the ridge. It was the most forward of two short 25-pounder guns that had been dropped by air at Nadzab on 5 September. These shortened guns were a redesign of the normal 25-pounder and didn't have the same range, accuracy or stability as the original. On this day the range was short but the gun only had nineteen rounds available, fired at one round a minute. 'That gave us 19 minutes to get along, as far as we could,' recalled Pallier. 'Keep moving, keep moving, we've got to use up that support,' Pallier urged his men. 'We used to hear the round whoosh then bang. I reckon it wouldn't be far from us going past.' The men were a bit past halfway when the last of the nineteen rounds was fired. He had counted the shots as had some other men, several of whom yelled out 'There she goes!' Pallier thought, 'What's going to happen now?'[49]

Captain Colin Stirling was standing alongside Mert Lee down below, watching the gun 'jumping all over the place' while Lieutenant Johnny Pearson directed the fire as accurately as he could at a range of 1050 metres.[50] Private Brian Cooke watched as the short black palms known as 'blackboys' that grew across the hillside were thrown into the air as the shells landed, looking so much like bodies.[51] Once the short 25-pounder had finished its role, the 3-inch mortars down in the valley, directed by observers up on Three Pimples Hill, continued to drop rounds onto the ridge. It was the narrowest of targets but at least the mortar shells would help keep the defenders' heads down. Most of the artillery shells and mortar rounds landed in front of the knoll, ensuring that the defenders would feel the effect.[52] From Gerry O'Day's viewpoint on King's Hill, very few of the mortar rounds hit the target, the bombs either falling short or going over.[53] Meanwhile the Vickers gun across on Three Pimples Hill was putting down accurate fire onto the knoll, giving the defenders yet another reason to keep low. 'It was the Vickers machine guns, the 3-inch mortars . . . and the snub nose 25,' Alf Edwards observed. 'They belted the bloody daylights out of them . . . they would be well down in their bloody foxholes.'[54]

Pallier was keen for even more fire support, so dropped three men off with a Bren gun, a 2-inch mortar and an EY grenade launcher at a small knoll halfway along the ridge. Johnny Cobble was on the Bren gun 'to try and pick up these bloody birds on Pallier's Ridge that were sniping back at us,' as Alf Edwards put it. 'Skipper, can I go on the supporting Bren gun?' Cobble had asked Pallier during the briefing on King's Hill. Private Bill Patterson was on the 2-inch mortar and Private Bob Malcolm was the rifle bomber. But now exposed to the Japanese defenders echeloned back along the left-hand side of their knoll, they never had a chance. 'The bloody machine gun got onto them,' Edwards said. 'They never fired a bomb from that 2-inch mortar. They had no hope, they copped the full blast.'[55] Patterson and Cobble were killed but Malcolm, who was lying down between them, was somehow not hit. He got his head to the ground and his tin hat over his arse, as a First World War digger had once recommended to him.[56]

Using his field glasses from back on King's Hill, O'Day could see that the Japanese had little holes dug along the narrow ridge beyond the knoll but it was difficult to pick out targets and his men could give little support without endangering Pallier's men. Conversely O'Day's men were taking fire from the distant knoll. Private Bill O'Dea had been attached as a runner from battalion headquarters and was lying down alongside Gerry O'Day watching Pallier's men move forward when he was shot in the face and killed.[57] A Japanese sniper had picked off Bill O'Dea at about 400 metres range.

•

Pallier had pulled his men up for a quick rest while they dropped off the three men at the intermediate knoll and 'had a couple of minutes deep breathing to catch our wind,' Hugh Norton related. The men gulped down a mouthful of water before moving on again. Further on one of them slipped but two others grabbed him before he tumbled down the slope. 'If he hadn't managed to pull himself up,' Norton said, 'he may have rolled for hundreds of feet to probable death.'[58] 'And then we got right along, pretty well underneath them,' said Pallier. Here the ridge widened out around the base of the Japanese-held knoll, now high above. 'It was such abnormal terrain that you couldn't form up like a normal attack and that's why we went along in single file one after the other. We couldn't even deploy much because we were strung out too much.'[59] For the final attack on the knoll, 'Pallier's idea was to go up, sort of from the right, up the centre and from the left,' Alf Edwards noted.[60]

Now only about 20 metres from the top of the knoll, with a near 45-degree climb up, Pallier yelled out to the men to fix bayonets if they wanted to.[61] Edwards said, 'I'll never forget that. And all you could hear was clang.' Then Pallier said, 'Let's go.'[62]

•

The Vickers gun was still firing onto the knoll, locked onto the tripod to fire along a fixed line with no up or down deviation. The gun was firing a lot closer than laid down in any manuals, just above the advancing men, and to traverse it the gunner just slapped the side of the gun with his hand to move it a degree or so. 'It was very close, you could see the bullets in front hitting the dirt . . . they took a risk; if they hadn't have done it, the

Japs [would have] had the knock on us,' Pallier said. 'That's what Pallier was working on,' Alf Edwards thought. 'His tactic was to get to a point and then he said the supporting fire lifted because we were virtually there . . . He said righto, boom and that was it.'[63] Over on Three Pimples Hill Stan Bisset watched closely as the men began the final climb up and cut off the fire. The Vickers gun crew immediately went to work shifting the gun to the prepared position to the right to cover any enemy troops further back on the ridge.

The men were climbing but it was a real struggle to get up and now a few rifle shots and a machine-gun burst could be heard from above, 'gradually increasing in intensity until it became one continuous roar'.[64] 'When the artillery had pounded the steep part it was soft and so steep you couldn't get a grip,' Pallier remembered, 'You'd never think men would make it.' Johnny Twine couldn't get a foothold in the soil and the strain was taking its toll as he dropped behind Hi Ho Silver. As he slid back he said, 'It's hard, Hi Ho.' Silver turned to him and just said, 'Son, I know it's hard but it's got to be done,' and as he said it he kicked a grenade away that had stuck in the loose soil. 'If that had have gone off in that split second Hi Ho would have lost a leg,' Pallier noted. The grenades were coming down right across the hill. 'There were that many that it seemed they had emptied a sugar bag full of them down the hill.' Another one stuck in the dirt next to Teddy Bear and 'he kicked it away while at the same time giving orders'.[65]

'The Japs began to jabber and an avalanche of grenades rained down on us,' Hugh Norton said. Norton was with 9 Section on the left and recalled how 'Chaps were kicking them out of the way and picking them up and throwing them down the hill.' Norton knew the men were very lucky to suffer so few casualties from them: 'If they had been as good as our own grenades are, half of us would have been killed.'[66] 'You could hear the Japs banging the grenade striker . . . all we could see was the smoke from these bloody grenades,' said Alf Edwards, 'and we were kicking them away so they would roll on further down the hill'. The Australians were also throwing their own grenades up. 'Digger Whitechurch, he was grenade mad,' Edwards declared. 'He would just pull them open, bang and let them go.' Edwards himself 'was always a bit precarious about a 36M . . . I always think that if I throw one of these bloody things I must not miscue or it'll come back at us.'[67] The men in 7 Section copped a few. 'We got some rolling back and they were Mills grenades,' Pallier observed. 'I can tell you, we see the Jap grenades and we weren't half as frightened of them as we were one of our own.' One of the first grenades exploded next to Pallier's left leg. 'When you get hit you don't feel it hit. It's a bit after you feel it, the effects of it.' Pallier was a lot closer to the top before he knew he was wounded. The grenade had splattered him with lots of little pieces, but one bit 'about an inch long' went through the side of his left knee. Teddy Bear was also wounded by a grenade when he was just about at the top but it didn't stop him.[68]

Two big strong men, two determined men, two experienced men, two well-armed men: Hi Ho Silver with his Owen gun and Teddy Bear with his rifle. Bear and Silver crested the knoll about 2 metres ahead of the others in 7 Section. 'Hi Ho had a tougher, harder look, Teddy was young,' Pallier said, 'well, we were all only boys then. He would be the last man in the world, probably you would think . . . to do what had to be done.'[69] Johnny Twine watched as 'Teddy and Hi Ho took off over the top like terriers.' Twine was 5 metres away, just coming over the crest when he saw

Teddy and Hi Ho facing a defender but both with their magazines empty. Twine watched as 'Teddy raced forward, bayoneted the Jap and threw him over his shoulder and away.'[70] As Edwards put it, 'Teddy says "stuff this" and the Nip copped about nine inches of bloody steel.'[71] To Private Harry Norton, Bear was 'like a hay tosser'.[72] It was the enduring image of the battle.

From over on King's Hill, Gerry O'Day watched as Teddy Bear led the others up and then 'in silhouette tossing Japs aside off his bayonet like sheaves of wheat'. Tim Moriarty also watched the unforgettable scene, although reflected that 'Bear normally looked the most peaceful fellow.'[73] Colin Stirling was down in the valley looking through his field glasses. 'It was like a scene from a movie,' was how he remembered it, 'one fellow hoisted a nip on his bayonet and turfed him over a precipitous drop. Then a few more.'[74] Pallier, with a much closer view, disputed some of the more exaggerated descriptions of the action.[75] Bear later told his wife, 'I know I'm in control of myself but I got to a stage when I knew anything could happen,' and told his son-in-law 'I was like a madman'.[76] Bill Russell wrote that Bear 'seemed, except when roused, a great jovial overgrown boy, always wearing the broad smile of one who feels that it is good to be alive'.[77]

As Pallier described it, you couldn't have hesitated. 'I can see the Japs now getting out of their foxholes, putting their bayonets on, couldn't get them on quick enough. If the [men] hadn't have fixed bayonets, if I hadn't have said that, they were dead men, as they'd emptied their magazines fighting up the hill.'[78] Bear reloaded and kept moving forward. Then an enemy machine gunner hit him in the knee. Bear told the journalist Andrew Butcher. 'I kept going but then he got me in the back. It felt as if someone had kicked me.'[79] Bear, who could hardly move, called out 'They're onto me with a machine gun!' Pallier called out for Bear to roll his way to get out of the line of fire. 'And he rolled, he couldn't crawl,' Pallier recalled. It probably saved his life and Bear would later name his son 'Noel' in gratitude.[80]

•

Only half of 7 Section were up on the knoll when Bluey White-church's men stormed in from the left and linked up with 7 Section.[81] 'The poor bastards, they got the shock of their life,' Alf Edwards reckoned, 'when they seen about 29 mad bloody Australians running over the top with bayonets fixed and screaming, any wonder they took off . . . what a show.'[82] We 'opened fire on their heads as they bobbed up above their fox-holes,' remembered Whitechurch. 'One of our men gave a shrill bloodcurdling yell that startled even us.'[83] 'The yell took us by surprise and inspired us,' said Hugh Norton. The men took up the yell and 'got stuck into the Nips.' One defender stood up in his foxhole and all who saw him opened up and Norton watched 'his tin hat jump up in the air at the impact of the bullets against his body'.[84]

Edwards let out 'a great godly bloody scream' as he went over the top right behind Whitechurch. 'I think it was more bloody fear than anything else,' he said. Edwards, who was the number two on Private Noel Sanderson's Bren gun, 'could see these Nips popping their heads out of bloody foxholes' but the Bren gun fire was falling short. Sanderson 'was a very big bloke . . . a very excited bugger . . . inclined to get very nervous,' Edwards added, and he kept on telling him to 'lift the gun, for Christ's sake, lift it up'. At the same time Edwards knelt and fired his rifle and 'saw one Nip's hat flying'. Then as he made his way along the narrow ridge looking for his section leader he was shot. 'Next minute, bang; well, it was like a bloody horse. Some Nip took a bloody pot-shot at me. I went arse over head.' Edwards slid down the hill with the bayonet of his rifle against his neck, the loaded rifle pointed at his head. He quickly moved the gun and took a look at the wound in his right arm where an inch of bone had been taken out by the enemy round. Lance Corporal Claude Lamport came down to dress the wound and then another two arrived, probably glad to get off the ridge. Then Hi Ho Silver arrived up top. 'Come on you bloody pair, get yourself up here!' he called out. 'It doesn't need three of you to look after him.'[85]

Back up top Private Gordon 'Happy' Davies 'appeared from nowhere' and told Pallier 'I think Pafrey's been hit.' Pallier told Davies to get Lofty Back to take over Pafrey's reserve section and to join the attack. He then heard Lofty shouting out 'Come on, come on!' to his men from over on the left. 'He drew attention to himself,' Pallier remarked. 'He was sort of out in front, urging them on,' an obvious target. A burst of machine-gun fire nearly cut him in half; the order had cost him his life.[86]

The enemy position was on a rounded knoll at the end of the razorback approach, and amid the din of the battle Pallier could hear his men yelling out as they charged forward. 'We'll get you bastards!' they called and 'We'll make you sorry!' and such. There were 'Japs sitting in foxholes, backs to us, throwing grenades over their shoulders,' Pallier saw. 'Round on the right of the pimple the boys were into them properly,' Hugh Norton said. Some of the defenders 'couldn't face the ferocity of our onslaught and rather than stay and take it jumped over the 150-foot cliff behind them to their doom . . . We had 'em licked.' Watching from down below, Alan Avery saw about ten defenders just run over the cliff, probably not knowing how steep it was. Thirty Japanese defenders died in the attack.[87]

Some defenders stayed to fight and continued to take a toll, with Pallier shot in the groin. 'The wound's in the front; where they go in wasn't too bad, it's where they come out,' Pallier noted. He had also been hit by another grenade but he still had a job to do. Having secured the knoll, he was concerned that the Japanese may counterattack and needed the weapon pits clear of the dead former occupants. 'Right, throw them out of the foxholes,' he ordered, and his men just grabbed the bodies by the shoulders and rolled them off the knoll. 'Those bodies rolling down, it was a funny sound,' Pallier remarked. With a lull in the battle, the men wanted a drink but most of their water bottles were empty. Their tongues were thick from thirst, so they resorted to drinking from the enemy water bottles.[88]

Alf Edwards had got to his feet and had made his way up to the top of the ridge. 'Bill Pafrey was up there, lying on his belly, shot through the legs,' Edwards saw, and he asked him how he was. 'Bloody shocking,' Pafrey replied. 'Look mate, I can't do anything for you, I've got a busted wing,' Edwards told Pafrey as he made his way across to Pallier. 'Permission to go ashore, sir?' Edwards asked him. 'Yes, Alf,' he replied, 'a job well done son . . . you made a name for the platoon'. Edwards then asked if he had 'any message for the crowd back on Kings Hill' and Pallier said to get some reinforcements across in case there was a counterattack.

Edwards headed back along the ridge to King's Hill with a wounded Teddy Bear behind him. 'Keep going, keep going,' Bear told Alf. At the knoll halfway back, Edwards found Bobby Malcolm 'as white as a bloody ghost'. When Edwards asked what had happened, Malcolm just indicated his two dead companions nearby. 'There they are,' was all he said. When Edwards got to King's Hill, he told Gerry O'Day, 'Mister Pallier said to get some reinforcements on that ridge as quick as you like.'[89] O'Day sent a platoon forward to relieve Pallier and to hold the position but there would be no enemy counterattack. When O'Day got back to headquarters that night he could see that Bill Landale was still distraught over being replaced as battalion commander; 'the situation had overcome him'. An unperturbed Mert Lee was getting on with the job.[90]

The first-aid people on King's Hill grabbed hold of Edwards and put a bayonet along one side of his fractured arm and bound it to the scabbard on the other side as a splint. Then they gave him a shot of morphine. The only way Edwards could then get down King's Hill was to slide down on his backside. Halfway down he came across some men who were on their way up with stretchers. 'No, no, leave him alone, he'll be alright,' one of them said. 'Come on, we've got to keep going, we've got to get up there.' The stretcher bearers had to bring back the dead and also Pallier and Pafrey, both unable to walk.[91] Pallier was relieved to get off the ridge: 'Your reaction is, well, you're wounded, you know you're out of it for a while. That's probably a bit of relief to tell you the truth.' Pallier was sent to the dressing station at Dumpu and put up on a small table. The ground was muddy with only a tent fly for cover, two Tilley lamps for lighting and primus stoves to boil the water. There were two doctors but it was 1.00 am the next day before they got to Pallier.[92]

Some months later Jack Bishop dropped by to see Pallier at the hospital. By reopening the supply line through to Bishop's battalion, Pallier's action had enabled the 2/27th to hold its ground in the following days. Pallier became the 2/14th Battalion intelligence officer and later was transferred to General Thomas Blamey's staff. He worked there for a month and then came back to the 2/14th. It was his home.[93] Alf Edwards ended up in a bed next to Teddy Bear in the 2/5th General Hospital in Port Moresby. 'He always took it so well,' Edwards said of Bear. 'That's the part that got me: he always had that big smile on his face.' With Edwards' arm in plaster, Bear used to write letters for him. 'I used to dictate them,' Edwards remembered, and 'we used to play what they call a game of cricket with cards. He was a good companion.'[94]

Both men would later rejoin the 2/14th, Bear as a newly commissioned lieutenant. 'The young uns, the reos, that was our baptism of fire, that one,' Edwards reckoned. 'After that we became fully fledged, accepted members of the platoon, you know, by the oldies.'[95] Noel Pallier later wrote to Bear after his sergeant was awarded a Distinguished Conduct Medal for his bravery on what would now be known as Pallier's Hill. Silver and Whitechurch had also been decorated. 'I'm damn proud to have been given the opportunity of leading such gallant men as Hi Ho, Blue & yourself & the rest of 9 [Platoon],' Pallier wrote to Bear.[96]

Chapter 5

'WE'D OUTFOUGHT THEM THERE'

The Japanese occupation of Pallier's Hill on the morning of 11 October had major ramifications for the 2/27th Battalion. That morning Private Frank Ranger was on his way back to the battalion with other men from 11 Platoon including Lieutenant Kel Crocker. They were escorting a 2/27th supply train heading for Guy's Post ascending the ridge to cross the saddle and go down to the Faria River when the Japanese on Pallier's Hill began firing on the native carriers. Fortunately none of them was hit but they dropped their loads and took to the bush. But as Private Mal Keefer came back down the track from the forward section he was shot in the groin, fracturing his pelvis. 'Quick Charlie, Mal's been hit,' Sergeant 'Lappy' Lapthorne called out to Sergeant Charlie Lofberg who treated Keefer, but, unable to move him, covered him with bushes to try to keep him safe. The group of about a dozen men stayed under cover among the scrub throughout the day and into the night, unsure of what had happened up on the ridge until the following morning. By then the native carriers had returned and it was only then that the men sheltering in the gorge knew the Japanese had been cleared from the ridge.[1]

Meanwhile Jack Bishop was reinforcing the key point at the end of Trevor's Ridge, soon to be named Johns' Knoll. When Bob Johns' platoon reached Trevor's Ridge on the morning of 11 October it was immediately sent forward to take over positions on the knoll so that B Company could move further east to cut further into the enemy supply line. 'The key position in the centre, which one of the companies had vacated, they put my platoon there,' Johns said.[2]

Johns' Knoll was the highest point on Trevor's Ridge and 'the peak of the knoll and much of the surrounding ground was covered in grass only,' Johns observed, 'with the tree line starting down the slope a bit.' Only six men could occupy the peak of the knoll and Johns had Corporal 'Paddy' Carey's section dig in there. Some foxholes and a slit trench had already been dug but Johns' men dug them deeper. The soil on the knoll was a heavy clay consistency so weapon pits could be dug to a good depth.[3]

At 3.00 pm Trevor's Ridge came under close-range mountain gun fire from further up the Faria Valley. It was a new experience for Jack Reddin as 'you normally expect to get some sort of warning' so you can take cover.[4] For Bob Johns it was similar to being under fire from the French 75 mm guns in Syria where 'the shell arrives at its target and explodes before the warning whine of its approach is heard' but Johns had no casualties in his platoon. It was a wet and uncomfortable night during which movement could be heard from the low ground to the east of the knoll.[5]

•

At first light all of Johns' men were awake and alert. An early morning patrol had run into some Japanese troops preparing to attack, which provided some measure of warning.[6] Two Japanese mountain guns opened fire at Trevor's Ridge at 11.45 am, soon joined by heavy machine guns and mortars. Clive Edwards sheltered on the southern side of the ridge beneath the crest. 'The game was on and Tojo opened up with 75 mm [and] about four woodpeckers [machine guns] in different positions and launched strong attacks upon our positions further up the hill and across his track,' he wrote. 'The worst news is that the Japs have got a woodpecker installed on Plateau Post which can make things nasty for us here.'[7] Plateau Post was on the lower slopes of Shaggy Ridge above the Faria River and a machine gun there could deliver enfilade fire along Trevor's Ridge.

On Johns' Knoll the mountain-gun fire came from the west, the mortar fire from the east and the fire of two Juki machine guns from the north. As Johns later noted, because the artillery was firing from the west and the Japanese infantry was gathering to the east to attack the knoll, any shells that went over Johns' Knoll, and that was most of them, 'went in amongst the Japanese. So they probably got more casualties out of their artillery than we did.'[8] Despite that, one weapon pit down the slope from Johns took a direct hit from the barrage and one of his men was killed. Then the support fire stopped and the attack came in from the east. 'There appeared to be thousands of them,' Johns wrote, 'They had little cover and we shot them down in droves.'[9]

Paddy Carey's section did most of the damage and forced the attackers to withdraw. The attacks continued throughout the day and during one of them the Bren gunner down the slope to the left of Johns suddenly stood up and cried out 'I'm hit!'

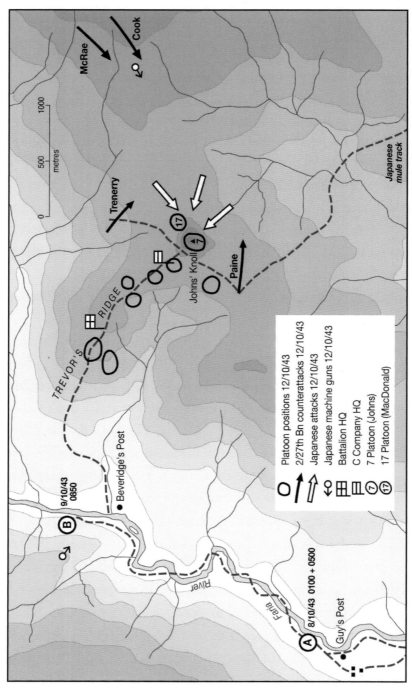

Map 6: Johns' Knoll, 12 October 1943 (Keith Mitchell)

Johns watched as he 'promptly was hit again and dropped'. Johns' batman, Ron Barnes, leapt from his own pit and, braving the enemy fire, ran down to retrieve the Bren gun, then returned for the spare ammunition. He later went out to get two cans of water for the parched men and one of the cans was leaking from bullet holes when he returned.[10]

Armed with his Owen gun, Carey remained on the peak of the knoll all day, right on the edge where it dropped off. He was in prime position to knock over any enemy attackers tackling what was a pretty severe slope. As Bob Johns observed, 'roll a grenade down there and the numbers they had, it had to explode amongst Japanese'.[11] Private Ray Fisher, who was next to Carey at the top of the knoll, watched the Japanese skilfully fire their knee mortars to explode the rounds in the air over the Australian positions. Fisher had laid out his equipment in front of him on the parapet of the trench and this had stopped one round coming in, but another exploded in the air above, catching him unawares. He was hit by the blast which riddled his clothing and smashed his rifle but only left him shaken and able to remain on duty ferrying vital ammunition forward.[12]

At midday Jack Bishop ordered 17 Platoon to move up to reinforce Johns by occupying the weapon pits vacated by casualties. 'Bob Johns' platoon got a bit of a hiding,' Private Keith Addison said, 'there were five or six empty holes'. Addison and Private Reg Hillier occupied back-to-back positions at the front of the knoll, each protecting the other with the body of the former occupant between them. Addison tried to use the dead man's Bren gun but it had been hit in the breech and did not work. Both men kept their heads down as a Juki machine gun cut a gutter across the top of the knoll with a tightly grouped stream of bullets.[13]

Addison could look down and see the Japanese slowly climbing up the slope on all fours carrying their rifles. They were trying to sneak up on the knoll but he could spot them with their long rifles with attached bayonets moving through the scrub. Addison would crouch down out of sight only 5 to 6 metres away before rising up on his knees to fire short bursts from his Owen gun at them. The gun was particularly effective at such short range and he preferred it to the Bren as you could fire it from the shoulder. As the attackers were knocked over backwards to roll back down the hill, Addison would quickly duck back down into his weapon pit.[14]

Holding back the constant attacks soon left the men on Johns' Knoll short of ammunition. 'They're running short of ammo on the right!' Reg Hillier called out. So when it went a bit quiet for a while the men would go around to any vacant weapon pits to recover any unused ammunition.[15] After the failure of the supply train to get through on the previous day, ammunition reserves were gone and the other companies on Trevor's Ridge had to give up all but a basic supply of ammunition to feed the demand. At 1.05 pm this ammunition was sent up to Johns' Knoll.

At 1.20 pm the mortar sergeant Sergeant George Eddy was also sent forward. He could see that the attackers were not far from Johns' Knoll and that he would have to shorten the mortar range to something that was 'not practicable, not taught, you couldn't do it'.[16] Although the enemy was too close to fire a 3-inch mortar, the mortar round could still be used in a grenade-type role after initiating the primary charge by banging the base of the round on the ground. Then when dropped over the edge of the ridge onto enemy troops some 6 metres away, the secondary charge would be initiated and the round would explode.[17] The soldiers who were throwing the rounds 'of course took a chance and so far as

I know they did not have any duds and the Japanese got their full benefit of the round,' Lieutenant Bob Clampett said. The twelve mortar rounds were very effective.[18]

At 1.35 pm Johns reported that his losses were heavy and that the Japanese were within 10 metres of the knoll. Half an hour later, Johns said that the situation was now critical and that he was considering withdrawal. Jack Bishop now realised that defending Johns' Knoll was not enough, he had to take the initiative. He ordered Lieutenant Bob Paine's 14 Platoon to attack on the right flank to cut the Japanese supply line and 'cause as much havoc as possible' and then ordered Lieutenant Rex Trenerry's 16 Platoon to do the same on the left flank. Paine's platoon moved out with Corporal Ron Box's section in the lead. The men killed one enemy soldier before the section came under sniper fire as it moved further around the knoll. Having cleared two ridges, Paine pulled his platoon back only to be immediately sent out again by Bishop. He told Paine that the platoon was to stay out all night if necessary. 'The boys took a very dim view of this,' one of Paine's men noted, a view not improved when it started raining as the men moved out along the side of the razorback. The Japanese opened up with light machine-gun fire and rolled grenades down onto them, wounding Ron Box and two others.[19]

On the left flank Trenerry's platoon reached the main track about 150 metres to the rear of the Japanese attackers at 4.00 pm. Six or seven groups of Japanese soldiers were spotted preparing to attack Johns' Knoll, and after Trenerry's men threw grenades among them they 'dispersed very quickly and ran into our own fire'. Trenerry then took five men down the track towards Johns' Knoll while another five men cleared the track the other way. Firing his Bren gun from the hip, Dave Blacker killed five while

Private Frank May took care of another four as they advanced towards Johns' Knoll. Up ahead the track veered around a big tree on a rise, which Private Wally Agett moved around with May close behind. As Agett cleared the tree an enemy light machine gun opened up from a dip on the other side of the rise, killing Agett who had just returned from leave to see his newborn baby in South Australia. May was also killed. May was Rocky Chellew's best mate but Rocky could do nothing for him as the enemy fire pinned the men down. He screamed back for the Bren gun to be brought up but everyone was staying under cover.[20]

Earlier Johns had told Bishop that he could hold if the ammunition was kept up and half an hour later added that the shortage may mean 'we couldn't possibly hold on much longer'. Fortunately Johns' casualties were still low and most of the enemy machine-gun fire was going over the top of the knoll. Low on small-arms ammunition, Johns' men used a 2-inch mortar and rifle grenades to ease the pressure as the attacks kept coming.[21] As Jack Reddin later recalled, 'very rarely is a battle waged on such a small section of our perimeter and the rest of us were all busily gathering ammunition from the rest of the companies and carting it up to keep Bob and the rest of his men well equipped'.[22]

The men on the knoll now realised that other Australians were counterattacking the Japanese but were not sure who they were.[23] Keith Addison could hear Paine's men moving out to the right and provided some covering fire for them down the valley.[24] About 7.00 pm Paine went forward, called out to Johns and headed his way. 'As we moved along the razorback everyone was very cold . . . and as it had been raining everyone was wet through and shivering,' one of Paine's men noted. During the sweep, Paine's platoon had killed nineteen enemy troops and no doubt contributed to the Japanese calling off the assault. The track was patrolled until 6.30 pm, when Trenerry met up with Paine before both platoons moved back to Trevor's Ridge. Trenerry's platoon had also killed 24 enemy troops and wounded many others, both platoons considerably easing the pressure on Johns' Knoll.[25]

•

Jack Bishop was also concerned about what Captain Seymour Toms' B Company was doing out to the east of Johns' Knoll as the phone line had been cut and Bishop did not want to leave the company 'out in the blue'. Two men were sent out to contact Toms and tell him to counterattack towards Johns' Knoll with two platoons while leaving one on the high feature he now occupied. Private Jack McManus and Lance Corporal Bert Scott went out on the left flank but had a tough climb up through the scrub and hadn't reached B Company before dark. They took shelter in the bush and heard enemy troops moving past during the night before finding the signal wire the next morning and following it to the summit of the ridge only to find that B Company had gone.[26]

The day of the Johns' Knoll attack had begun quietly for B Company. 'It was a glorious morning but things were quiet,' Lieutenant Tom Cook wrote. Then the phone line went dead and firing broke out down at Trevor's Ridge which continued all morning. Seymour Toms sent two sections out under Lieutenant Don McRae to find the line break, only to discover that the ridge to the west was now occupied by the enemy. McRae patched into the signal line and called back to Toms who sent Cook's platoon down to help. The Japanese on the ridge had seen McRae's men so turned their Juki machine gun around to face them. Cook sent sections left and right and it was Corporal 'Lum' Yandell's section on the right that got around to knock out the woodpecker. At least twenty enemy troops were killed on that first knoll. 'The gun was well dug in and there was a pile of dead round the gun,' Cook said. Down on Trevor's Ridge at 6.00 pm, Jack Bishop saw that 'Fire from the woodpeckers abruptly ceased.'[27]

Cook and McRae's men continued another 100 metres along the ridge until held up by three light machine guns in thick scrub. 'These opened up with some of the heaviest fire we've ever encountered,' Cook commented. Two men were killed and four wounded. 'We didn't know they were there, walked straight into it, killed in action like that,' Private Harry Ashton said.[28] It was now getting dark so a perimeter defence was established around the wounded men. Yandell and two other men then made their way through enemy lines to battalion headquarters at Trevor's Ridge to get help. They arrived at 7.45 pm and two hours later they returned with an aid man who had morphine for the wounded. At 5.30 am the next morning the rest of B Company joined them and the company headed back to the battalion.[29]

Expecting a Japanese attack against Trevor's Ridge, the 13 Platoon sergeant Cyril Johns had repositioned his men closer to the crest that day. 'We dug in, and I'm under a tree and I'm right up on the brow of the hill on the lee side,' Private 'Scotty' Innes recalled. After the Japanese realised their attack on Johns' Knoll had failed, the mountain guns opened up against Trevor's Ridge at 6.00 pm. 'Right on bloody six o'clock,' Innes noted, 'they must have lowered the sights or raised the muzzle of the gun or something'. A shell hit the top of the tree Innes was under. 'I heard the boom of the gun before the bloody shell hit and I dropped.' Corporal Max Ellis 'was pretty bad hit' with most of his thigh taken off and an arm wound. Private Jackie Spencer and Cyril Johns were also wounded. It was only when Innes went to help Cyril Johns that he realised how badly he had been wounded himself; his pants had been split from the crutch right down his left leg. A shell fragment 'took the kneecap and just sliced it right off. I don't know where me bloody boots went to.' Innes put on a shell dressing and then, using his rifle as a crutch, 'walked on that bloody leg for about a hundred yards' to the aid post. There were at least a dozen men already there and when he was asked what happened he said, 'Oh, bloody sniper got me . . . It was a seventy-five millimetre.'[30]

The attacks on Johns' Knoll had been going on all day with no respite and about three times it looked as if the position would be lost. But as Merv Weston wrote of Bob Johns, 'In the scorching steamy heat of that kunai-crested knoll he held on.'[31]

•

At 5.00 pm Bishop had sent a message back that he needed some native carriers sent forward with ammunition, no matter how late. So when Kel Crocker arrived at Guy's Post with the supply train at 5.30 pm he was told to press on to the battalion that night. It was pitch black and a hell of a job, having to move up the river in the dark and then crawl to the ridge in the mud, but Croker and his carriers kept going.[32] Up at Trevor's Ridge Clive Edwards observed that 'our ammo is dangerously low though a train is due in tonight—will it get here?'[33] There were 32 river crossings for the carrier line on the way up to the front as they followed the rising Faria River and the men had to fasten themselves together to stop being washed away into the dark.[34] The supply train arrived at 1.30 am the next day. 'About 300 of them deserved a medal,' Jack Reddin reflected. 'If you ever want to do a scary thing you'll travel that jungle in the middle of the night and across those rivers and yet that patrol of carriers reached our unit with vital ammunition and supplies which were there for us at first light if there had been another attack . . . That was a mammoth task.'[35]

Still full of adrenaline from the battle, the men up on Johns' Knoll stayed awake all night listening to the Japanese carrying out their wounded and burying their dead. Keith Addison remembered the sound of a dove cooing and took it as a sign that the enemy had gone. At 5.30 am the men from B Company came in between Reg Hillier and Addison on the north-east end of the knoll. Addison watched as they 'came up the long spur at dawn' but he was also wary. 'The Nips used to sometimes latch onto the end of a patrol and follow them in,' he wrote. So after the last man arrived Addison had the forward scout ensure they were all B Company men.[36]

In the morning a patrol went down to check the Japanese lines. At 9.40 am a badly wounded enemy soldier was brought in on a stretcher but died two hours later; another soldier was captured while trying to bury one of his mates. He had a broken leg and had been unable to flee. Addison saw the two prisoners come in and put a shell dressing on the leg of one, using a knife to cut his trousers. He then gave him water from an empty tin, not from his water bottle.[37] The prisoner who survived was Private Tsutomu Eigashira from 9 Company of the III/78th Battalion. The rest of his unit had only left a few minutes before he was captured.[38] About 150 Japanese were buried after the battle but this included 22 graves that the Japanese had dug and which may have contained multiple burials. 'We killed more of the enemy there than we killed anywhere else in any of our campaigns,' Johns said. 'We certainly had our revenge for those of our battalion that were killed at places like Gona.' The 2/27th had seven men killed and 28 wounded in the battle.[39]

The Japanese could ill afford the losses they had suffered. The day before the battle some of the 78th Regiment units had been sent to the north coast, further weakening the already under-strength regiment. Four infantry companies, a machine-gun company and two mountain guns were used in the operation against Johns' Knoll and many valuable men, weapons and ammunition had been lost.[40]

Jack Reddin later noted that the battle had been won by very good tactics from Jack Bishop and 'great courage by Bobby Johns' platoon'. Johns was the youngest officer in the unit but had acted like the oldest.[41] The young platoon commander felt elated after the battle, conscious of the fact that his platoon had withstood many attacks and 'had had some sort of victory, pyrrhic though it seemed at the time'. The platoon was given the honour of leading the way down the Faria River back to Guy's Post after the 2/27th was relieved two days later. 'The Japs didn't attack again,' Johns commented, 'We'd held . . . We'd outfought them there.' Back at Guy's Post, Johns went down with scrub typhus and 'that was the end of the campaign for me'.[42]

Chapter 6

'THE BRIG WANTS THAT HILL TONIGHT, MAC'

While the 21st Brigade battled its way into the Finisterres, Brigadier Ken Eather's 25th Brigade was also moving out of the Ramu Valley into the foothills around the Surinam River further east. Eather's Brigade had had a key role in the capture of Lae on 16 September and the three battalions were still recovering from that operation when they began the Ramu Valley campaign. That was more the case with the 2/33rd Battalion, which had suffered 149 casualties in a tragic air accident on 7 September.[1] Following a short rest after Lae, the battalion had flown up the Markham Valley to Kaiapit on 28 September and by 1 October had moved up the valley to Sagerak and then to Kaigulin on 5 October.

On 9 October forward elements of the 2/33rd located enemy positions dug in on a razor-edged spur overlooking the Ramu Valley known as Feature 4100. After a hot, tiring march up the valley, the rest of the battalion had reached the edge of the valley below the dominating spur by mid-afternoon on 10 October. Above them on the spur they could count some 82 Japanese observers, all of whom 'were gazing down into the valley like sightseers one sees on the lookouts at Katoomba,' Sergeant Bill Crooks wrote. They appeared to be dancing up and down on top of the hill and could be heard shouting out.[2]

It was late in the afternoon when the battalion commander, Lieutenant Colonel Tom Cotton, informed brigade headquarters that he had made his dispositions for the night and would move again at daylight the next day. However, Brigadier Eather did not want to wait and ordered the Japanese position to be attacked immediately. Cotton passed the message on to the commander of B Company, Major Dave MacDougal. 'The Brig wants that hill tonight, Mac,' Cotton told him.[3]

MacDougal had already had an extraordinary war. Sent to Malaya with the 8th Division in January 1941, some months later he was asked if he 'wanted to volunteer for a special job'. Along with another officer and 45 men MacDougal was sent to northern Burma to be trained by British commandos in guerrilla operations. They would become part of 'Churchill's butchers', as Tokyo Rose later christened them, operating with Chiang Kai-shek after he had appealed to Winston Churchill for help against the Japanese incursions into China. In January 1942 MacDougal had headed north on the Burma Road and across the Himalayas into China. Promoted to acting lieutenant colonel at the young age of 23 and sent to Guilin, he trained what was known as a 'Surprising Battalion' in the art of guerrilla warfare. In June 1942 his cadre was transferred to the border region of western China near Changsha, a place he remembered as 'Full of malaria, and dysentery, and everything else . . . And we couldn't get the Chinese to do anything.' MacDougal added that 'We were living . . . off the land.' At one stage only eleven of his 40 commandos were fit for service and all were 'fairly close to walking skeletons'. Chiang Kai-shek's soldiers 'were as frustrated and as sick as we were'. He flew to Delhi to meet with Commander-In-Chief India, General Archibald Wavell, who ordered the force be withdrawn after 'a disastrous sort of effort'. Wavell asked MacDougal if he would like a job with Colonel Orde Wingate's Chindits in Burma but MacDougal's response was, 'No sir, I want to get back to a regular battalion.'[4]

MacDougal returned to Australia, got married and took up a training role at the jungle warfare school at Canungra before being given command of B Company in the 2/33rd. After losing one of his three platoons in the Liberator crash at Port Moresby, his company had fought its way down the Markham Road and led the way into Lae. He had then worked his men very hard to ensure they would retain their battle discipline. After flying into Kaiapit, MacDougal had led the company on 'a hot and sweaty march' up the Ramu Valley and he now faced the imposing task of capturing Feature 4100.[5]

MacDougal's men were getting some much-needed rest from the day's march when they were suddenly told 'Get ready to move. Leave your blanket rolls, you won't need them.' Officers were a scarce commodity in the 2/33rd at this stage, MacDougal and the recently commissioned Lieutenant Ray Nielson being the only ones in the company. 'So 60 of us,' MacDougal wrote, 'with one Lieutenant, one Sergeant, and one Corporal as Platoon Command-ers headed up that 4100 hill.' Leaving their packs behind, the men began climbing at 5.00 pm along a jungle-covered gully up the side of the hill. It was the only cover available and went almost to the peak. The climb was slow through deep mud and thick rainforest, and they were at times on all fours until they reached the kunai grass near the top. There the men, who were all 'heaving, sweating and almost exhausted' from the climb, rested. 'There wasn't one sentry on . . . everyone went to sleep. They just dropped in their tracks.' Most of their water was also gone.[6]

About an hour and a half later MacDougal woke Nielson and they did a reconnaissance in the fading light. Though all the kunai grass had been burned off to black stubble on the slopes below the summit to create a cleared field of fire, Nielson had found a sheltered approach behind a grass-covered spur that ran to the summit. As soon as the signal wire was connected, Cotton was on the line. 'Where have you bloody well been?' he asked. When MacDougal told him they had been asleep, Cotton 'blew his gasket' before explaining that he had machine guns lined up to provide covering fire. MacDougal said he would go in without support. 'They won't know what hit them,' he told his commander. It would be the battalion's only night attack of the war in New Guinea.[7]

The attack went in at 9.00 pm with two platoons forward and the third holding a firm base behind. MacDougal positioned himself and two runners between the two forward platoons. 'We crawled out into the open, and we went up that slope, which was more than 45 degrees—it was nearly vertical.' The men could hear the Japanese talking and smell their cooking fires but as soon as they began the frenetic climb up the near-vertical slope below the summit, the defenders opened fire and grenades came tumbling down. 'Fortunately,' MacDougal said, 'the grenades just bounded down the hill, and burst behind us'. As the forward sections went to ground MacDougal and Nielson yelled out,

'Move, move in, don't hesitate! . . . Fresh mags on, fix bayonets, 11 Platoon, charge!' Nielson ordered his men as he threw two of his own grenades over the crest and led the way up.[8]

Private John McLaughlin was one of the first up with his Bren gun and managed to silence an enemy light machine gun. Nielson watched as McLaughlin 'balanced himself leaning against the side of the hill and blew the Jap's head off from a few feet away'. McLaughlin said he 'saw the Jap's helmet bounce six feet in the air with his head still in it'. MacDougal and Nielson continued to drive the men on. 'In, in!' they yelled as the two platoons moved over the crest and drove the defenders back, leaving six light machine guns behind. In front of the weapon pits the defenders had dug little trenches full of grenades with some twenty in each, most of which the startled defenders had never thrown.[9]

MacDougal then fired off a red and white flare from his Verey pistol to indicate the position had been taken. Meanwhile a Japanese machine gun opened fire from further back on the ridge and Corporal Dave Green was badly wounded in the stomach. 'He went out chasing the Japs, which was meritorious,' MacDougal commented, 'and he got caught in the crossfire somewhere.' At 10.00 pm MacDougal phoned headquarters requesting help for Green and the adjutant asked, 'How badly is he hit?' MacDougal replied 'He's really pretty bad' and asked 'can John Follent come up?' Captain Follent, who was the medical officer, began the climb up with some stretcher bearers while MacDougal formed a perimeter and prepared for a counterattack that never came. The rain certainly did come, filling the weapon pits and making it a miserable night.[10]

After a difficult climb in the dark, Follent and the stretcher bearers did not arrive until 6.00 am and two hours later began the descent with Green but he would die on the way down.[11] The loss was felt keenly by MacDougal because Green had saved his life during the advance on Lae. It was 'a really sobering moment for us all at the time of our triumph,' MacDougal later reflected. That morning MacDougal lined up the six captured enemy light machine guns with their own Brens and opened fire on another group of enemy troops about a kilometre away on the side of the spur. 'We had a pot shot at them,' said MacDougal. 'No one dropped, but they scattered very quickly.' Following the successful attack the 4100 Feature was renamed MacDougal's Hill.[12]

The Japanese had dug some 40 weapon pits on the feature, most facing south and west but MacDougal had sent his men up the near vertical eastern lip of the crest. Tom Cotton was pleased, telling MacDougal, 'That was great, Dave, the brigadier is very pleased. It's nearly worth a DSO.'[13]

•

Soon after dawn on the morning of 12 October two shots rang out over the 18 Platoon positions among the foothills north-east of MacDougal's Hill. The first bullet hit Private Frank Cassidy in the head, the bullet parting his scalp and opening the skull directly above the middle of his eyes but only wounding him. The other bullet hit the barrel of Corporal 'Chesty' Barrett's Bren gun, 'rendering it useless'. The men dug deeper holes and keen eyes looked to the shoulder of timber ahead searching for the sniper but the shots kept coming, fifteen in all, hitting three hats, two rifles and a walkie-talkie but without causing any more casualties. When Bill Crooks and Private Graham McGhie crawled up the slope with a 2-inch mortar to bring fire down onto the tree line, a bullet hit McGhie's bomb holder and another took the heel off Crooks' boot. 'Two to one, Tojo!' the other men yelled out. Soon thereafter came a burst of fire from only 50 metres away, from below the knoll and much closer than the tree line. A camouflaged trapdoor then suddenly opened and the bold Japanese sniper crawled out and ran for the timber. Every member of 18 Platoon opened up on the fleeing figure as the men shouted out their deadly encouragement. 'Cop this, Tojo', 'Go you beauty—you'll never make it' and 'How's this for size, you bastard?' The sniper scampered to the safety of the tree line.[14]

Following the capture of MacDougal's Hill, Cotton felt the battalion had got as far as it could go into the foothills. However, Eather disagreed and supported a further move. Don Company, as good as wiped out following the Port Moresby air crash, would get the job. The company had been rebuilt at Lae around a company from the 2/2nd Pioneer Battalion and 'they became our new Don Company,' as Dave MacDougal noted.[15] Captain George Connor was the company commander.[16]

On 13 October Connor's company was briefed about an attack north-east of MacDougal's Hill and Flight Lieutenant Ian Olorenshaw had been attached from the RAAF to direct the air support.[17] Using sapling poles, a line of half towels gathered from the men was pushed out 20 metres in front of the Australian positions to mark the front line for the supporting aircraft. At 9.00 am two RAAF Boomerangs, nicknamed Bib and Bub, arrived overhead and reported that the enemy position was about 900 metres deep around a series of well-defended bare knolls.[18] Just after 9.00 am twelve USAAF Kittyhawks approached in a line from the south-east over the Australian lines at a height of about 15 metres and over a 20-minute period each aircraft made three strafing runs. 'Hot .50-calibre expended cartridges came tumbling down' on the Australians who dived back into their weapon pits and covered themselves with groundsheets to avoid the burning brass. However, most of the Kittyhawks had fired too late and those enemy weapon pits on the nearer half of the ridge went untouched. Observing from up above, the Boomerangs reported the enemy had run for cover and Eather could hear the wireless chatter, so told the battalion commander, 'You've got them on the run, Cotton.'[19] 'Ah, we're just going to walk on to it,' Bill Crooks thought.[20]

At 9.55 am the men from Lieutenant Dave Tudehope's 16 Platoon moved crab-like along the left side of the ridge in extended order, hidden in defilade until they reached the knoll. They then switched across to the right flank as the Vickers and Bren gun support fire was 'just clearing our heads', as Tudehope observed. The platoon sergeant Johnny Beck could be heard calling out, 'Spread out 16, spread out, don't bunch' but the terrain forced them together. Then about eight or nine Japanese defenders appeared over the top of the knoll, yelled out, fired a quick volley and threw a 'shower of grenades' down onto the attackers who were still scrambling up on their hands and knees. 'The hill was like a wall,' Dave Tudehope remembered, and there was no easy way up. Those watching from further back saw the attack 'stagger, stop, and then saw the falling, rolling bodies of the men of D Company—and then there was nothing more to see'. Dave MacDougal, who could see the men 'silhouetted coming up the slope against sky', was amazed 'to see a line of men get to the top of the ridge and gradually go off one at a time'.[21]

We 'got almost to the top and I got my Bren guns firing over the hill, and then all hell burst loose with grenades,' Tudehope said. 'You could see them going by you with the orange flame going out of the tail.' When the defenders ran out of grenades they 'started to throw clods of earth and stones' and Tudehope was wounded. Two men made the crest of the knoll, Private Laurie Jones and Private Gordon Burton, the latter 'kneeling there calmly and picking them off,' Tudehope recalled.[22] Jones and Burton remained on top for 10 minutes before the call came from Captain Connor: '16 Platoon, gather up your wounded and get back out of it.' Only nine men from Tudehope's platoon remained unwounded and three of those had suffered shell shock from the grenade blasts. Sergeant Johnny Beck, one of the few D Company survivors of the Port Moresby air crash, had been wounded for a fifth time and this wound would prove fatal.[23]

Further back Dave MacDougal told Ray Nielson, 'Come on we'll give them some supporting fire.' MacDougal grabbed a Bren gun and Nielson lay beside him to change magazines. 'We were naughty boys, we shouldn't have been there,' MacDougal said, but he had already seen that 'Uncle Tom [Cotton] and some of our BHQ were operating the mortars!' Behind MacDougal the rest of Nielson's platoon were spread out refilling Bren magazines and passing them up as MacDougal fired until the barrel was glowing red. Japanese rounds were whipping past and when Nielson brought his arm up to feed a new magazine he was clipped on the elbow and wounded.[24] The attack was called off at 11.45 am after three men had been killed and another eleven wounded. That night the 2/31st Battalion took over the 2/33rd positions.[25]

Ray Nielson was taken to the dressing station near Dumpu and stayed overnight. They were also bringing in mountain-gun casualties from Trevor's Ridge and he lay there all night on a stretcher under a tarpaulin. The bloodied doctors were kept busy with the other wounded and Nielson felt he shouldn't be there with what he called 'a lousy bullet nick' so he 'buzzed off' the next morning. He was not the only one. When Dave Tudehope woke up he said, 'I'm out of here' but was spotted by surgical staff who raced after him and brought him back.[26]

After the Ramu campaign Dave MacDougal lost his job due to a 'little man'. While Colonel Cotton was away the replacement battalion commander accused MacDougal of insisting that the medical officer come forward after Captain Follent had been sent for to help the mortally wounded Dave Green. Putting the medical officer in such danger was apparently against regulations.[27]

●

Higher up the command chain, General Vasey had to contend with his division now playing second fiddle to operations at Finschhafen, where units of the 9th Division had made an amphibious landing on 22 September. The division now required significant logistical support. As the New Guinea Force commander, Lieutenant General Sir Leslie Morshead wrote to Vasey on 18 October, 'With our now much increased commit-ment for 9 Div and the difficulty of building up reserves at Lae and Nadzab our resources are greatly strained.' Morshead added that 'I well appreciate the urge to move forward and to do things', but 'now it is a case of holding your horses'.[28] Two days later Vasey replied that 'I have no desire to get myself committed into these hills until I am convinced of our relative strengths' but then added that the Japanese have 'very little strength between here and Bogadjim'. Vasey thought it practicable to capture Bogadjim by an overland operation but considered that he needed his third brigade and more artillery support to do so. 'I feel compelled to adopt an inactive role at the moment,' he told Morshead.[29]

Vasey's thoughts at this time are interesting. The 9th Division commander, Major General George Wootten, had served as a brigadier under Vasey during the final battles of the Papuan campaign and Vasey told Morshead that he had sent 'a boy on a man's errand' in relation to Wootten. Vasey's own understanding of how to fight an enemy in country where there were essentially no flanks was lacking. He still thought you had to have enough strength to either create your own flanks or to attack enemy flanks and, as Wootten was also learning at Finschhafen, you could not afford to fight that way in New Guinea. Holding the vital high ground was the key to success with the available resources.[30]

Vasey was dabbling with deep penetration operations using his two commando squadrons but only as patrols. He never took on board the lesson that he should have learned at Kaiapit: that a small, lightly armed force moving swiftly could negate conventional military thinking and defence lines. Having now drawn the Japanese defenders in the Finisterres onto his forces holding the foothills north of Dumpu, he had the opportunity to strike swiftly further west towards Yokopi and Daumoina and threaten the coast at Bogadjim, which would cause panic in the Japanese command with such a large force committed at Finschhafen. Two fully supported commando squadrons could have provided that strike force, with an infantry brigade following up to hold key high points, keep the supply lines open and respond to any enemy flanking moves. Vasey's second brigade could be kept in the Ramu Valley to protect the airfields at Dumpu and Gusap. Vasey didn't need a third brigade. He just needed to take a risk and trust his men if he wanted to be proactive with the resources he had. The actions at Pallier's Hill, Johns' Knoll and MacDougal's Hill had clearly shown the ability of his smaller formations in such country. By mid-November Vasey's window of opportunity had passed and he was told to supply 1000 native carriers to Finschhafen, thus further limiting his options.[31] Vasey's 'big brigade' thinking would now confine his division to a sedentary role through to the end of 1943 and beyond.

Morshead was also at fault for not fully appreciating that a push towards Bogadjim, whether it was reached or not, would put extraordinary pressure on the Japanese supply line to Finschhafen and take much of the pressure off Wootten. The limitations of Vasey and Morshead, with their knowledge and experience founded on their ability to work with large formations in open country, were clear.

Of course there was a greater strategy at play, with American landings on west New Britain and on the north coast on the Huon Peninsula at Saidor scheduled for the Christmas–New Year period. But if Bogadjim could be threatened by Vasey in October–November, then the Japanese would be trapped on the Huon Peninsula without a reliable coastal supply route and that could only benefit later operations.

Chapter 7

ONTO SHAGGY RIDGE

On the afternoon of 14 October the 2/16th Battalion moved up the Faria River to Trevor's Ridge to relieve the 2/27th which began the move back to Guy's Post late in the afternoon. Although the heavy afternoon rain prevented the Japanese from observing the move, the track down Trevor's Ridge soon became 'a running stream of mud'.[1] 'It simply poured with rain as we waited, blue with the cold, for the Bn [battalion] to snake out into single file along an appalling track,' Clive Edwards wrote. It was already dark when the men reached the swollen Faria River and they had to form human chains at the numerous crossing points as they made their way down the river. 'Drowning was certain if we broke the chain,' Edwards noted.[2] 'There's all sorts of boulders and stones moving along the bottom and you can lose your footing very easily,' Jack Reddin added. 'We lost one man who lost his grip and lost his footing.' That man was Signaller Ron Blake, his body found the next day. He had been a brigade signaller attached to the 2/27th and was the third signaller to lose his life in the previous four days.[3]

With the 2/27th Battalion back at Guy's Post, attention shifted to the massive bulwark that towered above and would soon be known as Shaggy Ridge. 'It was an incredible feature,' Jack Reddin observed, 'a feature that most of us had never seen anything like before in our life.' It wasn't a mountain but more like a long narrow mountain range with no individual peak, just 'an outcrop of rock or a pimple as we used to call it'. The north-eastern side of the ridge was open, covered in thick kunai grass with the odd narrow patch of timber bleeding out of the side of the ridge. The even steeper south-western side caught the coastal weather and was thickly covered with rainforest. 'It is as steep as hell on both sides and is only flat for a couple of feet on top,' Bob Clampett recalled. The only feasible way up was via the southern shoulder. As Reddin put it, 'You just have to see it to believe it.'[4]

Shaggy Ridge was named after Lieutenant Bob 'Shaggy' Clampett, who had taken the first 2/27th units up onto the ridge on the same day as the rest of the battalion was making its way back from Trevor's Ridge to Guy's Post. Clampett had been given his nickname in Syria soon after he had received his field commission when, after six weeks in the field without a haircut, Clampett and four other newly commissioned officers had been invited by the battalion commander to the officers' club. However, Clampett's company commander, Captain Tom Gill, had one look at him and said, 'Clampett, you cannot go with the CO with your hair as it is . . . you're just like those so and so goats out there, those shaggy goats.' The name stuck.[5]

As the intelligence officer, it was Jack Reddin's job to name terrain features that were unnamed on the map. As he was discussing operations with the quartermaster, Captain Jack Lee, he mentioned 'old Shag's going up the ridge, what will we call it?' 'Just call it Shaggy Ridge,' Lee replied. Reddin thought Clampett's 'unruly hair sort of matched the terrain and so I thought that was a jolly good idea so we named it Shaggy Ridge'.[6] 'I wonder if that name will ring a bell,' Jack Bishop wrote home.[7] On 14 October Bishop told Clampett, who had only just taken over A Company after Charlie Sims had been evacuated with pneumonia, to put together a composite company and go up the ridge. Clampett gathered together 9, 11 and 18 Platoons, each one from a different company. Clampett's 'strict instructions were to keep the Japanese occupied' with patrols but, in contradiction, on 'no account to cause any casualties to ourselves'. The main task was observation.[8] 'We already knew there were Japs on top, we'd seen them there when we crossed the river,' said Reddin.[9]

On 16 October Clampett sent out a patrol to the top of the ridge shoulder which found a four-strand barbed-wire fence with tins hanging off it for early warning, but it was decided to go no further than this 'ordinary agricultural fence'. Nonetheless, the Australians had been seen. 'The Japanese were approximately 30 to 40 yards ahead but they looked down on us from a height of roughly the height of a two-storey building,' Clampett recalled. He reported back to headquarters and said that he thought his company could capture the Japanese position atop the ridge but it was 'again reaffirmed that under no circumstances were we allowed to attack'. Clampett therefore just maintained his position on the shoulder of the ridge, observing and patrolling, although 'not necessarily in an orderly manner, but in a frequent manner, both day and night'.[10]

'Just across to my left there is a ridge. It is covered with long kunai grass on my side and dense timber on the other . . . I have to climb it tomorrow,' Jack Bishop wrote in a letter home.[11] On the afternoon of 17 October he set off with Jack Reddin to climb Shaggy Ridge but Bishop only made it one-third of the way before he had to return to his headquarters at Guy's Post. Reddin also got to accompany a number of war correspondents up onto the ridge. 'So I started off at the bottom with seven or nine of these journalists and only one was with me when we reached the top.' That was Merv Weston, a top-grade squash and tennis player with the fitness to match. 'All the others faded on the way up,' Reddin stated, 'long before we reached the top.'[12] On 20 October Reddin was ordered to accompany a platoon up through the scrub on the left-hand side to meet up with Clampett's company on top of the shoulder. As the men climbed 'the rains came down and everything got slippery' so Reddin decided to just take two men up with him, leapfrogging their way up the steep slope. When they finally reached the top 'there was Shaggy's men training their guns between our eyes'. 'I knew Shaggy Ridge well,' Reddin observed, 'at least how to get up there'.[13]

Although it was now confirmed that the Japanese were on the ridge, Brigadier Ivan Dougherty's opinion was that 'there was no desperate hurry to clear them out'.[14] However, it was decided that the 25-pounder guns down below could have an impact so Jack Reddin got the job of taking the artillery observation officer Captain Bluey Whyte up onto the ridge. 'He got us all to retreat just a few yards,' Reddin said. 'Seemed pretty scary to me at the time, while he sorted out how to get artillery onto the top.' Whyte got under an overhanging bank near the barbed wire and when he had the range right he called for Fuse 231 on the shells, which delayed their detonation. 'This resulted in a horrible mess, with many dead Japs and trees blown apart,' Whyte noted. 'There were great holes in the ground where the shells had gone in and exploded, forcing shrapnel up through the ground.'[15]

On 22 October a patrol moved along the ridge to an area of bamboo clumps which had been thinned out by the Japanese over the previous week. Les Thredgold and Private George Vandeleur were out front and watched about a dozen enemy soldiers digging in and cutting timber. Les crawled forward to the barbed-wire fence and watched one of the soldiers splitting bamboo with a machete and taking it up the hill where another soldier was sitting down with his rifle covering the track up. To Thredgold it looked like they were making a fire lane down the track through the bamboo. They had also laid out dried leaves and bamboo behind the barbed-wire fence to make a warning sound when trodden on. Then 'one cheeky Jap . . . came down and he dug a hole behind us or just over the side of us'.[16] While Vandeleur covered him, Thredgold worked his way back but when his toe caught in a vine the soldier 'saw it move then he looked at me'. The soldier jumped into the hole he had been digging and yelled out to the men higher up the ridge. 'Our position was blown,' Thredgold said, so they pulled back to the rest of the platoon. As they withdrew they came across Bluey Whyte. Thredgold told Whyte 'to get down quick smart,' afraid the Japanese would open fire on them. But it was Whyte who would do the shooting. He found a spot where he could see the enemy position and he had the artillery open fire, which 'blasted the place to smithereens,' remembered Thredgold.[17]

On the next morning of 23 October the men of Lieutenant John Garnock's 9 Platoon crawled out under the barbed-wire fence and found that the forward enemy post had been vacated so he had his men occupy it. Garnock counted 30 foxholes in the area, four of which had been hit by the artillery fire. A patrol then moved about 250 metres further on until the men could hear Japanese voices, at which point they returned. On 24 October a five-man patrol from 18 Platoon moved up to locate the new enemy positions. The lead scout was Private Bruce Truscott who was 'a new chap' who had only been with the battalion a few weeks but was keen to prove himself. He led the patrol across the same ground that Garnock's platoon had covered on the previous day. They had only gone about 100 metres to where there was a dip that formed a saddle on top of the ridge, with a sheer cliff on the south-west side and the steep open kunai slope on the other, when the crack of a rifle shot was heard and Truscott was fatally hit. Some Japanese troops had moved in overnight and set up an ambush. Les Thredgold was back with the rest of the platoon when Private Des Blake came running back to tell them 'they've got Bruce'. It would be five days before the body of the first Australian killed on Shaggy Ridge could be recovered.[18]

That afternoon Clampett's company was relieved by Major Ron Johnson's C Company. Johnson was a 'wild looking bloke' and an aggressive company commander who had been wounded five times. Lieutenant Peter Langsford's 14 Platoon moved up to occupy the ridge just back from the saddle where Truscott had been shot. Bruce Deering was the forward scout when the patrol arrived and said, 'No Nips here' before taking off his pack and sitting down on the track. Private Roy Freedman was behind Deering, both men hidden from enemy view by the cloud that gathers on most afternoons. But suddenly the mist lifted like a curtain and fire broke out from further along the ridge, wounding Freedman in the wrist and Deering in the thigh. 'They went bang, bang, bang and I got one,' Deering recalled. Both wounded men were pulled back below the skyline out of the line of fire.[19]

A few nights later, when the men were moving back along the crest at night, Sergeant Harry Hood went over the side at a point where the path along the top took a twist. Private Don Duffell heard him go over and just managed to stop himself before he followed. Fortunately Hood was able to halt his fall and get back up onto the top.[20] The men then dug a path along the south-western side of the ridge just below the crest, and weapon pits were dug into the jungle-covered slope under cover from enemy snipers. However, there were still dangers. Private Norm 'Lofty' Emmett was a big man with a big foxhole and when it rained heavily, it weakened the sides of his position. He was just below the ridge when his hole collapsed one night and down he came with only the many trees on that side of the ridge preventing him tumbling to the valley below.[21]

After Harry Hood had taken his tumble it was decided to avoid moving at night other than to change over the forward three-man Bren gun post every two hours. A string was tied to the waist of one of the forward men who could tug the string to alert the post further back and vice versa. Don Duffell was up there one night but when he pulled the string it came free so he had to make his way back to wake Private Jack Jose who was due for the next shift. Jose was a jittery little fellow and when Duffell shook him he awoke with a fright, called out 'They're here!' and punched Duffell on the jaw before trying to strangle him. Duffell therefore had trouble calling out the password, which was Woolloomooloo, a word the Japanese would have trouble with. Meanwhile 'Lofty' Emmett woke up and towered over the two struggling men with his bayonet, calling out 'Move aside, I'll get the bastard!' Then Private Herb Flanaghan said, 'No, move away, I'll give him a burst with the Owen.' Just then the cloud lifted, throwing some moonlight onto the situation and probably saving Duffell's life. The strain was too much for some. After only one night, one of the older men told Duffell, 'Don, I know we volunteered but I couldn't stand another night up here.' It was arranged that he be sent down.[22]

After the retreat of his unit from the Finisterres, Kenji Ueda ended up in the front line on Shaggy Ridge with 5 Company, II/78th Battalion. His section was ordered to move along the ridge to a place 'where the crest of the ridge had three small hills and . . . dig a defensive line'. The most forward of the three hills was the Pimple, the strongest position on Shaggy Ridge. As Ueda observed, 'It was an odd position as the ridge was so narrow there were spots on the track along the crest where only one man could walk.' Ueda noted that when the Australians moved along the ridge towards their position, there were no serious attacks, 'just probing, bombing, machine gunning'.[23]

•

Above Shaggy Ridge a flight of Boomerang aircraft from RAAF No. 4 Squadron operated on most days, spotting and strafing Japanese positions for the Australian artillery and the American fighter-bombers. In the last week of October there were constant missions out to the Bogadjim road from the coast, along which all reinforcements and supplies for the Japanese troops in the Finisterres came. Flying behind the enemy lines Flying Officer Ron Dickson had accepted that his plane would be shot at when carrying out such missions. 'It happened on every flight in varying degrees of severity,' Dickson wrote. On one of his early missions he could not resist strafing the staging point for the Japanese trucks at Daumoina about 3 kilometres north of Yokopi. 'It was just too irresistible to pass them by,' but his flight commander Ian 'Pip' Olorenshaw later told him 'You came back with so many holes in your aircraft, I don't know how you remained airborne.'[24]

On 22 October Dickson was on a two-and-a-half-hour mission directing an artillery shoot in the Faria Valley and then back to the Bogadjim road where he 'indulged in strafing anything and everything in sight along the road'.[25] On this day the flight moved from Nadzab to Gusap, giving the aircraft a longer loiter time over the Shaggy Ridge area. The next day Dickson was up again doing the same work, his longest mission to date at 3 hours and 15 minutes. On 28 October he was again over Daumoina to check out the transport park but he did not strafe the area as he was diverted to look over the Ramu River area further west near Koropa: 'I would not have been asked to go there just to view the scenery.'[26] There was considerable concern that the Japanese would push down the valley.

The Boomerangs would always operate in pairs, with one doing the work down low and the other providing top cover against air attack. The men on the ground would nickname the pair of Boomerangs Bluey and Curley or Bib and Bub depending on what cartoon they favoured. On 29 October Dickson's wingman was Flying Officer Norm Trumper and the mission was to try to locate the Japanese mountain gun at the head of the Faria Valley. Dickson got lucky when he spotted a Japanese officer in the open next to a patch of jungle pulling his arm across his body as if it was attached to a firing lanyard or something so he radioed Trumper, who was providing top cover, that 'we should do our best to give this place a bit of attention'. Dickson 'approached low and at the last moment rose up and focused on the Jap site' with his strafing run before dipping low on departure. However, Trumper did not follow Dickson's example and took his own line of attack to the target, carrying it out as if on the gunnery range with a shallow dive from about 30 metres and then pulling straight up after strafing the target. To Dickson this method made Trumper an ideal target for any ground fire and his misgivings about his wingman's strafing technique were confirmed on landing back at Gusap. 'All who saw his plane were appalled at the damage done to the aircraft by the ground fire,' Dickson wrote. 'It was quite remarkable that he survived this encounter.' To Dickson, Trumper 'was an accident waiting to happen'.[27]

The next day Dickson and Trumper were up again looking for the Japanese mountain-gun positions. They had two locations to investigate: near the head of the Faria River valley and around the adjacent Kankiryo Saddle. As the Boomerangs approached the area 'the mountain ridges were engulfed in dense cloud' so while Trumper flew top cover, Dickson looked for gaps in the cloud. Trumper then followed Dickson down through the cloud to maintain contact. After circling around the upper Faria Valley Dickson was able to mark a suspected gun position on his map before heading for Kankiryo, flying through a narrow gap between the cloud base and the tree line along the top of Kankiryo Saddle into the Mindjim River valley to the north.[28]

Dickson's dilemma was how to fly safely across Kankiryo Saddle below the low cloud base while at the same time having a good look for likely gun positions. He would approach the saddle from the Mindjim Valley and after crossing the Kankiryo Saddle to the Faria Valley, 'despite the opening available being very tight', he would go up through the clouds, head back to the Mindjim Valley and repeat the process. With only a brief opportunity to view the small ground clearing on each pass, Dickson had to make a number of runs and soon realised that it would not be possible for Trumper to keep contact with him. Each time he would reach the Faria Valley and then break up through the clouds, Trumper would be there waiting for him but after a number of runs he broke through the clouds and Trumper was no longer up there. At first Dickson was not concerned but after a few more runs 'it dawned on me he could have come to grief'. Dickson tried the radio with no response and then searched what ground he could see below for any sign of a crash and it soon became clear that Trumper 'must have gone in'.[29] Trumper's Boomerang had crashed near the northern end of Shaggy Ridge on the west side of Kankiryo Saddle on a feature later known as Prothero Two. His broken Boomerang was found three months later when Australian troops occupied the feature.

Trumper had been shot down by ground fire from Kankiryo. As Lieutenant Kumao Ishikawa later wrote, 'We could only watch in silent frustration the enemy spotter planes that would come flying up as if weaving at extreme low altitude in the valley from Irie Village to our position.' But Ishikawa knew that if his men fired, they would give away the location of 'our secret position'. The frustration only grew at 'the enemy pilots whose faces could be glanced at between trees' and Ishikawa finally received permission from his battalion commander, Captain Shoichi Kagawa, to try to shoot an aircraft down. Ishikawa had ten men aim at a Boomerang flying over his position but thought 'the first salvo was fired slightly below him and before he passed over us three or four more salvos were fired'. But on this first occasion there was no result. That came in the following days when an explosion was heard and one of his men 'came rushing in short breaths, tears on his face'. 'Commander, we did it!' he excitedly told Ishikawa; the men had finally brought the Boomerang down in flames. 'The pilot had been burned in the lower torso, asked for water then passed away,' Ishikawa wrote. Several days later, Ishikawa received a message of praise, a bottle of sake and twenty packs of cigarettes from General Nakai, 'which pleased us all'.[30]

•

With his battalion about to be relieved from Shaggy Ridge, Jack Bishop cobbled together a plan that would hopefully see the Pimple captured before his men left the ridge. Just after dusk on 3 November he sent D Company out in heavy rain to try to find a way up the open north-eastern side of the ridge to attack the Pimple the next day. 'We didn't like the job much but off we went,' Clive Edwards wrote. The men would cross the area that was under enemy observation in darkness. 'It was a slow and queer march in pitch darkness on only a narrow track,' Edwards noted. Having already been on an earlier patrol where the men 'finished up by hanging tooth and nail to sheer slopes where a slip would have landed us in the Faria far below', Edwards was well aware of the challenge.[31]

The men were overloaded for such a climb. 'We carried our tents and everything because we expected to remain on Shaggy Ridge,' Edwards wrote. 'I had to carry Tiny Bastick's rifle because he was lugging six mortar bombs, and the extra weight didn't improve things any.' It took five hours to reach a point from where they could make the final push up onto the ridge. 'It was a ticklish position for we are parked on a slope of about 50 degrees and dare not show our noses over the ridge,' Edwards realised. Les Thredgold had his men stick their bayonets into the ground and tie themselves to them as they lay down on the side of the ridge for the night. Lieutenant Gordon Macdonald then took a patrol higher up and 'reported that any attack was impracticable'.[32]

Meanwhile the men on top kept the attention of the defenders on the Pimple. At 9.25 am the guns down in the valley opened fire and at 10.00 am Peter Langsford took a ten-man patrol out along the top of the ridge to see if the artillery had forced the Japanese off the Pimple. The patrol advanced until the men were under the cover of the rock face below the Pimple but noise could be heard above and there were two bursts of machine-gun fire, which made it clear that the Japanese were still there. The patrol split in two and Corporal Tom Excell took four men around to the right side of the rock face while the other five men went left where the shale thrown up by the recent shelling soon halted progress.[33]

On the right side Excell's group moved through the shattered timber below the Pimple and then came across a clear patch with two tents and a machine gun set up slightly above and to the left. Excell and Private Willie Smith moved behind the enemy position at a higher point of the ridge and threw five grenades and fired a burst from an Owen gun. A series of machine-gun and rifle shots followed. The other men from Excell's party were fired on so slid down into dead ground before hearing a dull thud like a man falling. Excell and Smith did not return and after half an hour the other men withdrew. Their bodies would remain unrecovered for two months.[34]

'One day they got serious,' said Kenji Ueda, 'They were equipped with automatic sub machineguns and came at us suddenly . . . they fired shots like rain drops.' Ueda's five-man section kept their heads down but some men from another section 'were very brave, they stood up and shot at the enemy, but they were all soon cut down'. Ueda's men then 'started shooting our rifles into the sky, and we soon learned that the Australians would never charge us as long as we fired our rifles'. Ueda thought that if it seemed his section was holding the position in any strength the Australians would not attack them. He would not have known there were only two Australians on the ridge but 'as long as we seemed to be holding our position in strength, they would not come close'.[35]

•

The morning after the loss of Excell and Smith, the Australian artillery and mortars opened up on the Pimple, trying in vain to drive the Japanese off. Clive Edwards thought that 'they must be jolly well dug in and won't worry about the muck'. Rex Trenerry took his platoon along the side of the ridge and then up through a thickly timbered patch of jungle but although he could see the Japanese, the jungle petered out into open kunai and the lead section came under fire.[36] Trenerry reported back that the rest of the way to the top was impossible. Meanwhile Guy Fawcett was spending a long time on the walkie-talkie with Jack Bishop 'trying to convince him of this fact but it sounds as though he's taking some convincing'. As Edwards noted of Bishop, 'it's alright for him to say the country is passable'.[37] In the end Bishop saw reality and called off the attack. 'We couldn't go further,' Private Alan Bullock stated, as it was 'too steep above'.[38]

Meanwhile Kenji Ueda's section had pulled back and established another position where the ridge was wider and Ueda's section held the left flank, on the open side of the ridge 'some distance down off the ridge proper'. While the men were still digging in about 10.00 am, 'about 30 Australian soldiers emerged from the jungle below us,' Ueda said. 'Each time they showed themselves, we shot at them, but we never got any of them.' It would have been Trenerry's men that Ueda's section fired on. The next day Ueda's men were out of their dugouts and cleaning their weapons when they were fired on 'from a hill behind us'. Ueda stated, 'It was my fault that two of my men were killed right then and another later.' After driving the Australians off, Ueda decided to move back closer to the rest of the platoon.[39]

On the afternoon of 7 November, a patrol along the top of the ridge by Lieutenant Colin Fisher led him to conclude that the Pimple was 'unassailable' because only two or three men could approach it at a time and they would come under intense fire. The main enemy position was well dug into the rock and had proved immune to shelling. Private Horrie Beames was shot in the back and killed while two other men were wounded as the patrol withdrew.[40] 'This time we were well prepared and had more men than them, so we easily defeated them,' Ueda wrote, 'We knew we had killed at least one Australian soldier.'[41]

That night the Japanese positions came under mortar fire 'and all we could do was to hide in the bottom of our holes and wait for it to end,' Ueda wrote, but in the face of 'almost overwhelming strength, none of our men ran. They were brave men.' Ueda noted that there were three artillery pieces and a Juki machine gun available, 'but we had to save them for a critical situation as, as soon as we used them, the enemy would spot their position and destroy them'. The Japanese also had their 50 mm light mortars but the rounds for them had 'super quick fuses and it was very dangerous to use them in the jungle as it would explode even if the grenade hit a small branch just over your head'. Ueda also thought that the Japanese hand grenades were 'almost too dangerous for us to use in the jungle'.[42]

•

On 9 November the 2/33rd Battalion took over operations up on Shaggy Ridge. Coming down off the ridge was a challenge and Don Duffell slid down on his back using his heels as brakes. During the descent the grenade discharger cup tore away from his webbing and was lost and Duffell was later fined two pounds for loss of equipment. As a 'six bob a day tourist', that meant four days' pay.[43] Although the artillery and air strikes against the Pimple continued, the 2/33rd didn't make any attacks. On 19 November an artillery round dropped short, startling Private Frank Heinze who jumped into the air and then slipped off the ridge, tumbling down the kunai-covered east side for some 20 metres before he was able to pull up. 'Am I alright, Doc?' he asked the medical officer John Follent, 'I thought I had broken my bloody neck.' Follent assured him he was fine but knew Heinze was right; Heinze would die during the difficult stretcher carry down off the ridge.[44]

With his battalion out of the front line for a break, Jack Bishop had time to sit on a ridge in the foothills and pen another letter as he took in the panorama: 'On my left is a narrow valley, and beyond it once again these everlasting hills. The valley loses itself in infinity in both directions, and along its floor winds a great river . . . it is the Ramu.'[45] They were interesting days for the 2/27th commander. In late November Bishop took a phone call at his forward headquarters from Brigadier Dougherty who informed him that General Vasey wished to say goodbye. When Bishop asked where Vasey was headed, Dougherty replied, 'He isn't going anywhere, but you are.' Bishop's time as a battalion commander had come to an end. 'I was to return to the gilded staff,' Bishop wrote. His value as a staff officer now saw him promoted to full colonel and appointed as a general staff officer to the 6th Division, the formation that he had first served with in the Middle East. On 12 December, while sitting on an aircraft on the way back to Australia, Bishop wrote what would be his final letter from New Guinea. 'Life and events are moving far too quickly for me. I said farewell to the grandest lot of lads with whom I have ever been associated,' but 'at least I shall not have to climb Shaggy Ridge again.'[46]

Lieutenant Colonel Keith Picken, who had adminis-tered command of the 2/7th Battalion during the latter part of the Salamaua campaign, took over from Bishop, arriving on 5 December. For the 2/27th it was a quiet time with the 2/16th Battalion having now taken over on Shaggy Ridge and its approaches. Vasey wrote to Morshead on the same day and, in regard to Bishop, told him 'I am sorry that the change had to be made.'[47]

Chapter 8

KESAWAI

By late October the 2/6th Commando Squadron had forward outposts within two hours of the Japanese road head at Yokopi, watching for any enemy move towards the Ramu Valley. Gordon King's headquarters and Gordon Blainey's A Troop were based at Kesawai, some 20 kilometres north-west of Dumpu where there was a small airstrip, a supply dump and huts for native carriers. About 10 kilometres further up the valley at Isariba, Derrick Watson's C Troop had a strong outpost with a Vickers gun and a week's worth of supplies. 'That'd be typical Watson,' said King, 'You see he was an old infantry or machine-gun guy.' Bob Balderstone's 9 Section was 2 kilometres further north at Ketoba and patrols from here were able to contact 2/2nd Commando Squadron patrols even further west. King was concerned that his men were so spread out and reliant on a very exposed line of communication that ran round the foothills. It was the 'type of thing we never trained for, I mean our defence was always mobile defence, it was our only method of defence'. In retrospect King 'thought he should have been more proactive about the whole thing and put an end to it because it was just stupid'.[1]

The outposts were certainly vulnerable but Kesawai was considered safe enough until it came under air attack on 26 November. The greater surprise was that the attack came from American aircraft. Alex Mackay could hear fighter planes in the morning, test firing their guns across the valley before they headed back towards Kesawai where one plane swooped down as if in a victory roll, followed by the others. Mackay, who was having a shave at the time, quickly dived into a trench as machine-gun rounds struck the ground.[2] Eight Kittyhawk fighters strafed the village for 13 minutes, setting two huts on fire and killing Signaller Frank Sutcliffe who had stayed at his post to send out a radio message to call the attack off. He ran for cover at the last minute but it was too late. A native helper, Safiang, was also killed and two other men were wounded in the attack.[3] Padre Arthur Bottrell had been standing in the shallow creek when he noticed 'one of the planes turn in a half-roll, flatten out and begin a dive at the camp out of the sun' and wondered 'What's he playing at?' He soon found out as 'streams of red-hot tracer, incendiary, armour-piercing .50 bullets; the whole pot pourri of shells packed in the belts of Browning machine guns' was fired off.[4]

Gordon King watched the attack and thought, 'Christ what are they up to?' King, who was laid up with scrub typhus in a hut beside the creek, quickly got into the creek bed for shelter. However, 'being in the creek for a while didn't do me much good'.[5] Wally Hagan and Trooper Fred Cross also dived into the creek, clinging to the bank and burying their heads under water.

Hagan 'crawled out to find our camp in tatters, trees two-foot thick bored through with point five bullets'.[6]

When the American flight leader arrived a few days later to apologise, 'he was received in stony silence'.[7] A steadily deteriorating King found enough strength to add the necessary harsh words to that silence. 'Inexperienced, go go, trigger happy, macho, big shot' was how King later summed up the offender.[8] Alex Mackay thought the officer may have been stupid enough to think that the Salvation Army flag under the eaves of one of the huts was a Japanese flag.[9] Captain Lou Longworth later noted that the 'Splintered and devastated huts at Kesawai were mute evidence of the deadly accuracy with which the US Airforce had strafed the village in error.'[10] Four days after the attack King was evacuated with scrub typhus, leaving Blainey in charge. King had no qualms about that. 'Gordon Blainey was I think the best soldier of any rank with whom I ever served.'[11] King also had his admirers and days later he was promoted to major.

•

Although the Australian commanders had failed to take the opportunity to strike north from Kesawai towards Madang, their Japanese counterparts were very concerned at the threat so decided to strike first. Their plan was for a simultaneous attack on a broad front to envelope Kesawai from three directions before attacking the Australians at Dumpu. The I/78th and II/78th battalions would be involved plus two battalions from the much fresher 239th Regiment, part of the 41st Division. The regiment had been moved down the coast from Wewak to take part in the attack. The 78th Regiment would attack Kesawai on 8 December

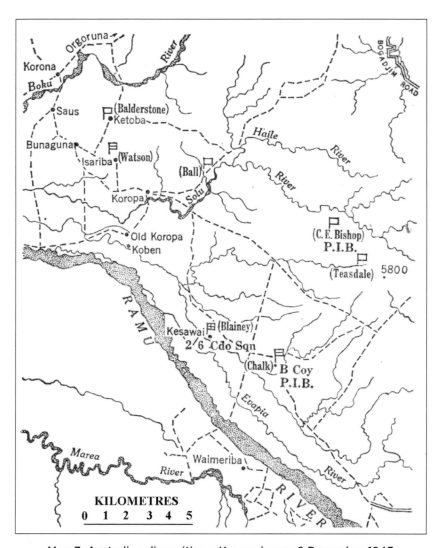

Map 7: Australian dispositions, Kesawai area, 8 December 1943
(Dexter, *The New Guinea Offensives*, p. 690,
Copyright Australian War Memorial)

while further west the 239th Regiment would attack Ketoba and Isariba before moving on Kesawai. During the night preceding the attack there were to be raids on the Australian headquarters area at Dumpu 'to stir up' the enemy but there is no indication that this happened.[12]

On 8 December reports came in that enemy troops were digging in on a ridge north of Kesawai after an attack by two Japanese companies. Once the ridge had fallen, a parachute flare was fired and a large Japanese supply party came forward.[13] Another report added that 'More enemy are dribbling down over rear ridges all the time.'[14] On 9 December there was a strafing attack by twenty Kittyhawks on the Japanese force which claimed two planes shot down by ground fire although both had actually made emergency landings, one with a shot-out oil cooler and the other with engine failure after the hydraulics were hit. 'But' as the Japanese later conceded, 'the force in using a thousand rounds of the scarce ammunition introduced a new problem for the succeeding battles.'[15]

Trooper Johnny Rich was the 2/6th Commando Squadron's expert on booby traps and just on dusk each evening he would go out from Kesawai to lay them along likely approach routes. The booby traps utilised grenades with either a trip wire attached to the firing pin or using the more efficient Murray switch. When Rich went out at dusk on 8 December he was accompanied by the sergeant major, Dave Devaney, and Trooper Bert Sublet. At 7.10 pm a 'nasty burst of gunfire split the camp' and the commandos at Kesawai dashed to their positions on the perimeter. 'Fingers tightened on triggers; hands palmed grenades; muscles taughtened on grim faces,' Padre Bottrell later wrote. Soon thereafter Sublet raced back into the perimeter gasping 'Ambush! . . . Down the track . . . they got Dave and Richy!' Within half an hour, reports came in from the perimeter of enemy movement in the kunai grass. Gordon Blainey knew that Kesawai village was a 'hopeless' defensive position and within another 15 minutes he had informed brigade headquarters that he was pulling out. At 2.00 am the Japanese attacked the vacated position.[16]

Further west Derrick Watson had built a strong position at Isariba, 'a tiny village perched on a small hill with a cleared top, ten yards wide by one hundred long, and ringed with slit trenches for defence,' as Captain Longworth observed. However, Watson was away at Ketoba when Isariba was attacked. The 70 men at Isariba had taken up their defensive positions at 4.00 am and 'awaited the dawn and what might come'. The first attacks came in just after dawn on 9 December and lasted for an hour and a half. The only ground available for Japanese supporting fire was rendered untenable by a Vickers machine gun backed up by rifle bombers, but towards noon the attacks increased and Gunner Shorty Booker was wounded by a mortar shell. Orders were then given to withdraw and, as the men moved out of the village at one end, the enemy troops came in at the other. Trooper Jack Ralston remained to guard the track while the rest withdrew until Sergeant Alf Miller came back, fired a shot over Ralston's head to get his attention and then waved for him to come out as well.[17] When a PIB scout said the villages to the east were occupied, the Isariba group headed south for the Ramu River with the wounded Booker carried by four natives. All night the men hacked a way through the thick scrub and kunai grass on a compass course that brought them out at the Ramu River at dawn.[18] From there the group headed east along the river to the Australian lines. Watson 'was pretty cranky I think with us, his headquarters, because he thought he hadn't been properly warned,' King later stated. 'He'd set himself up there to fight a long drawn out war . . . He was prepared to stay there and defend Isariba, Ketoba, forever.'[19]

North of Isariba, Bob Balderstone's position at Ketoba came under attack at 8.45 pm on 8 December with heavier attacks at 2.30 am the following morning. With ammunition low, Balderstone pulled his men out 10 minutes later. A RAAF Boomerang spotted them later and dropped a message to cross the Ramu River and follow the south bank east where local natives helped them back across the Ramu to Dumpu without losing a man.[20]

Out at the Solu River camp on 8 December, Lieutenant Charlie Ball saw a party of Japanese moving along the Solu River so took his section towards Isariba to warn the men there of the approaching threat.[21] As he approached Isariba the next morning Ball could hear the fighting had started so decided to make his way south to the Ramu River. On the way he came across the artillery survey camp and told the fourteen artillerymen there to join his party 'but to keep out of our way in case we had to fight'. Traversing the swampland towards the Ramu was tough going as Ball had to avoid a well-used track. He had earlier destroyed his wireless, the weight of it and the wet batteries being too cumbersome. Upon reaching the Ramu, the men crossed together and found succour at a native village where they could rest up, eat, and dry their clothes. Ball then decided to head east to the Australian lines where his party was seen by another patrol and helped back across the river. On the morning of 11 December Ball's party reached Dumpu where the men had to have the socks cut off their swollen feet.[22]

Higher up the command chain General Morshead was concerned that the 2/6th had withdrawn, telling General Vasey that 'These squadrons should hold ground when and where it should be held.' He was not alone in his inability to differentiate the roles of commando squadrons and infantry battalions. Morshead also told Vasey that 'It has taken the enemy a long time to make a move' and, although still unsure whether it was a blocking move or the prelude to a larger attack, that 'No doubt you will welcome his attacking.' Not for the first time, Morshead also denied Vasey's request for his third brigade to be brought forward from Port Moresby.[23]

•

Back at Dumpu, Brigadier Eather reacted to the threat of an enemy push into the Ramu Valley by ordering two companies from the 2/25th Battalion to hold the east bank of the Evapia River. By the morning of 10 December there were two companies positioned behind the Evapia River while Major Cam Robertson had taken the other two companies further forward to reoccupy Kesawai. Both companies were well under strength, each of around 85 officers and men with Lieutenant Terry Feely and four signallers attached to provide artillery support. On reaching Kesawai, Robertson's A Company formed a perimeter in the village with the creek at the rear while Captain Dick Cox's C Company with an attached Vickers gun dug in on a sharp 500-metre-long ridge overlooking Kesawai on the northern side. One-man circular weapon pits and two-man trenches were dug and every man had an alternative weapon pit with fire lanes cut for all automatic weapons.[24]

At 1.00 am on 13 December the Japanese set fire to a grass-roofed hut and this was the signal for the attack on Kesawai to commence. Up on the ridge 13 Platoon came under small-arms fire

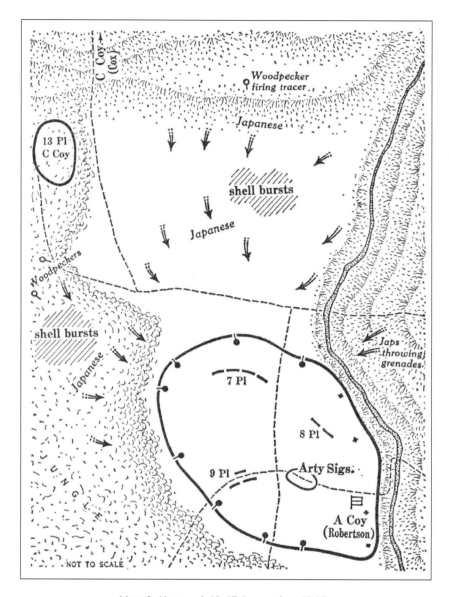

Map 8: Kesawai, 12–13 December 1943
(Dexter, *The New Guinea Offensives*, p. 699,
Copyright Australian War Memorial)

followed by grenades thrown by attackers who had crept up close during the night. The Australians replied with the Vickers gun and three Bren guns, stopping several strong attacks to the front while those up the steep slopes on the flank were held off with grenades. Other enemy soldiers crawled forward chattering and clicking their rifle bolts to attract Bren and Vickers fire to enable these key Australian positions to be identified for counter fire from a Juki machine gun positioned on a knoll further back. The well-drilled Australian infantrymen held fire until the enemy charged to within 30 metres, at which point the Brens and Vickers mowed them down. Three of the six Vickers crew were wounded in the fighting but the gun kept firing. Four Bren gunners were also wounded.[25]

Private Roy Carpendale was with 13 Platoon up on the ridge. He was on the left end of the line in a pit with Private Allen Joyner on one of the Bren guns, which gave them a good field of fire into the gully below the ridge. During the first attack the Juki got onto them and Carpendale was badly wounded. 'I'm hit!' he called out. 'So am I,' Joyner replied. When Carpendale asked him where he had been hit, Joyner just said, 'everywhere'. Carpendale got out of the weapon pit into a dip in the ground and crawled back, his wounded side like a dead weight.[26]

At the same time as the ridge attack, the Japanese attacked the Kesawai perimeter with about 120 men. Lieutenant Merv Searles' 7 Platoon opened fire on a party of 30 enemy troops moving across their front looking for a flank that wasn't there. The Japanese then attacked Lieutenant Roger Thomas's 9 Platoon but these attacks were also thwarted. The attackers then dug in while heavy machine-gun fire from three Jukis was brought to bear on the village. Grenades were also thrown into the perimeter, the flashes of the fuses being struck and their glowing arc as they were thrown clearly visible against the night sky. Improvised grenades, made up of a block of explosive with a fuse attached, were also being used but were relatively harmless without a heavy metal sheath around the explosive charge.[27]

By 2.00 am the phone line back to battalion headquarters had been cut but the artillery line was still intact so the forward artillery observer Terry Feely was able to bring down accurate fire around the perimeter. After Feely was mortally wounded while observing the fall of shot, Cam Robertson took over and by sound-ranging brought the fire to within 100 metres of the perimeter in order to protect Thomas's platoon from further attacks. Further back, at the Evapia River, the men of the other two 2/25th companies 'were standing to, and those not occupying fox-holes paced restlessly about, upset and worried about their cobbers up front'. At 2.45 am the line back to the artillery was finally cut but the shelling continued onto the last recorded target in line with Feely's directions before he was wounded. Two key assumptions were made by the Australian gunners: that the Australians would not advance from their perimeter during the night and that the atmospheric conditions would remain stable and not affect the shell trajectory.[28]

Finding no open flank, the Japanese tried to encircle the Australian position while a Juki fired into the perimeter from higher ground to the north. By 4.30 am the attackers were closing in from all sides, the attackers calling out to draw the Australian fire and identify their positions. One of the more erudite attackers called out 'White dingoes over there! Honourable Japanese gentlemen over here!' before a Bren gun shut him up. Meanwhile Lieutenant Russel Saunders was killed moving between the sections of his platoon.[29]

Up on the ridge Dick Cox had established communication with Robertson via a walkie-talkie and explained that he had been attacked by about 300 troops in two waves and that things were desperate. With ammunition low and the day soon to dawn, Cox considered his position to be untenable. Enemy troops had also outflanked Cox's position and were impacting Robertson's company in Kesawai. Cox suggested both companies get out at dawn and Robertson agreed. At 5.30 am Cox pulled two of his platoons off the ridge with the stretcher cases while 13 Platoon acted as rearguard. Roy Carpendale walked out with his arm in a sling. The company pulled back about 1500 metres before the rearguard joined them at 7.50 am.[30]

Robertson had his men moving out of Kesawai at 5.40 am with 8 Platoon leading the way, followed by 7 Platoon with five stretcher cases, while 9 Platoon occupied the creek bank as the rearguard while the Japanese moved into the village. One of the stretcher cases died on the way out as the men withdrew through thick jungle and swamp with water a metre deep. At 7.00 am the two companies met up at the agreed rendezvous and from here Robertson was able to contact the artillery to have the evacuated position shelled. The two companies made it back to the battalion lines along the Evapia River that day. But the Japanese were already spent. The effects of constant rain, exacerbated by widespread malaria and dysentery, weakened the troops while water-damaged equipment and ammunition plus a shortage of the latter had their effects.[31] Five Australians were killed at Kesawai and fourteen wounded, while the Japanese admitted to losses of 67 killed and 136 wounded for the entire operation.[32]

•

General Vasey used the attack to once again ask General Morshead for more resources. 'My views are much firmer that his activities are the preliminary of something considerably bigger,' Vasey wrote. At this stage Vasey was prepared to give up control of the area west of the Yogia River, 15 kilometres west of Dumpu and behind which he had the 25th Brigade stationed, but he was worried about the gap between the 25th and 21st Brigade. He also had concerns about the strength of his seven battalions, each of which averaged only 486 other ranks, with two below 400. 'The effect of these deficiencies is well illustrated by the encounter a night or two ago against a post of 2/16 Bn,' Vasey told Morshead. What Vasey was referring to was a Japanese raid on a five-man section from the 2/16th Battalion on the night of 10 December that caused four casualties and forced the section to abandon the post. Vasey wrote how 'the disparity compelled them to leave the post temporarily'.[33]

Although the Official History refers to this attack as taking place against the forward section on Shaggy Ridge, it was against an observation post at Green Hill, which was south of Shaggy Ridge near Bert's Post.[34] At 11.00 pm on 10 December gunfire was heard from the position and it was reported that the five-man outpost had been attacked by a seven-man enemy patrol using bayonets, and four of the Australians had suffered stab wounds. The section commander, Corporal Gwyfryn 'Porky' Yorweth, said that one of the enemy had been killed in the attack.[35]

The raid was carried out as part of the attack on Kesawai. First Lieutenant Hirohichi Uemura, the commander of 11 Company, which was defending Shaggy Ridge, had asked Warrant Officer Kataoka to carry out a reconnaissance of the area south of Shaggy Ridge. Kataoka selected two men, Yamamoto and Uchiizumi, to accompany him and the three men set out after dusk on 10 December and at about 10.30 pm reached Green Hill where they sighted the two tents of the Australian outpost. Yamamoto and Uchiizumi were keen to attack and, although Kataoka's orders were to reconnoitre, with the chance to take revenge for day after day of shelling foremost in mind, he agreed. However, the men had been travelling lightly and none of them carried rifles or bayonets; the only weapons they had were Kataoka's sword and two grenades. Kataoka cut down two bamboo stalks and proceeded to sharpen them into spears with his sword and handed them to the two unarmed men.[36]

The three men then returned to the camp where the five Australians were asleep in the two tents with no sentry posted. They also noticed a kitchen area so, as Kumao Ishikawa related, 'first they went there and ate delicious stuff to their heart's content'. Kataoka then ordered his two men to stand guard over the first tent while he investigated the other. Finding the men in the second tent sound asleep under their mosquito net, Katoaka cut the ropes on both ends of the net, planning to attack with his sword when the men woke up and became tangled in the net. Kataoka then re-entered the first tent, asking the other two 'Shall we begin?'[37]

As one of the Australians finally woke up and slowly tried to get up, Uchiizumi stabbed him with his spear. The Australian called out, waking another soldier who was stabbed by Yamamoto. Then, as the third Australian emerged from the tent with his gun, Yamamoto grabbed it and clobbered the Australian with it. Then one of the Australians got hold of Uchiizumi and 'they tumbled around in the grass, screaming horrible cries like wild animals' until Uchiizumi broke free. Meanwhile the noise had woken the two men in the second tent but as Kataoka had planned they became tangled in the mosquito net. Kataoka attacked them with his sword but was then distracted by desperate calls from Yamamoto. As shots began to ring out, Kataoka and Yamamoto fled the scene, later meeting up with Uchiizumi and returning to the Japanese positions on Shaggy Ridge.[38]

Four of the five Australians had been wounded, one having had what he thought was a bayonet go through his ankle and another also stabbed. A third had a minor bullet wound. Private George Fritz may have been responsible for the bullet wound after he had stumbled out of the second tent with his Bren gun and tripped over, pushing the barrel into the ground. When he pulled it out and opened fire, 'the barrel peeled back like a banana' and the gun made a popping sound like a Japanese woodpecker machine gun.[39] The position now became known as Yorweth's Knoll.

Chapter 9

MISSING

On 15 December the 2/27th Battalion had returned to the Faria River valley below Shaggy Ridge. 'Our task was to dig in and stay put,' Jack Reddin noted. 'On no account were we to mount a major attack or attempt to move forward.' However, the battalion was able 'to send out exploratory recce patrols to pinpoint enemy positions across the river'. On the morning of 18 December a five-man patrol left Trevor's Ridge with orders to pinpoint a Japanese wired position for an artillery shoot. A section from 16 Platoon led by Corporal Doug Kemp accompanied by privates Murray Smith, Kev Jordan, Henry Smith and Fred Perkins made up the patrol, which was to return before dark. Jack Reddin watched them head out. 'At first light the patrol disappeared in the jungle on the opposite bank,' he observed as the men crossed Mainstream east of the Faria River and headed north up a spur.[1]

'The day dazed on,' Reddin wrote, 'then suddenly the crackle of gunfire flicked across the valley—then the blanketed explosion of grenades—then the deeper silence that follows the shock of sudden action—a tense waiting'. He pondered that 'Somewhere in that unbroken jungle—lying like a fur coat over some huge misshapen body—were the Jap strong points . . . Bad luck the first patrol had been seen.' It went quiet for about half an hour but 'Then it came again—the whiplash of rifle fire, the crackle of automatics and the dull boom of grenades—nearer this time— then an uneasy silence.' It appeared that two positions had now been located but Reddin knew it was 'bad business' for a small scouting patrol to be caught out twice. 'Send up a prayer for them. The Japs must be pretty wide awake.'[2]

Then there was a loud explosion from across the valley 'and a single column of black smoke spiralled up through the trees,' Reddin wrote. It was 2.20 pm as he jumped to his feet and grabbed the phone to call the artillery observation post. 'Arty O pip quickly,' he asked as he pulled his compass from its pouch and took a bearing on the smoke plume. 'Is that you, Blue?' he asked, once connected. 'Get a bearing on that column of smoke; can you see it?' After Bluey Whyte confirmed he had a bearing, Reddin told him 'For heaven's sake don't start anything till we give you the OK, we've got a patrol out there.' Whyte thought the blast was too loud for a mortar or even a 25-pounder round and, given the small-arms fire and grenade blasts, the worst was feared for Doug Kemp's section. 'The day wore on but no sign of the patrol,' Reddin wrote, 'eventually darkness and still no patrol'.[3]

•

When the morning of 19 December dawned, there was still no sign of the patrol. Then at 8.30 am, just as another patrol was about to leave, a lone survivor staggered back into the Australian lines. 'Black and bloody, with his clothing in tatters—without a weapon—one of the patrol—Kevin Jordan—had returned,' Reddin wrote. Lieutenant Colonel Keith Picken, Reddin and the battalion medical officer were soon on the spot to talk to Jordan but all they got from him was a blank stare. 'I'm sorry, sir,' Jordan finally said, 'I can't hear a word you're saying.' Upon examination it was confirmed that both Jordan's eardrums had burst from the explosion. 'It's a miracle he's still alive,' the medical officer said. So Kev Jordan would tell his story with a pen and paper.[4]

After crossing Mainstream the patrol had followed the track almost due north up a spur for about an hour before cutting in onto another track, which went west down the side of the ridge. Doug Kemp marked the spot so they wouldn't miss the intersection on the way back. At this stage Fred Perkins and Murray Smith were out in front followed by Doug Kemp and Henry Smith with Jordan bringing up the rear. As the first three men moved over a small crest, the Japanese opened fire. Jordan took cover behind the crest with Henry Smith. Then Perkins came back to them, dragging Doug Kemp who had been hit in the thigh and chest; Kemp told them that Murray Smith had been killed in the ambush.[5]

Henry Smith took charge and 'told us to beat it back quickly as the Corporal was in a very bad way'. The three unwounded men took it in turns to help Kemp back but missed the turn-off onto the main track and 'before we realised this we ran smack into another Jap position,' Jordan said. At that time Smith and

Perkins were in front carrying Kemp while Jordan was at the back. He watched as the patrol was ambushed a second time and saw Henry Smith get hit and thought he had been killed. Perkins and Kemp hit the dirt and 'Kempy started to throw his grenades, which attracted another burst from the Japs.' Jordan got behind a tree and fired seven or eight shots in the direction of the enemy position and then the next time he looked at Kemp and Perkins, Jordan was 'sure they were both dead'. The Japanese stopped firing and, thinking everyone else was dead, Jordan decided to get out but he 'took only one step and the sky fell in'. He had exploded a landmine on the track and was knocked out by the blast. It was towards evening when Jordan regained consciousness; he managed to crawl out and find his way back to the river where he waited until the morning to re-enter the Australian lines.[6]

Convinced by the story that the other four men on the patrol had been killed, Picken told Reddin to get the artillery 'to blast the hell out of the position'. 'OK Blue, all clear. Give them the works,' Reddin told Bluey Whyte over the phone. The artillery had just received a supply of new air-burst shrapnel shells and Whyte would try some of them on this target. 'It's not often we get a pinpoint target in this blasted jungle,' he told Reddin, 'We will square shoot the area commencing 1000 hours.' Picken then told Guy Fawcett, 'Guy, get the fighting patrol to cross the river and move into a position from which they can quickly as possible clean up when the shelling stops.' Whyte called down 260 shells onto the target.[7]

When the shelling stopped around midday on 19 December, Lieutenant Henry McDermott took out a 26-man patrol from 18 Platoon. The patrol found two empty bully-beef tins where Kemp's patrol had stopped for a feed and also found the body of Private John Newton from the 2/25th Battalion, who had been missing since 25 November, and his identification disc was removed. But the patrol went too far north from where the shelling had taken place and returned at 7.00 pm without finding the Japanese position.

•

The following morning, 20 December, the phone rang at battalion headquarters. 'OC Don Coy to CO,' Guy Fawcett said, 'Sir, another miracle has happened.' A second member of the Kemp patrol, Fred Perkins, had turned up at the forward positions. Keith Picken asked if he was OK and Fawcett replied, 'I'll bring him up to you right now.' Jack Reddin was there when the sturdy young eighteen-year-old, a recent reinforcement from NSW, arrived at headquarters. It had been Perkins' first time in action and he stood in front of Reddin and Picken with an 'impassive face, calm eyes, rock steady'. 'Tell me about it from the beginning,' Picken asked the young private.[8]

As Jordan had said, after the patrol left the Australian lines it went north until coming across another track, which was followed down the side of the ridge. Perkins was the forward scout as they crossed a small knoll but when the Japanese opened fire from only about 12 metres, Perkins was unscathed and managed to drop down and roll off the track. But he could see that Murray Smith was dead. 'One through the head, sir', Perkins told the colonel. Doug Kemp had seen that his good mate Murray Smith had been shot so came running up and tried to drag him back. Kemp was hit as Perkins shouted at him to go back because Smith was dead. Nonetheless 'he still tried to drag Smith back and he was hit again and fell into the scrub on my side of the track'. Perkins then managed to get to Kemp and, although he had to abandon his rifle, he was able to help Kemp back over the small knoll out of the line of fire. Henry Smith found them and took a look at Kemp's wounds; he had been hit in the chest and in the thigh. 'We had better get him back quickly,' he told Perkins. Henry Smith had also been wounded in the leg during the ambush but was still able to walk.[9]

Helping Kemp, the three men made their way back but missed the turn off onto the track they had come in on and continued on for about 30 minutes until they struck another enemy position. This one had a square of barbed wire around it and, thinking they had reached the Australian lines, Perkins and Henry Smith proceeded to crawl under it. Perkins got through but Henry Smith was badly wounded by a light machine-gun burst across his midriff. Although he was also wounded, Doug Kemp started throwing grenades but Perkins then saw that he 'was hit several times more and was killed'.[10]

'We were lying there in the grass with no shade or cover and the slightest movement brought a volley of shots,' remembered Perkins. Then Henry Smith suddenly shouted, 'I can't stand this any longer!' before jumping up and charging the enemy position. Perkins watched as 'they mowed him down'. Then Perkins heard the explosion behind him as Kev Jordan stepped on the mine. Perkins didn't know what caused the blast and he couldn't look back as he 'was lying in full view of the Japs, protected only by the very short kunai grass'. Every time he did move, even to get to his water bottle to quell his thirst, Perkins was fired on, so he just kept very still. Eight bullets went overhead but then 'one bullet went into the ground an inch from my head,' he told Picken. At this stage the only weapon Perkins had left was a solitary grenade so after that bullet just missed, he threw it, 'and then they didn't fire at me anymore'.[11]

As the afternoon wore on it started to rain and eventually it got dark. As Perkins told Picken and Reddin, 'I can't explain why I didn't crawl out during the night and in fact I went to sleep.' When he woke up it was too light to move, but, although Perkins could hear the Japanese talking and having breakfast, they didn't come out. By now Kev Jordan had returned to the Australian lines and the decision had been made to shell the position. When the bombardment started it was very accurate and, as Perkins related, 'the Japs did a lot of yelling and screaming' and they must have taken casualties. Perkins couldn't see through the smoke and dust and also had to keep very flat on the ground with shell fragments and chunks of wood flying about and huge tree limbs falling. 'No I didn't get hit, it was a miracle.' When the shelling finally stopped Perkins could hear a lot of groaning and crying and he remained undisturbed for the rest of the day. That night he crawled out under the wire, avoiding the tins full of small stones attached as a warning. 'I couldn't help making a lot of noise getting out,' he said as he found a way 'through the fallen branches and shell holes'. But he wasn't fired on and was able to shelter in the scrub until it was light enough to return to the Australian lines.[12]

When he later found the scraps of paper he had written about the patrol, it certainly brought back poignant memories for Jack Reddin. 'I will never forget my admiration of that young man,' he wrote of Fred Perkins, 'how he kept his cool, his dignity, his mental balance'. 'And I think of Kemp's indomitable courage and determination in his attempts to save his scout, and then later his courage and determination to fight on despite his wounds. And I think of the wounded Smith's torment, lying in the kunai grass, and his final charge to certain death.'[13]

•

Meanwhile Lieutenant McDermott had been ordered out again to find the correct position, this time with 21 men. They left early on 20 December and, knowing that they had missed the turn off the track on the previous day, the patrol turned off the ridge top track. 'We went down a little track sideways' and at about midday 'we ran into a big barbed-wire entanglement,' Les Thredgold said. 'Well, there were Japs everywhere.' Private Norm Stock was the forward scout with Private 'Freddy' Faul, 'a corker little lad', second in line when a machine-gun burst split the tree in front of Stock, wounding him in the chest and face. 'Get behind another tree, Norm, or they'll get you!' Thredgold called out.[14]

Thredgold, who was about 25 metres back, quickly organised the three Bren guns to provide covering fire. 'I think that was the only time I gave the fire order in the front line,' he later noted.[15] Under that covering fire, Thredgold went out and grabbed Stock and somehow got him back. He then called out to Faul, 'It'll be alright, we'll get you out.' When Faul looked back at him he was laughing, clearly unperturbed at his predicament. 'When I get the machine guns to open up on this machine-gun nest, you jump over the bank,' Thregold told him. Faul did as he was told and jumped over the bank, only to find it was actually a cliff and he got caught up in a tangle of vines. It took them over half an hour to get him untangled before they pulled back to the battalion lines. When they returned Thredgold and McDermott were told to go back to battalion headquarters to see the colonel. It was 2.00 am before they got to see Picken and he was not in a good mood. 'I'll tell you when to attack,' he told McDermott, 'You are on a recce patrol, not a fighting patrol.'[16]

•

Following the action at Kesawai, the 2/25th Battalion increased patrolling into the Finisterres west of Shaggy Ridge. A number of patrols sent out to the Solu River area confirmed that the Japanese had pulled back into the mountains and there was no immediate threat of further attacks into the Ramu Valley. On the morning of 19 December a patrol of 30 men under Captain Charles Milford set out on a five-day patrol to follow up the enemy line of withdrawal into the mountains. That afternoon the patrol saw signs of enemy movement and later spotted the light of a fire on a wooded slope about a kilometre ahead. Milford had the men remain on the reverse side of a hill overnight before detaching a section under Lieutenant Martin O'Rourke to investigate on the following morning. O'Rourke found evidence that Japanese troops had been there but had now moved on.[17]

Meanwhile Milford proceeded along the Solu River with most of the men before leaving the river and following a track along a knife-edge spur that had had considerable use. The spur fell away sharply on both sides as it approached a wooded ridge. It was late in the afternoon as the lead section moved out onto the ridge where there was a cleared patch of kunai grass about 40 metres in diameter with some burned-out huts on the western side. As the men spread out to investigate, the rest of the patrol waited down the track below the crest.[18]

Corporal Philip Morel, who was in charge of the lead section, apparently noticed something on the right side of the clearing and motioned the rest of the section to halt. At the same time, two Japanese machine guns opened fire from well-concealed positions in fairly thick scrub and kunai grass on the eastern side of the clearing. Morel was seen to go to ground as the enemy opened fire and threw grenades into the clearing. From where the rest of the patrol was, on the steeply rising spur below the crest, it wasn't possible to fire on the enemy position. Two men were missing—Phil Morel and Private Sydney Lawson—both of whom had been armed with Owen guns. But no Owen gun fire had been heard during the ambush and no groaning could be heard. Half an hour after the ambush two men crawled up to near the crest and called out 'Are you there, Phil?' but received no answer. At 4.30 pm Milford ordered his men back down the spur and he followed an hour later. After contacting battalion headquarters, Milford was ordered to bring his patrol back and one and a half hours later Sydney Lawson also returned. Lawson had been wounded in the hand during the ambush but had escaped by rolling down the steep slope on the far side of the clearing. He had heard no sound from Morel before his escape.[19] Morel's service record was stamped 'became missing and is for official purposes presumed dead'.[20]

•

A Japanese diary found at Crater Hill on 1 February 1944 mentioned that the diarist had heard that an enemy soldier, who had been taken prisoner on 22 December 1943 and had died, had carried a letter from a friend 'who mentioned that his mother was worried about him and wanted to send him some sweets for Christmas'. 'Mother love exists even in foreign countries,' the diarist wrote.[21]

The diary entry refers to one of the four Australians who had gone missing in the area in the preceding days. Although their remains are still missing, Murray Smith and Henry Smith are officially listed as killed in action while Doug Kemp and Philip Morel are listed as missing but presumed dead. Therefore Murray and Henry Smith are not on the alphabetical list of Australian army personnel who remain missing in Papua and New Guinea. Murray Smith, Kemp and Morel are listed on the memorial to the missing at Lae War Cemetery while Henry Smith is listed on the memorial to the missing at Bomana War Cemetery outside of Port Moresby. The 2/27th Battalion padre and Fred Perkins went back to look for Doug Kemp's body after the war but, as Les Thredgold noted, 'we never ever found Doug. No one else found him so we don't know what happened to him, whether they took him as prisoner, whether he was murdered or what happened . . . the two Smiths as far as I'm concerned, they were killed.'[22]

Kemp was 23 and single and seemingly more likely to have carried a loving letter from his mother, who was his next of kin. The 29-year-old Morel was born in New Zealand and was married to Elizabeth Morel at the time he went missing.[23] Murray Smith was only 20 and also single while Henry Smith was 21. One of these four men died in captivity.

Chapter 10

THE ONE-MAN FRONT

Like the rest of the 21st Brigade, the 2/16th Battalion had required major rebuilding following crippling losses in the Papuan campaign. Originally a West Australian battalion, the 2/16th received substantial reinforcements from the disbanded 16th Motor Regiment, a New South Wales unit. Private John Bidner was a section leader in 16 Platoon alongside Private Ray Mantle, Lance Corporal Jimmy McCulloch and Private Andy Murray, all former 16th Motor Regiment men.[1] 'There was a sprinkling of old fellers in the 2/16th and they were the saviours,' Ray Mantle observed.[2]

The 2/16th had led the advance of the 21st Brigade along the Ramu Valley but it wasn't until 14 October that the battalion moved forward to relieve the 2/27th. The early 2/16th patrols up the Faria River didn't find the enemy and this didn't please the battalion commander, Lieutenant Colonel Frank Sublet, who told the next patrol, 'You had better find them today or else.'[3]

On 16 October Lieutenant Roy Buchanan's 8 Platoon patrol made contact at a bamboo village at the river crossing upstream of the Mainstream junction and five Japanese were killed. The next day another patrol returned to the village, known as Irie to the Japanese, and 18 Platoon made contact along the supply track, killing two enemy soldiers.

On 18 October 17 Platoon moved up to Irie where the men found rice, indicating that enemy troops were close. There was a mountain gun in the area shooting up onto the ridge and Allied aircraft were strafing the area, the hot cartridges dropping down amongst the Australians. A patrol led by Sergeant Jack 'Springy' Longman moved to the river and took cover among some trees, then watched as an enemy scout came across the river but, although six rifles opened up, he wasn't hit. Having drawn the Australian fire the Japanese replied with heavy fire from the west bank that included a Juki machine gun. Private 'Tich' Pearce took cover with his mate Lance Corporal Merv Fleay kneeling behind him. Pearce fired off six magazines from his Owen gun as leaves and branches fell down around him as the tree was slowly chopped to pieces by the slow-firing Juki woodpecker. Pearce knew they had to get out but when he turned back to tell Fleay to get going he saw a purple mark on his head where a sniper had struck. Pearce had lost his best mate, the country boy with whom he shared a foxhole, who would always say 'I wonder how the cattle are going.'[4]

•

Following the move back into the Finisterres, Lieutenant Kumao Ishikawa's unit reached Irie village where Ishikawa came under the command of the labour company commander, Captain Shimojo. With Shaggy Ridge to the west and the Faria River to the east, the village 'was an ideal defensive stronghold'. A 75 mm mountain gun was placed under Ishikawa's command, 'a priceless artillery piece for our infantry defending Kankirei'. However, when the engineers had constructed the gun position they cut down the trees in a 60-degree arc ahead of the gun, making the location obvious from the air. 'It was as if the gun position was deliberately let known to the enemy,' Ishakawa wrote, 'risking being devoured by machine guns to say nothing of enemy artillery.' But the Australian patrols 'did not appear to go beyond threatening reconnaissance'.[5]

The Australians had only just set up an observation post called River OP at the Mainstream and Faria River junction when six shells from the mountain gun were fired at the position on the morning of 19 October. The Australian forward observers, Lieutenant Ross Macfarlan and Lieutenant Johnny Pearson, then called down counter-fire, dropping 70 shells onto the Irie area.[6] The position soon came under 'a ferocious gunnery attack like never seen before,' Ishikawa recalled. The first shells exploded in the trees but soon were hitting the ground, endangering the gun. Still under shellfire, Ishikawa pressed Shimojo to move the gun position, knowing how vulnerable it was to observation. Having no success, he went to the signals dugout to contact the regimental commander, only to find the line back to headquarters cut by the shelling. Then there was 'an ear-splitting big noise', and 'a blow as if clobbered by a plank pierced my left shoulder'. Ishikawa was bleeding and feeling faint but a medic got to him and patched him up.[7]

Ishikawa made his way back to Kankiryo to meet with the commander who was concerned for Ishikawa and also for the mountain gun, which he ordered to be moved. 'Though not entirely satis-fied,' Ishikawa found a new emplacement for the gun in a densely forested area at Kankiryo. 'We kept cutting down trees to the bare minimum to keep secrecy from the enemy,' Ishikawa wrote, because with 'spotter aircraft flying at will, it was a foregone con-clusion that our gun will be annihilated in one attack.' A sturdy timber frame was constructed over the gun and foliage was laid across this frame to camouflage the position. A reinforced log bunker was also constructed as an observation post with 'an unobstructed panoramic view'. Ishikawa's main targets were in the Faria Valley and up on Shaggy Ridge but even with the tenfold magnification of the artillery telescope he had difficulty spotting the fall of shot. Unfortunately for him there were no smoke rounds available for ranging, unlike for the Australians who used them to good effect. Ishikawa had few enough normal rounds and had to be frugal in their use. 'We could not fire to our satisfaction. But, given the valuable ammunitions transported with immense effort, we had to endure it.'[8]

•

Following the loss of Norm Trumper's Boomerang on 31 October it was decided to dive bomb the Kankiryo area. Lieutenant Erick Kyro was a P-39 Airacobra pilot in the 41st US Fighter Squadron based at Nadzab whose aircraft was named Sisu, Finnish for 'guts', a nod to his heritage. The Airacobra did have a bomb rack but it was normally used to carry a fuel drop tank to increase its limited range. The Airacobras were often used for short-range escorting of transport aircraft from Port Moresby to Buna, Wau and Nadzab and bombing missions were rare. During the Kokoda campaign small firebombs had been strapped onto the drop tanks and used as a makeshift bomb against the narrow, suspended Wairopi bridge over the Kumusi River. For the dive-bombing role against the mountain gun positions at Kankiryo, the armourers mounted a 500-pound bomb onto the shackle directly below the cockpit that was used for the drop tanks. 'The plane flew normally as the bomb did not weigh much more than a full 75-gallon fuel tank,' Kyro noted. The missions would be flown using only the internal fuel tank.[9]

At 4.00 pm on 1 November, RAAF Boomerangs guided two Airacobras to Kankiryo but the attack was unsuccessful because the target was partly hidden by cloud. Another attack was carried out the next day using eight Airacobras, including Kyro's. The aircraft flew a circling pattern over Kankiryo, taking turns to dive bomb the area after following a Boomerang down to the target. There were no clearings, no smoke and no apparent enemy ground fire 'to give us a clue what to aim at,' said Kyro. He followed a Boomerang down as it dived at a canopy of trees, but 'we could not see anything down there . . . all we saw on the mountainside was an extensive, ocean-like canopy of lush green tree tops'. Kyro resumed his place in the formation and once all eight aircraft had dropped their bombs, they returned to Nadzab.[10]

The Airacobra attacks did not stop the Japanese mountain guns so on 5 November a high-level air attack was organised on the Kankiryo area using four squadrons of medium bombers, 36 aircraft in all. At 10.10 am the bombers were over the target area at the head of the Faria River valley below Kankiryo. Australian artillery fire had indicated the general target area using smoke rounds and the bombs were all seen to fall in the target area. However, it would not stop the Japanese guns.

•

On 7 November, the 2/16th was relieved by the 2/25th Battalion. It seemed as if each new battalion had to go through the same experience of shellfire at Trevor's Ridge to learn the same lesson. The 2/16th men were not far down the track before the 2/25th had three casualties from the seven mountain-gun rounds that were sent their way.[11] The 2/16th set up headquarters at Guy's Post at the base of Shaggy Ridge. 'It rained and not having shelters erected, everyone got wet,' Private Jack Smith wrote.[12] Three weeks later on 29 November the 2/16th relieved the 2/33rd Battalion up on Shaggy Ridge. Corporal 'Bud' Harley had a good mate in the 2/33rd, Corporal Gordon Hancock, but had been told he had been killed in the tragic air accident in Port Moresby on 7 September. When an exhausted Harley reached the top of Shaggy Ridge after carrying the Bren gun up, the first guy he saw was Hancock, who had been injured in the crash but had recovered.[13]

Jack Smith was sent up the ridge to establish a forward aid post. 'It's a terrible climb,' he wrote. 'The Japs are holding the highest point about [140 metres] in front of our forward posts. To attack the Jap means a single-man front on the narrow ridge.' The forward company reported that 'This is the first time that it could be truthfully said that [the battalion] was holding a one-man front.'[14] Private Frank Murphy made up half the front line, sharing a weapon pit at the base of the incline below the Japanese-held Pimple, a prominent edifice at the top of a steep rocky slope. The main section position was about 25 metres further back along the ridge, and ahead of Murphy's outpost was a trip wire attached to a grenade hidden inside an empty bully beef tin.[15] On the ridge you dug a hole, got in it and didn't move at night. 'Only the Japs moved at night,' noted Private Vic Leicester. The men at the forward posts could hear the Japanese talking and the 2/16th men enjoyed shouting out the odd remark such as 'You couldn't hit a shithouse!' or from the enemy side, 'Ten mile Bogadjim!'[16] (Bogadjim was the closest village to Shaggy Ridge on the north coast.) Further back Jack Smith helped pitch the forward RAP tent on the only available flat space where 'the wind whistles across the ridge and is very cold'.[17]

Major Robert Alison had been the C Squadron commander in the motor regiment and now commanded C Company of the 2/16th. On 2 December he briefed a five-man patrol tasked with locating the forward enemy positions somewhere behind the Pimple and assessing their strength. 'Intelligence tells us they're gone,' Alison told them. 'Proceed till fired on, then withdraw.' Bud Harley was the point scout on the patrol, and when he passed Private Charlie Bloomfield at the forward post on the way out that morning Bloomfield called him over. 'They've told you they've gone, haven't they?' he asked. When Harley agreed, Bloomfield told him 'You watch yourself.'[18]

The patrol moved out in single file with Harley leading, but, due to the fallen bamboo and low undergrowth, progress was slow. The men had to crawl forward on their hands and knees and after 200 metres one man was dropped off to provide cover against any enemy flanking move. To Harley the approach to the dominating Pimple was like a quarry face and the climb was a challenge. When he got near the top he could hear enemy voices and also saw a slit trench with a clean and shiny rifle sticking out. Harley crawled up to within 4 metres of the slit trench, at which point a Japanese soldier stuck his head up. Harley fired the Owen gun he held in front of him and then headed back, bumping into Private Dawson 'Joe' Blow, who was behind him. The two men quickly jumped down the quarry face where Blow stood still for a while. 'C'mon Joe,' Harley told him. 'A man has to wait for his hat,' Blow replied as his hat slid down the slope after him. With a Japanese patrol further down the ridge trying to cut them off, the Australians headed back to their own lines for a meal.[19]

Food for the Australians normally meant canned bully beef, preferably heated up in a fire after a hole was pierced with a bayonet to let out the fat. The men could often get tomatoes or mangoes from a native village to make a stew with the bully beef, while native potatoes added some variety if you could get hold of them. Water was always scarce on the ridge, as it had to be carried up, so the men would spread their raised groundsheets over the top of their weapon pits so the regular afternoon rain showers ran off to be collected.[20]

•

Further along the ridge Kenji Ueda observed that every morning and afternoon there would be a break in the Australian activity. 'Then, a little smoke would appear from their position. Sometimes we could see them having tea or coffee.' One of the Japanese soldiers would then call out, 'Hey, the Australians are taking another tea break.' Although the Japanese wanted to fire at them, 'we couldn't as our location would be exposed,' Ueda recalled, and added that 'we had nothing like the luxuries they had'. The Japanese troops survived on minimal rations as if in a 'locked society'.[21]

The lack of tents made life particularly difficult for the Japanese. 'We slept in heavy rain for months,' remembered Ueda. 'When we slept, we leaned over on our rifles.' With food supplies often non-existent, the Japanese ate anything they could find on the ground. 'We ate bananas and grass, flowers and anything else,' according to Ueda. This proved fatal for some men who had eaten toxic beans and potatoes. One of Ueda's own men found some potatoes, which he cooked into a soup of sorts. When Ueda tried some, 'I spat it out straight away, but later the pain came, bad pain, and I couldn't stop drooling like a cow for a week.' Another of Ueda's men was not so fortunate. He had eaten much more and 'suffered from terrible pain for half an hour' before he died.[22]

Japanese troops at Kankiryo were hindered by steady rain, 'red worms which bore into the skin' (leeches) and food shortages after rations were cut in half. Due to the time in the front line and the lack of Vitamin B, starving and beri-beri riddled patients 'appeared one after another and fatigue was prevalent throughout the entire force'.[23] There was nothing to take the men's mind off their plight. Kumao Ishikawa had not received a single letter or read a newspaper in the ten months since he had left Korea.[24]

The Japanese concentrated on small surprise attacks at night. Moving in the darkness of the jungle was a challenge, and each man would carry a branch with some phosphorescent fungi attached. Kenji Ueda took part in one patrol where the men held hands to stay together but 'after five hours walking, we couldn't even find the enemy,' he said. 'So we went back to where we started.' After some initial success, such as at Yorweth's Knoll on the night of 10 December, 'it became very difficult because the Australians rigged up wire and microphones all over the jungle'. One night attack commanded by Lieutenant Tokunaga was detected and he lost a lot of men.[25]

Kenji Ueda's time on Shaggy Ridge came to an end prematurely, a victim of the ridge itself. He was returning from the front line to company headquarters, following the main track along the ridge when he fell down a steep cliff and hit his head on a rock.

'Fortunately I was wearing a helmet and my head was OK,' he said. But he had broken one of his kneecaps and was knocked unconscious. Fortunately another soldier found him several hours later and after a doctor came up to look at him he was sent back to the hospital in Madang. It was a hospital in name only, with 'ten tents there and nothing else,' leaving any other wounded and sick outside on the road. During his first week at the hospital seven soldiers with malaria were brought to beds near Ueda and all were dead before nightfall.[26]

From the middle of November through to late December heavy monsoon-like rain caused major problems for Japanese operations on the Huon Peninsula from the Finisterres to Finschhafen. Many men drowned crossing the swollen rivers between Madang and Sio, delaying any movement. Rising seas also made barge transport and unloading difficult while coastal defence guns were swept down and buried in sand. All the bridges but one along the Japanese supply road from the coast were washed away stopping all traffic and communication. Native billets couldn't stand the rain, clothing could not be dried, malaria and dysentery cases increased, and the Japanese were unable to repair airfields and roads. 'Ordnance material became rusty and damp in great numbers' while munitions failed due to lack of waterproofing.[27] By 23 December, 6 Company, which was responsible for the defence of Shaggy Ridge, had only 35 effective troops left out of the 192 men that had departed Japan.[28]

•

Throughout December Shaggy Ridge became 'the most popular AIF tourist resort' as a 'continual stream of visitors and more curious onlookers' visited the now famous one-man front.[29] Most of the time the ridge was covered in mist and this restricted visibility to 100 metres or less but 'On a clear day it was possible to see as far as the sea near Madang.'[30] General Vasey visited the ridge on 12 December, moving along the ridge to the forward weapon pit where Frank Murphy and Private Bill Ryan were keeping watch. 'G'day,' Vasey said and pulled out a pack of cigarettes and offered each of them a smoke. He then squatted down for a smoke and asked Murphy and Ryan how things were and if they were getting their mail and enough food.[31]

Vasey also met with the acting battalion commander, Major Garth Symington. Symington had been in command since 30 November after Colonel Sublet had left for a training course in Australia. Symington told Vasey that 'the boys were fed up with just patrolling' before saying that 'I think we could take Shaggy Ridge.' 'I don't think you could,' Vasey replied. 'Two colonels have told me it was not possible to take it from the front.' After Symington repeated that he thought it could be done, Vasey said, 'Thanks Symington, that's interesting.'[32]

On 17 December Symington had a call from Brigadier Dougherty. 'Garth, did you tell Vasey you could take Shaggy Ridge?' 'Yes I did,' Symington replied. 'You had no right to do it, now you have to do it,' Dougherty told him. On 18 December Symington discussed his plan with Dougherty who told him that the attack was not to take place until after Christmas Day as he 'wanted all Christmas comforts to get up to the troops'. Later Symington learned that Dougherty had wanted to make a brigade attack on the flank so was not at all pleased with the change of plan. Symington got little help from his brigadier in planning the attack so he dealt directly with division where he knew some people. He was very pleased to get significant artillery and air support but appreciated that the men would have to do the job on the ground. He was quietly confident that they would.[33] Vasey also seemed quietly confident. Passing through Dumpu on the way to the airfield on 21 December he told some of the men that 'we'll let them have their Christmas, but we'll give them a good New Year's present'. Dougherty, who had suffered a badly sprained ankle, flew out of Dumpu with Vasey and would not be present for the attack.[34]

Captain Ron Christian's B Company would make the initial attack. The companies took turns in occupying the forward positions on Shaggy Ridge and it happened to be Christian's company's turn at the time of the attack. On the morning of 26 December Christian was flown over the ridge in an RAAF Wirraway. 'The enemy was very well entrenched on the pimple,' Christian observed, 'Beyond this were two further known strong posts called intermediate snipers pimple and green snipers pimple. All three features were natural fortresses and honeycombed with foxholes well protected by strong posts.'[35]

Although Dougherty had left Symington to organise things himself, he did make contact directly with Ron Christian, asking him if he thought he could capture the Pimple. Christian replied that 'given sufficient air and artillery support we could do it' so Dougherty 'allowed me to plan the whole exercise. Christian's company was to capture the Pimple and advance along the ridge for about 400 metres before handing over to D Company to move through and consolidate. The initial attack would be supported by bombing and strafing from sixteen Kittyhawks, over 3000 rounds of artillery from two 25-pounder batteries, a section of 3-inch mortars with some 300 rounds and a section of Vickers machine guns with 10,000 rounds. As Christian recalled, Dougherty 'kept his promise about support and for that stage of the war it was unbelievable'.[36]

With so little room for manoeuvre, only one platoon could make the initial assault and that would be Lieutenant Arthur Geyton's 10 Platoon. Geyton was new to his command so the platoon sergeant, Tom 'Pinky' McMahon, suggested he should plan the assault and Geyton agreed. It was hard to argue with the fiery redhead. On 21 December McMahon carried out a patrol to the Pimple and was able to pinpoint the enemy positions.[37]

•

The most intriguing member of 10 Platoon was an American airman, Second Lieutenant Tommy Roberts. His journey to Shaggy Ridge began during the depression in 1932 when he left his home in Indiana, Ohio, and headed west where a ranch owner named Howard Boyce offered Roberts a job on his Colorado ranch. Roberts worked with Boyce for seven years, hunting coyotes and guiding the hunters who came to stay at the lodge. One of those hunters was David Hutchison, an airman who became a close friend and arranged for Roberts to join the Army Air Corps in 1942. Both men were based in Colorado and continued to hunt together.[38]

In November 1943 Tommy Roberts shipped out to Australia. By now David Hutchison, known as 'Photo Hutch', was a colonel and able to get Roberts a posting to the 25th Photo Reconnaissance Squadron. When Roberts mentioned that he wanted a crack at the Japanese, it was Hutchison who managed to overcome all the red tape due to his close relationship with General Vasey. 'When Roberts first came to me in New Guinea,'

Vasey said, 'he was introduced by a colonel of the US Army Air Corps and after the introduction Roberts, a pilot, told me his intention and asked my permission.' Roberts had told Vasey that 'Before I start shooting them in the air I want to shoot them on the ground.' Vasey agreed, so Roberts joined 10 Platoon on Shaggy Ridge about a week before the attack.[39] 'He staggered into the Australian lines carrying a pack bigger than himself,' Private George Ford remembered. 'He was the most cheerful bloke in the camp on Christmas Day 1943,' Private Danny Leu added, and he soon proved he was a crack shot with his American rifle.[40]

•

Since flying into Kaiapit in late September and trekking up the valley, Norm Stuckey had been constantly moving among the Australian units around Shaggy Ridge. 'The going was hard and the heat terrific,' he wrote. Like most of the men in the Ramu Valley, he was suffering from something, in his case infected insect bites that had laid him up for a week in mid-November. But 'I am still taking pictures' and 'am looking forward to hearing how my pictures are turning out'. His pictures were turning out very well. Stuckey didn't know it but his skill as a photographer was also causing issues at a high level back in Australia. Stuckey had worked as a press photographer for Sir Keith Murdoch in Melbourne before the war and Murdoch was now requesting he be released from his current work. This request had been made after another of Murdoch's *Melbourne Herald* photographers, Laurie Richards, was requested by the Ministry of Munitions. Stuckey did not want to come back and in the end got to stay, but although his photographic skills were gaining him recognition, he could not see the results for himself. On 10 November he asked that his film supplies be sent up wrapped in newspapers as he hadn't read one since 1 October. He knew some of his photos had been published but he was like a blind artist unable to see his own work.

On 19 December General Blamey visited the Ramu Valley to meet with General Vasey, and Norm Stuckey had the job of taking photos, meaning he could also listen to the plans for the upcoming operation. On 23 December Stuckey wrote in a letter, 'Sunday I intend to proceed to Shaggy Ridge where it is planned to push the enemy from a feature they have held for some time. This should provide us with some good material.' But on 26 December he was told, 'I think it would be wise to warn you against writing about future intentions such as the Shaggy Ridge business' and to 'keep the information strictly to yourself'.[41]

Down 'by a green volcanic lake in the foothills of the Finisterres' the war artist William Dargie looked out across the wide plain of the Ramu Valley to the clouded peaks of the Bismarck Ranges bordering the other side of the valley. Higher up on the sharp ridges 'one is never far from the skeleton of the earth,' Dargie wrote, 'eroded slopes of intrusive granite that has cooled and crystallized at some great depth, green rocks and flakes of red jasper, all exposed now that primary drainage has washed the great mass of their covering earth down to form the river flats below'. Like Stuckey, Dargie would record the sights and scenes of the Ramu Valley campaign, but he would use sketchbook and canvas.[42]

After a roast turkey and plum pudding lunch on Christmas Day, Ron Christian briefed his platoon and section leaders on the afternoon of 26 December. His company would attack the ridge on the following morning.

Chapter 11

THE PIMPLE

At dawn on 27 December the forward Australian troops on Shaggy Ridge pulled back about 250 metres in anticipation of the supporting bombardment. At 8.00 am two Boomerangs strafed the Pimple to indicate the dive bombing target for 16 Kittyhawks. Each plane dropped a single 300-pound bomb and, although four clearly missed, the other bombs looked on target. 'It was a beautiful sight,' Tommy Roberts wrote, 'you could see the bombs growing larger and larger, whistling as they came—then the terrible concussions.' It was a new experience for Roberts being on the ground so near to the target. 'The earth rocked and shook, trees were broken and tossed like jackstraws.'[1] 'The Kittyhawks were spectacular,' Captain Allan McInnes simply observed.[2]

At 8.16 am the artillery barrage began. Eight 25-pounder guns fired about 2100 rounds, the largest artillery concentration that the 2/4th Field Regiment had fired thus far in New Guinea.[3] The forward observing officer Lieutenant Ross Macfarlan, accompanied by three signallers, had spent a number of days observing the area and ranging the guns from an observation post in a tree. There was also an alternate post further back which gave an extensive view over most of the ridge and as far as the north coast. From this post Colin Stirling had seen the Japanese at Kankiryo Saddle but they were hard to hit as 'you couldn't get the angle with the range' to drop a shell on the target. The artillery was now targeting the Pimple, but because it was a solid rock outcrop, the shells only chipped away at the target, creating a lot of loose shale.[4] 'The spur was completely hidden in the pall of smoke,' Tommy Roberts wrote.[5]

For some 45 minutes from 8.30 am the Kittyhawks returned to strafe the ridge north of the Pimple, firing 12,855 rounds of .50 calibre. 'The Kittyhawks re-formed and came back to pepper the top of the hill with bullets,' the war correspondent Kenneth Slessor wrote. Four Vickers machine guns added another 10,000 rounds from 8.51 am.[6] More artillery and mortar fire followed. 'By the time the mortars had finished, the barrels were half way down into the shale and mud,' Frank Murphy recalled. Murphy got a face full of dirt from stray shell fragments landing nearby while another large shell piece dug into the ground beneath his boot with steam rising up around it.[7] At 9.00 am Lieutenant Lance Logan, who had a grandstand view of the bombardment from Feature 5500 west of Shaggy Ridge, sent out the simple message, 'Boy are they pasting shit out of Shaggy.'[8] Down at Kankiryo, Kumao Ishikawa noted that 'from early morning, the enemy gunnery soldiers commenced firing in unison with full power'. Ishikawa could only see the front-line positions along the ridge in glances 'between smokes from exploding shells' and it offered 'a savage scene as if the entire mountain was changed'.[9]

•

As the artillery barrage crept forward, the men from 10 Platoon moved up to the start line at the base of the scree-covered slope below the Pimple, carrying bamboo ladders to assault what one observer called 'Nature's Bastille'.[10] Unfortunately the ladders could get no purchase on the loose scree and were abandoned. George Morris, the company sergeant major, had shown up just before the attack with a coil of rope over his shoulder and said it was best to go up the scree on hands and knees.[11] Prior to the attack Garth Symington had told Morris, 'I don't want to see your red hair up there.' However, from his advanced headquarters on the ridge, Symington could see the red heads of both Morris and McMahon through his field glasses climbing up the face of the Pimple.[12]

The rock wall had been stepped out every metre or so prior to the attack but the bombardment had removed any trace of the steps and it was very slippery going up as the stone on the hill kept giving way.[13] Pinky McMahon was the first one up and immediately went to ground on the ridge crest in front of the Pimple. He knew there was a dip in the ground here which was in defilade from the bunker in front of the Pimple but he wondered why no one else had followed him over the top and was hollering out 'Come and give me a hand!' It appeared another position off to McMahon's right on the side of the ridge had started a crossfire that had cut off the rest of the men.[14]

Although he was on his own, McMahon was trying to keep the enemy occupied. He started throwing his six grenades into

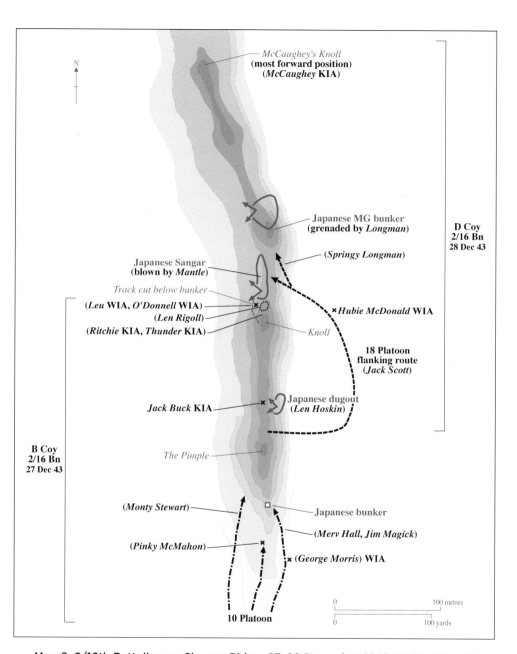

Map 9: 2/16th Battalion on Shaggy Ridge, 27–28 December 1943 (Keith Mitchell)

the bunker but although he was landing them inside they were thrown back at him before exploding. McMahon would then try to brush them over the side of the ridge but he was too slow with one and it exploded, badly damaging his left hand. Down below, George Morris and Corporal George Walker had a grenade land between them, peppering them with shards. McMahon thought that the grenade that wounded Morris may have been one that he had brushed away over the side of the ridge. Without the use of one hand McMahon had to put any grenade under his boot before pulling the pin and throwing it with his good hand. Once out of grenades, McMahon held his Owen gun out in front with his good hand to fire at any attempt to get at him with a rifle shot. Fortunately he was in a blind spot where the defenders in the bunker had to poke their heads up to see him and then 'hold their rifles up high and fire without looking'. Apart from the hand wound McMahon had also been wounded in the side of his head and when he wiped it he got blood in his eyes making it difficult to see. Time was running out for the daring redhead.[15]

Faced with the imposing climb up through the loose shale of the cliff face, Corporal Monty Stewart had taken his section around to the left across the wooded slope while Corporal Merv Hall took his section around to the right across the exposed slope. Stewart had George Fritz behind him but Fritz was having trouble getting forward with the Bren gun so Stewart got about 10 metres out in front. He was climbing at the tree line where the shattered trees from the Pimple formed a mass of tangled wood that he could step on, but it was slow going as his backpack caught up in the branches. As he came almost level with the bunker, Stewart could see it was set back from the top of the scree slope in front of the Pimple and dug into the side of the hill. From the front the bunker had a long firing slit on the left and a doorway to the right where an enemy defender was sheltering. Stewart was looking at the bunker and hanging on to a branch but he couldn't get his feet set in order to bring his Owen gun to bear and he didn't want to spray the shot.[16]

Before Stewart could get set to fire he saw Merv Hall suddenly appear on the skyline racing in towards the bunker from the right. The defender in the doorway did a back flip and catapulted back into the bunker as Hall moved in throwing grenades and firing his Owen gun. From Pinky McMahon's viewpoint it looked like one of the defenders had jumped out of the bunker with a bayonet and 'Merv shot him as his feet hit the ground.' When a second defender emerged, Hall's Owen gun jammed so he struck him down with the gun butt before throwing a grenade into the bunker. Private Jim Magick was close behind Hall, 'rattling away' with his Bren gun, providing covering fire. The bunker was captured and all occupants were killed while Hall was wounded in the forehead.[17]

Jack Smith had moved forward with the leading section. The track up the ridge was 'covered with smashed branches and bamboos knocked down by the artillery,' he wrote. 'In places it meant lying down and rolling under tangled debris.' Once up, Smith got busy treating the wounded.[18] As 10 Platoon moved forward towards the top of the Pimple, Monty Stewart again took his section along the left side of the ridge through the shattered trees. The 25-pounders were still lobbing shells in front and there was the odd tree burst behind and Stewart thought he was lucky to get through.[19]

Danny Leu was just behind Stewart as they stood up to fire on a second bunker just over the top of the Pimple, but as they broke the skyline a machine gun in the bunker opened up and Leu was hit in the chest, puncturing a lung. To the right of Stewart, Private Dinny O'Donnell was also wounded when a grenade exploded in front of him, leaving his face a mess. Stewart's section then kept down below the crest and sheltered in the scrub at the side of the Pimple. As the defenders started to throw grenades Stewart had to hang onto Danny Leu with one hand and use the other to hold onto some scrub while also brushing the grenades away down the slope to explode harmlessly. After one exploded close to his left leg and peppered his left thigh, Stewart managed to prop his haversack out in front for some added protection. 'It's getting dark,' Leu observed, but with the help of stretcher bearers he was dragged back along the side of the ridge. After being relieved by 11 Platoon half an hour later Stewart caught up with the wounded and helped carry Leu's stretcher further back to the aid post.[20]

As the wounded men made their way back along the ridge they passed Norm Stuckey who took photographs of all of them. Private Harry Raiskio, the big Finn with a wounded arm, Pinky McMahon nursing his busted hand, George Morris lying down with a cuppa, Merv Hall with his head heavily bandaged, a battered Dinny O'Donnell and a stretcher-bound Danny Leu. Stuckey then watched as the native bearers began the long carry down the ridge with George Morris on a stretcher. Stuckey had already taken some photos of the D Company men as they waited back on the ridge and he then went forward with them as the men relieved B Company. He took photos of men from Lieutenant Jack Scott's 18 Platoon burying four enemy dead in the bunker below the Pimple, as well as some views back down the ridge before heading down the ridge with his exposed film packs. Earlier that morning Stuckey had thought he may get no worthwhile photographs that day but had ended up taking some of the best of his career.

Having set out at first light through mud nearly up to his knees, Stuckey was well on his way up the ridge when he was stopped in his tracks. 'Imagine my surprise on getting halfway up the 5000 odd ft climb to be told that orders were that I wasn't to proceed,' he wrote. A major from public relations told Stuckey he had to wait for the commander's permission to go further. Stuckey knew that would be after the attack was over so he got on the phone to the commander, presumably Major Symington, who reiterated his previous orders that the photographer was not to proceed. Stuckey kept talking, earbashing the commander until he finally relented. 'It was only my initiative that got me there,' Stuckey wrote. While Sergeant Darrell 'Joe' Kinna, the cine-cameraman, who was on a hill some 3 kilometres away 'got sweet fanny adams on what is considered the most important action of the Divvy in this show', Stuckey took 60 photos that day, starting with the bombardment of the Pimple and finishing with the Australians in occupation of that key position. After descending the ridge and making the long walk back to Dumpu, Stuckey was spent. 'By jove I had a big day on that job,' he wrote, 'I was just euchred [exhausted].'[21]

•

As the men from 12 Platoon moved up, they faced the same problem as the men that preceded them. Frank Murphy found climbing up the face of the Pimple a case of advancing 2 metres and then sliding back one, flat on your face in the loose shale. To

Murphy it was like a ski run and when he reached the top he had to tip his Bren gun upside down to get the dirt out.[22] The area had really taken a hammering. 'It was like rubble up there,' Private Allan Cook said.[23] The signaller Private Rolfe 'Blackie' Butler had trouble early as he had laid the cable right up to the start line and a bomb had dropped short and blown it away. It had to be laid again and then extended up onto the Pimple, right over the top of the first bunker. The delay meant that the signallers were late getting the phone line up to the forward units, much to the chagrin of Captain Christian.[24]

Back at the top of the scree slope Private Jack Buck leaned over the eastern side of the ridge to fire on a slit trench further down and was shot through the mouth and killed.[25] Allan Cook was nearby and thought it a fluke shot, as the enemy defender had just put his rifle up through the slit in the groundsheet covering the trench and fired blind. Tich Pearce went past and saw Buck lying face down with a hole in the back of his head from the exit wound as though he was looking out over the Faria River. 'That Jap kept popping up to have a shot, and used a groundsheet over his foxhole to flick off the grenades,' said Monty Stewart. 'You had to lean over and drop a grenade on the position, but it would be flicked aside with the covering groundsheet,' Cook added. One of the men brought up a length of bamboo from one of the ladders abandoned at the cliff face and they tied a grenade to the end and attached a length of vine to the pin before lowering it. The first time they tried to pull the pin the vine broke, but although the next one worked the Japanese defender kept firing back.[26]

Tommy Roberts had gone in with B Company, struggling up the scree slope in his flying boots and finally discarding them. Once up on top he had been running around 'like a chook with his head cut off' according to Frank Murphy. To Roberts it was 'like back home bear huntin'. Armed with his semi-automatic Garand rifle, he had finally found a spot on the ridge not far past where Jack Buck was killed and was watching the ridge side. Murphy was also there when one of the Japanese defenders emerged from his foxhole and ran across the slope trying to escape. He slipped and slid about before Roberts fired at him with the Garand until he hit and sent him tumbling down the ridge side. Murphy had his Bren on the ground but, by the time he brought it up to fire, Roberts had done the job.[27]

Murphy then moved up with 12 Platoon to form a perimeter up to the knoll above the second bunker. It was actually a stone sangar (a bunker built above ground), solidly positioned on top of the ridge at a point where both sides of the ridge were almost sheer so it could not be outflanked. Christian and Symington came up and decided the battalion would hold what it had got and at 11.00 am D Company took over. When Private Jack Ritchie and Private Tim O'Brien came forward to relieve Murphy and Bill Ryan in the forward Bren gun position, Murphy showed Ritchie the field of fire to the north along the side of the ridge and to the west into the undergrowth. He then added, 'if you want to have a go at it, go around to the left'. Then he asked, 'Have you got all that?' 'Yeah,' Ritchie replied. Then Murphy made a final point, telling Ritchie, 'whatever you do, don't put your head over the ridge or you're a goner'. They were the same words that Murphy had been told when he had earlier taken over the position from Jim Magick. From the top of the small knoll in front it was only about 12 metres to the bunker. Murphy then headed off down the ridge but had not gone more than 25 metres when he heard a single rifle shot ring out and also heard the shout of 'Bloody hell no!' from the forward position. Ritchie was dead, shot in the head as he chanced a look forward, falling back into O'Brien's arms. O'Brien later told Murphy that everything Ritchie had been told not to do, he did.[28]

An hour after the Pimple had been captured Johnny Pearson was up there directing artillery fire, bringing the shells down only 50 metres ahead of the forward positions. During the first phase of the attack 3362 rounds were fired onto an area approximately 400 metres long with practically no width. The guns down in the valley got so hot that the gunners would burn themselves on the cradles, let alone the barrels.[29] A Boomerang flying over the ridge reported that there were 'Japs streaming back towards [the] saddle'.[30]

The challenge for D Company was how to get beyond the second Japanese bunker, a task that the intelligence sergeant attached to the field security section at brigade headquarters thought he had the simplest of answers for: Sergeant Eric Thunder, who could speak Japanese, arrived at the forward position in the afternoon and, although he was told not to put his head up, 'he got up and verbally abused the enemy in their own language,' Private Ray Mantle observed. 'He lasted less than 10 seconds' before being shot. The men were told that his body must not be captured and they retrieved it the next day.[31]

That afternoon the forward platoon began to dig a trench around the western side of the ridge towards the enemy bunker. The new plan was to get close enough to use Molotov cocktails against the bunker, which was constructed of stone and sat astride the razorback of the ridge with a sheer drop on either side. The men worked all through the night on the trench and by morning they were close enough. Meanwhile, at about midday, Corporal

Len Rigoll had got forward over the knoll into a small recess where the bunker couldn't fire at him and was able to keep an eye on the position. The Japanese would throw grenades but Rigoll would kick them over the side of the ridge and he remained there until 4.30 am the following morning.[32]

•

Down in the Ramu Valley a more measured approach was being taken to eliminating the difficult Japanese positions on the ridge. The 2/5th Field Company had been asked to provide blast bombs, each made up using a steel cylinder filled with nearly 3 kilograms of gelignite with the base plate from a hand grenade welded onto one end. A hole was drilled through the base plate so that, when a grenade was screwed on, the detonator would drop through the hole into the gelignite. The gelignite-filled cylinders had been made up by the workshop at Nadzab and put on the next flight to Dumpu. Then it was up to Captain 'Dinky' Giles to attach the grenade but he found that the hole in the base was too small for the detonator to fit through. With no time to fly new bombs up, Giles drove a jeep to a remote spot and sat with the bomb between his legs as he drilled out each hole hoping that this would not ignite the gelignite.[33]

Sappers Len Hoskin and Jackie Jamieson were given the job of taking six blast bombs up the ridge. Two native carriers helped them but 'The further we climbed the more I discarded equipment,' Hoskin noted. He was amazed at the endurance of the carriers. 'With his pack and my gear they must have been carrying [35 to 45 kilograms] and to see them walk up these steps without a pause or a bend in the back was something to see. It must have amused them greatly to see us struggling up.' Finally Hoskin came to a point where 'I looked up and saw these rough steps cut into what looked to me to be a vertical cliff.' It was the incline up to the Pimple. Hoskin then handed over his Owen gun and made the climb up on his hands and knees.[34]

The target for the first blast bomb was the position dug into the eastern side of the ridge from where Jack Buck had been shot and which had defeated all attempts to silence it with grenades. It had been cleverly dug back into the ridge at right angles, meaning that the blast from an ordinary grenade had no effect on the occupants. Under cover from a Bren gunner, Hoskin had a look at how he was going to employ the bomb. The idea was to drop it into the small opening at the top of the position, a hole only about 45 cm long and 15 cm wide, just enough room to poke a gun out. Hoskin would not be able to climb down to it so he would have to lean over the side of the ridge with two men holding onto his legs in order to drop the bomb in. Hoskin told the two leg holders to heave him back in a hurry when he shouted out. His first attempt missed and, as the attached grenade had an 8-second fuse, the bomb was a long way down the cliff before it exploded. With the second bomb, 'I pulled the pin, counted to four in the best military manner . . . shouting out at the same time as I let it go.' As he was pulled back up, Hoskin was pleased to see the bomb 'drop truly into the opening and that was that'. Some men went down and dug out two dead Japanese, one of them an officer. The bodies had not a mark on them; the blast had killed them as they sheltered around the corner of the position dug into the side of the ridge.[35]

•

Determined to get the advance moving along the ridge, Garth Symington had met with the D Company commander Captain Vivian Anderson on the afternoon of 27 December to plan the attack for the next day. With 16 Platoon now in position to attack the stone sangar at the second pimple, the plan was for Lieutenant Jack Scott's 18 Platoon to move down the open eastern side of the ridge and then across the slope to a position below the third pimple before climbing the ridge and capturing the position. Scott, who had only just returned to the battalion following an attack of malaria, was one of the most experienced men in the battalion, having served throughout the war with the 2/16th. After being badly wounded in Syria and again on the Kokoda Track and for a third time at Gona, Scott had been commissioned.[36]

Symington discussed the bold plan with Scott who agreed that a flanking move was the best option. The platoon would move down to a sloping plateau, which was wide enough to move along before they began the ascent. 'They had to go over the cliff from where we were and scramble around the ledges,' Len Hoskin said. The men had earlier used shovels to dig into the side of the ridge to which they attached ropes, giving them something to hold onto to get around the side of the ridge. To get down they just 'had to slide down the hill' and, having reached the plateau, Scott noticed that the battalion padre, Charlie Cunningham, was there. 'What do you think you're doing here, Pard?' Scott asked him. Without slowing up, Cunningham replied, 'Wherever my boys are going, I go too.'[37]

Meanwhile, the men from Lieutenant Sam McCaughey's 16 Platoon had spent the night digging around the stone sangar at the second pimple. The sheer drop on either side prevented any normal attempt to outflank the post but during the night the western side of the ridge was cut away to get around the sangar to the trees where the snipers couldn't get them. The digging was difficult as the ridge was full of rock. 'It was a very hard slog,' Ray Mantle said. McCaughey was quite young and, like his company commander, he had come across from the 16th Motor Regiment. He was one of those digging and the sweat was pouring off him. Mantle was McCaughey's batman and knew he could be 'a cranky bastard' so was certainly determined to get his platoon moving along the ridge.[38]

The sangar was about 3 metres square with some wood to hold the roof up and a small hole at the side for entry. There were still four blast bombs available and Ray Mantle was handed one of them. 'Here, you get rid of this,' he was told. Mantle positioned himself at the side of the bunker, pulled the pin on the grenade and threw the bomb into a hole at the side. The explosion blew the side out of the sangar and Mantle lost his hat in the blast. McCaughey's men then climbed along the side of the ridge in single file, hand over hand with their rifles slung over their shoulders, until they reached the next bunker where they waited for Scott's men to arrive from below and deal with it.[39]

At 10.50 am Scott reported that his platoon was in position down the slope at the base of the third pimple. From the time Scott's men had left the ridge it had taken about four hours to reach the foot of the cliff beneath the enemy stronghold. Scott had a walkie-talkie to talk with Captain Anderson, who was controlling the supporting fire on the enemy positions and at 11.05 am Anderson called for artillery and mortars to drop smoke onto the third pimple to cover Scott's move up the ridge. Scott couldn't see the enemy position but Anderson had a clear view along the top of the ridge from his position and was able to tell Scott 'You're directly below your objective, you are now on your own.'[40]

Scott realised that to scale the cliff with all his men, 'laden with all our gear and ammo would be too difficult, and would destroy the element of surprise'. He told his men to take a break and gathered the three section leaders and the platoon sergeant, Jack 'Springy' Longman, for a short conference. A small mobile section carrying only Owen guns, spare magazines and grenades would make the attack, led by Jack Longman, a natural athlete known as 'spring heel Jack' or Springy for short. An original member of the battalion, Longman was very cool under fire and nothing seemed to unduly worry him. 'She'll be right' was his standard answer to everything. Scott would bring the rest of the men up on the left-hand side where there was more leverage, but which was also subject to enemy fire. He hoped that 'by the time we got there they would be too busy with Springy and his boys to do much about it'.[41]

As the men gathered beneath the rocky overhang, Scott was quite confident they could not be fired on from above. However, they were vulnerable to any grenades that may be rolled down and that soon happened. 'Look out, there's a grenade!' someone shouted and three men went one way and the rest the other. The grenade exploded among the three men, Private Clarrie Trunk, Lance Corporal Hubie McDonald and Private Bill Broughton, and Hubie was blown off the ridge side, coming to rest on a small ledge lower down. Trunk was hit in one eye and also badly wounded in the leg above the knee. Jack Scott ripped the leg of Trunk's pants and patched his wound but was unaware that McDonald was also wounded. 'I was not aware that he had gone over the edge,' Scott later wrote, 'I was fully occupied with trying to keep our bearings.'[42] Len Hoskin watched from up on the ridge as 'Another chap copped it and rolled back down the cliff and fortunately landed on a ledge and was just lying there apparently badly wounded.' Hoskin then saw the padre, 'hanging on just fingers and feet work his way around to the ledge'.[43] 'Your family has already lost one son, I am going to see to it that they don't lose another,' Cunningham told McDonald, whose brother Terry had been killed during the Kokoda campaign.[44] But Cunningham would need more help to get the wounded McDonald back up the ridge.

Just after midday Vickers and Bren guns opened up to cover the final climb up the ridge. There were also some smoke rounds, which landed very close to Scott's men to provide further cover from observation. Half a dozen men formed a pyramid so Longman's section could scramble up the overhanging cliff far enough to get a hold in cracks and crevices on the rock face. Scott watched as Longman pulled himself up with his left hand while firing his Owen gun with his right as he went over the top. Longman crawled up while the machine gun was firing and put a grenade with a short 2-second fuse into the bunker embrasure which silenced the position. With the way now clear, the rest of the men climbed up further to the left where some steps had been dug. Private Jim Knight positioned himself on the lip of the cliff where he could fire his Bren gun directly into the enemy position and beyond with great effect.[45]

Further back on the ridge Len Hoskin watched the extraordinary assault by Scott's men. Jack Jamieson was with him, the men 'as safe as a bank' protected in the lee of the sharp ridge. 'What we witnessed in the next hour or so was as incredible and spectacular as anyone could ever wish to see,' Hoskin wrote. From only

50 metres away he could hear Scott's orders and the men calling out to each other. 'The officer leading the attack stood on the top perfectly skylined and was issuing orders and pointing to both sides for riflemen this way, machine gunners over there, when we saw him grab his shoulder and stagger but he still stood there doing his job although he had been hit,' Hoskin added.[46] Scott remained on duty and was later awarded the Military Cross for his inspiring leadership, which had opened up the way forward along the ridge.

Bud Harley was up on the ridge when Padre Cunningham came up to him and said, 'Bud, can you spare me half an hour?' Harley agreed and asked, 'What can I do for you, Padre?' Cunningham told him that 'You can help me bring back Hubie McDonald.' They grabbed a stretcher and headed down. 'Hubie was on a small level neck of land, on his back, with a field dressing on his thigh, [and] another chap was with him,' Harley wrote.[47] The other chap was Bombardier Morrie Bellairs, an artillery signaller. Bud Harley got McDonald in a fireman's lift and carried him out to where he could climb up to the track. He then called out for a rope and tied it under his own arms, got McDonald back in the fireman's lift and where he couldn't crawl he was pulled up the slope.[48]

•

Scott's men had no sooner taken up defensive positions at the third pimple when Sam McCaughey's platoon 'came storming along the track and occupied positions forward of us'.[49] Lance Corporal Jim McCulloch took the lead section forward, helped by the bombing and shellfire that had cleared some of the undergrowth. Most of the enemy positions were down in the trees, dug into the western side of the ridge protected from artillery fire, and held by young soldiers dressed in three or four shirts due to the cold at night. The constant noise and confusion seemed to keep the defenders' heads down as McCulloch's section moved along the ridge. John Bidner had half a sugar bag full of grenades and the remaining three blast bombs, which he would hand up to the men in front who would drop them into the enemy dugouts down the slope. One man at a time would go forward. McCulloch did one, Private Wally Offer another and Bidner did one of the blast bombs himself. Having edged his way forward on his backside, Bidner sat on top of the ridge, pulled the pin on the grenade, held the lever and then dropped the blast bomb into the entrance hole at the top of the dugout. He then leaned back as the earth rose in front of him.[50]

For one of the defenders the thought of being blasted out was too much. McCulloch watched as he ran back along the open side of the ridge until someone fired a burst sending him rolling like a ball down the side of the ridge. Another bewildered defender came out of his dugout near what would come to be called McCaughey's Knoll and stood out in the open on a boulder until a Bren gun burst nearly cut him in two.[51] Snipers were the biggest threat to McCaughey's men. McCulloch spent an hour trying to get a peek at one but every time he lifted his head a shot would ring out. They finally got compass bearings on the trajectory of the rounds and the sniper was shot.[52]

The platoon advanced about 150 metres along the ridge to McCaughey's Knoll. They stopped when they realised the Japanese had dug in underneath the knoll and were throwing grenades. One of the men was wounded.[53] Further back on the ridge Scott's platoon had come under sporadic sniper fire so he moved his men off the summit and on to the reverse slope. This brought its own problems as that side of the ridge was heavily timbered and even though the trees were now only skeletons there was still the danger from tree bursts. The Japanese gunners would aim at the trees so that when the shells exploded the shell fragments would rain down on anyone sheltering below. The men got busy with their bayonets trying to cut the trees down and Scott sent a message back for some axes to be brought up. He then decided to go back to company headquarters himself but was only half-way back when the enemy mountain gun opened up. A shell then landed 'not far behind me and blew me forward down the gravel slope and into the lap of CSM Stan Hounslow'.[54]

The Australian artillery was also busy. Private Allan Bidner was alongside the forward observation officer who was moving along the top of the ridge directing fire onto an enemy sniper. The sniper was firing at anyone who stuck their head above the top of the ridge. Bidner could hear the shells going by as the observer brought them as close to the top of the ridge as he dared. To Bidner the shells were 'so close you thought you could reach out and catch them'. There were also targets down in the Faria River valley where Japanese troops could be seen digging trenches. 'You just watch this mob,' he told Bidner as a ranging shot landed near their position and then the next one hit right among them.[55]

Down at Kankiryo, Kumao Ishikawa could see the Australian assault moving along the top of the ridge, closing in on the headquarters bunker. 'Under such a ferocious shelling, even in the reinforced bunker, built as it was with timber, very few of the men who fought in this position would have survived,' he thought. A gun further back along the ridge and a battalion gun were already firing along the ridge in support of 11 Company, but one of Ishikawa's men urged him to also fire their gun in support. However, Ishikawa knew he couldn't do so without cutting down more trees around the gun position and exposing it to Australian observers. He went looking for an alternate gun position but then heard the crashing of Australian shellfire onto Kankiryo. He raced back to the observation post to be told that, after he had left, Lieutenant Nakao had come to the gun position in a distressed state asking why the gun wasn't firing while the men up on the ridge were being attacked. Some trees were cleared and then 35 rounds were fired. The Australian observer up on the ridge then brought down counter-fire and, with the shells landing close by, Nakao 'ordered us to leave temporarily,' Tsutou Kobayashi said. Then 'one round directly hit our gun and destroyed it'. When Ishikawa arrived he found that amidst the fallen and split trees, now open to the sky, lay the dead and the dying gun crew. The gun 'had received a direct hit in the axis of the bore, the barrel being split like a peeled banana,' Ishikawa wrote. If that was indeed the case it is more likely a Japanese round exploded in the barrel.[56]

•

Despite the loss of the gun down in the valley, the Japanese gun further along the ridge fired 30 rounds on the morning of 29 December, aiming at the tree tops at the back of the ridge. 'The shrapnel spread everywhere,' Jim McCulloch said.[57] The men would cut down the trees to prevent tree bursts using Bren or rifle fire. About ten well-placed shots would drop the top but there were a lot of trees along the ridge and it was a dangerous place to be.[58] Jack Scott moved his men to the open eastern side of the ridge during the shelling and let the shells go over the top.[59]

The mountain gun shelling resumed in the afternoon and there were more tree bursts, one blast catching Wally Offer and knocking John Bidner out. Ray Mantle was in a foxhole near Sam McCaughey when Offer was hit and he heard his lieutenant call out for a stretcher bearer. Then McCaughey said, 'Bugger it, I'll do it myself' and left his foxhole to help Offer. When Bidner recovered he got to his feet and staggered up to the top of the hill back to where McCaughey was helping Offer when he heard the mountain gun fire again. He and McCaughey went to ground next to each other but McCaughey copped the full blast. He turned to Bidner, saying, 'I've had it, Blondie.' Despite the shellfire Private Ross Younger helped get McCaughey under cover where Private Jim Mortimer treated him, but the brave lieutenant died on the knoll that would now bear his name.[60]

Bidner made his way back to the aid post where Bud Harley asked him 'What's wrong?' Bidner then showed him the hole he had in his back. He was put on a stretcher and his wound was dressed but the medical officer, Captain John Zwar, was concerned and said that he had to be taken off the ridge that night for further treatment. The native carriers were asked to do it so they cut longer poles and made up a saggy stretcher to enable Bidner to be carried safely down to the main dressing station where he was immediately operated on.[61]

•

On 30 December C Company relieved D at McCaughey's Knoll. A Japanese sniper was making life difficult so the men dug a crawl trench and one man went forward at a time to try to spot the sniper. Bud Harley occupied the position for a while and tried the old trick of putting his hat out on a branch to attract fire, but when the sniper fired, his shot was only an inch away from Harley's head. The patient watching paid off, however, when the sniper was shot at dusk as he was coming down from his tree.[62]

The next day there was more shelling from the mountain gun and Major Alison suggested to Symington that they pull back from McCaughey's Knoll and allow the air force to bomb the reverse slopes. After Symington said he thought the men should stay, Alison went to see Brigadier Dougherty about it, and later on Symington 'was given a dressing down by Dougherty at his HQ'.[63] Some days later the battalion did pull back to Intermediate Sniper's Pimple, from where they could still see through to the coast and control the ridge but were much safer from the Japanese artillery fire.

The battle for Shaggy Ridge was for the moment stalled. The Japanese considered that they had lost a most vital position to the enemy but they still held most of the ridge. They had lost twenty men and ten were wounded but 33 men remained to defend the ridge top.[64]

Chapter 12

18TH BRIGADE

The pressure was now on to find the Japanese mountain guns that caused the Australians to pull back from McCaughey's Knoll and Green Sniper's Pimple. It was a priority for the flight of RAAF Boomerangs operating off the secondary strip at Gusap. The loss of Norm Trumper in October clearly showed the dangers involved in flying around Shaggy Ridge and the pilots had to be constantly aware of their aircrafts' limitations. As Flying Officer Alex Miller-Randle later wrote, 'an aircraft, unlike a car or helicopter, cannot stop and back off'. Miller-Randle considered that 'flying up a valley close to tree tops was extremely dangerous because it was very difficult to judge the incline'. That incline could often exceed the aircraft's maximum rate of climb and the valley usually narrowed as it approached the head of the valley, making turning back impossible. These were exactly the conditions faced in flying up the Faria River and Mindjim River valleys to Kankiryo Saddle. Flying downhill also had its dangers. After flying a Wirraway down the Faria Valley to make a supply drop over Trevor's Ridge, Miller-Randle misjudged his descent and returned to Gusap with branches, twigs and leaves around the control surfaces of his right-hand stabiliser.[1]

Miller-Randle, 'an out of condition, puny-muscled flyer', was taken up to Shaggy Ridge on foot so the artillery observers could show him where they thought the guns were located. 'All the way up,' he wrote, 'on any piece of ground that showed even a suspicion of being flat' were men 'lying on or under groundsheets for protection, resting and sleeping'. After warnings about sleepwalking and grenade explosions, Miller-Randle 'slept like the dead' and headed back down the next day. 'Coming down was not a whole lot easier. I was wet and covered in mud, and walking in the rain, drizzle or mist,' he wrote. Every so often an enemy shell would go over the ridge, searching for the Australian positions and Miller-Randle 'began to appreciate how damned important it was to find those guns and destroy them'.[2]

On 31 December he flew a mission to Shaggy Ridge with Flight Lieutenant Eric 'Bob' Staley. 'On that day, Bob and I went out specifically to find the guns.' One aircraft flew as top cover while the other stayed low, flying along the open eastern side of Shaggy Ridge looking 'under the foliage for gun ramps or caves'. At one point while Miller-Randle was flying top cover he realised that Staley's aircraft had disappeared. 'Panther one. Do you read me? Over,' he radioed, but there was no reply. 'Eventually with heavy heart I returned to base.'[3]

Across to the west of Shaggy Ridge on Feature 5500, Trooper Allen Osborne, who was manning a 2/6th Commando Squadron outpost, had a bird's eye view as Staley's aircraft dived up and down over the Prothero feature at the northern end of the ridge. 'He was obviously looking at something,' Osborne recalled. Then at one point the plane dived down but didn't come back up. Osborne watched and waited before scraping a line on the ground with his foot in line with where the plane had disappeared. Then he could see a smoke plume rising away to the north and could hear the aircraft's ammunition exploding.[4]

A patrol was sent out and when Osborne reached the crash site the next day he found the Boomerang's engine and half of one wing had burned out but the rest was intact. Staley had been thrown out of the plane on contact and an empty pistol holder with Staley's name on it was found on his body. The Japanese had already been there. Next day another Australian patrol reached the site, scratched out a grave and buried the brave pilot.[5]

Staley had suffered the same fate as Trumper in October, shot down by ground fire as he tried to spot the Japanese gun positions around Kankiryo. A citation was later found among captured documents stating, 'Sergeant Major Fujita and five men from 6 Company on anti-aircraft firing duty in Kankiryo area shot down one enemy plane on 31 December 1943. They are hereby commended for the exploit.' The citation was signed by General Nakai.[6]

•

With the new year, Brigadier Dougherty's 21st and Brigadier Eather's 25th Brigade would be relieved. Battle casualties within the brigades had not been unduly serious but they had been severely weakened by non-battle losses, particularly malaria. The military term for this loss of unit strength was 'wastage' and the average wastage in the 7th Division during the Markham and Ramu campaigns was 3.66 per cent. Of this figure only 0.13 per cent were battle casualties and thus for every battle casualty during the campaign the division had 28 non-battle casualties. The wastage figure for the division had steadily risen with every month in theatre. In September it was 0.9 per cent, October 2.29 per cent, November 4.08 per cent and by December wastage was averaging 5.44 per cent. The December figure reflected an average of 711 men out of action from a total average strength of 13,074.[7] 'The place was full of malaria,' Vic Leicester observed. 'The lines got pretty thin.'[8]

The third of General Vasey's brigades, Brigadier Fred Chilton's 18th, would replace the 21st while Brigadier Heathcote 'Tack' Hammer's 15th Brigade, a militia unit, would replace the 25th. The AIF battalions were made up of men who had volunteered for service worldwide while militia troops were limited to Australian territory only, including Papua and New Guinea. Like many other senior AIF officers, Vasey was not keen on having a militia brigade under his command. 'I have a militia brigade, under Hammer, with me now,' he wrote to Major General Horace Robertson, the commander of the militia-based 2nd Division in Australia. 'Seeing them makes me more sympathetic than ever towards you.'[9] The 2/2nd Pioneer Battalion would remain under the command of 18th Brigade and one battery from the 2/4th Field Regiment would also remain in place.

The 18th Brigade had an unmatched record during the fighting in the earlier Papuan campaign. It had had the key role in the victories at Milne Bay, Buna and Sanananda but, like the other two brigades in Vasey's division, it had suffered grievous losses and had been completely rebuilt before the current campaign.

After the promotion of the former commander Major General George Wootten to the command of 9th Division, Chilton had taken over the unit.

•

Most of the reinforcements used to rebuild the 18th Brigade had come across from the disbanded 5th Motor Regiment in July 1943. The 2/9th Battalion absorbed 190 of them.[10] Corporal Frank Rolleston was an experienced old hand with the 2/9th. 'In my opinion some of our very best soldiers were reinforcements,' he wrote. 'There were some who boasted that they were originals of the battalion, but some of these saw little or no actual fighting.'[11]

The 2/12th Battalion absorbed six officers and 191 other ranks.[12] 'They should be very good troops,' Captain Kevin 'KB' Thomas wrote.[13] They had gone from a light horse regiment to a motor regiment and 'then they turned them into ordinary foot slogging infantrymen,' Captain Angus Suthers observed. 'These fellows turned out to be top liners and what they did at Shaggy Ridge was unbelievable.'[14] The battalion commander, Lieutenant Colonel Charles Bourne, had asked the padre Roy Wotton 'to help in blending the old and the new' and by the time the 2/12th had completed its training 'the unit was a true unity and the old spirit was as evident as ever'.[15]

Major Ian Cameron, the C Company commander, was another of the new officers. 'Experience wasn't everything,' Lieutenant Alwyn Francis wrote. 'There's Cameron you see out of a motor regiment and he's a company commander in one of the crack regiments of the AIF.'[16] Corporal George Schollick went across to A Company where he 'immediately took a liking to those gaunt veterans with the Atebrin complexions'. Schollick felt it was 'rather an insult to any of these battle-scarred veterans' for him to be in charge of them, and handed in his stripes.[17]

Major Colin Fraser had served with the 2/12th in the Middle East as a company commander. On return to Australia he had been appointed as the military intelligence staff officer at New Guinea Force headquarters during the Papuan campaign. Fraser didn't appreciate being away from the battalion during that time so he applied to return to the 2/12th for the next campaign. Soon thereafter Fraser found himself back with the 2/12th as second-in-command.[18]

Private Jack Beard had previously been a bandsman and hence a stretcher bearer, so when the reinforcements were asked 'Are there any stretcher bearers amongst you?' Beard stepped forward. There were four bearers allocated to each company, one to each platoon and one at company headquarters. Guns were always issued to the bearers but weren't normally carried in action. Some of the officers gave them their revolvers as they didn't want to be identified as an officer by carrying them and that's how Beard got his.[19]

At Port Moresby the 2/12th Battalion carried out day-long 50-kilometre route marches for months to build up their stamina.[20] 'We'd go out on a route march at seven o'clock in the morning then come home at four and there's no hotter place in the world than Moresby,' remembered Lance Corporal Bill Etchells. 'You'd only march a couple of miles and the sweat would come through the creases of your boots.' They kept this up for two months until someone realised that the cooks, who were not doing most of the marches, 'were doing better than the bloody blokes that were going out all the time'. When the men were pricked with a safety pin and couldn't feel anything, it was apparent that 'half the blokes had bloody beri-beri', Etchells added. 'Rough; I don't think I've seen anything as silly in my bloody life.' The training was then modified to a half day of exercise followed by a half day of sport.[21] The men were also told not to wear helmets and most men aged over 30 were left behind in reserve. Only the young and fit went across to the Ramu Valley.[22]

As with the other two battalions of the brigade, the 2/10th Battalion needed so many reinforcements after Milne Bay, Buna and Sanananda that there was no way they could be obtained from training camps. Ten officers and 360 other ranks from the 11th Motor Regiment joined the battalion on the Atherton Table-lands in north Queensland.[23] As Private Stoddart Diggles put it, the 2/10th had been 'reinforced in mass'. It was understood there was no alternative to ensure the battalion's survival and there was no bitterness about it.[24]

•

Just after dawn on 2 January 1944 the US 126th Infantry Regiment landed at Saidor on the north coast of the Huon Penin-sula. After a naval bombardment of some 2000 5-inch shells and 4.5-inch rockets, there was negligible resistance to the landing and a key stepping-stone had been secured for General Douglas MacArthur's drive towards the Philippines. For the Japanese command it was a hammer blow to their strategy of holding back the Australian advance along the north coast, cutting the coastal supply line and isolating some 15,000 Japanese troops east of Saidor. From Rabaul the 8th Area Army commander General Hitoshi Imamura gave orders for those isolated troops to retreat west via the perilous mountain tracks that bypassed the American lodgement. 'A general retreat followed, with [the] situation so confused that no one knew where he was going,' Corporal Tadao Hashimoto, a 78th Regiment signaller, later told his captors.[25]

From east of Saidor, Lieutenant Masamichi Kitamoto heard 'a roar of airplanes and cracking of machine guns as the enemy planes strafed the camp . . . I looked towards the sea. About fifty ships with white waves in their wakes were sailing towards the west.' Kitamoto led a patrol to report on the landing and reached the perimeter two days later. By that time the American airfield engineers were already hard at work constructing a new airbase.[26] On 2 January the 41st Division commander, Lieutenant General Goro Mano, flew from Wewak to Alexishafen to take command of those forces from Madang to the Ramu Valley including the defenders of Shaggy Ridge and Kankiryo.[27]

The closest force available to the Japanese to act against Saidor was the 78th Regiment at Shaggy Ridge. 'For the purpose of preparing the way to smash an enemy force of about 20,000', units of the Nakai Detachment began moving north towards Saidor on 4 January.[28] 'It is said that the division is to go through the mountains,' one of Nakai's men wrote. 'Is 20 Div to be finally annihilated?'[29] With the threat of a further landing at Madang, Nakai also sent units to Bogadjim.[30] So while the Australians were flying in two fresh brigades to deploy in the fight for Shaggy Ridge, Nakai was losing a significant proportion of what meagre forces he still had available. He despatched five of his infantry companies to Saidor and Bogadjim, leaving him only seven weakened companies to defend the Shaggy Ridge area. The companies sent to Saidor could only ever be a token gesture and were too late to have any effect. The only thing that prevented the 15,000 Japanese troops east of Saidor from being cut off was the decision by the Americans at Saidor to remain in their coastal beachhead focusing on constructing an airbase and supply centre to support the upcoming operations further west.

•

Following the loss of one of the mountain guns on 28 December, the Japanese decided to move a gun up onto Prothero and position it to fire on a flat trajectory directly along Shaggy Ridge. To better protect the gun, a position was selected on the very edge of the ridge but in an area where the ridge extended out somewhat, allowing a site facing along the west side of the ridge to be chosen. Being on the edge of the escarpment meant that any bombs or shells landing to the south or west would be landing a long way down the slope of the ridge while the higher ground to the left made it almost impossible for the Australian artillery to hit the position. Any shells flew over the defiladed gun and impacted some 300 metres to the rear. The Prothero area was also covered in thick vegetation to provide camouflage and blast protection. The bunker was dug out of the ground and covered with logs, earth and vegetation for further protection and camouflage. When Bluey Whyte later saw the position, he said it was 'beautifully constructed' and 'strongly resembles a log cabin'. An improved phone line was also run between the gun position and the forward positions on the ridge.[31]

On 1 January men from the Obatake Unit, part of Lieutenant Colonel Shigeo Kageyama's battalion from the 26th Field Artillery Regiment at Kankiryo, woke at 4.00 am and headed up to Prothero to begin the construction of the bunker. The men worked all day, returning to Kankiryo at 5.00 pm. The following day they did the same and had the bunker ready for occupation. Meanwhile all the gun components of a Type 94 75-mm mountain gun had been brought forward to Kankiryo and the unit carried these up to the new position on 4 January. The gun broke down into eleven parts, the heaviest of which weighed 95 kilograms. That afternoon the men returned to the former gun line and brought ammunition up to the new position. More ammunition as well as personnel belongings were taken up the following day and a tented camp was established.[32]

On 2 January Captain Shoichi Kagawa was evacuated and Captain Kakuji Yano took over command of II/78th Battalion. '[Yano] was a military man who reminded me of an ancient Samurai with distinguished records,' Kumao Ishikawa wrote. On 9 January, First Lieutenant Shinichi Katayama's 6 Company relieved 11 Company on Shaggy Ridge.[33] 'Katayama was short in stature but a handsome man with a boyish face,' Ishikawa observed. 'He had a character of an ideal military man with superb fighting spirit and sincerity with exemplary conduct.' He would need all those qualities to defend Shaggy Ridge with a much weakened company against a fresh brigade.[34] Captain Yano 'did not hesitate to entrust to Katayama the fate of the strategic Byobu Yama', as the Japanese called Shaggy Ridge.

•

On 1 January the first units of 18th Brigade flew into Dumpu. 'We landed without incident in a cloying, steaming heat,' Private Bill Spencer recalled.[35] The 2/12th Battalion flew in on 2 and 3 January. 'They're fairly noisy but they're comfortable old planes,' Alwyn Francis noted. 'They just cruise along slowly and safe as houses virtually, unless something attacks them.'[36] As the 2/9th moved up from Dumpu, 'Shaggy Ridge could be seen clearly, rising 1700 metres into a thickening mist of afternoon rain cloud,' Spencer wrote.[37] When Frank Rolleston's company took over, he heard one of the departing 2/16th men quip, 'Goodbye Shaggy, you bastard.'[38] The men had been issued blankets, but because they had got wet on the previous night at Guy's Post many men threw them away on the way up as they were so heavy. Later they wished they hadn't as it got quite cold up on the ridge at night. 'One guy on sentry duty was lent a jumper and said he would stop out there all night if he could keep it,' Private Gordon Davidson said.[39] 'The Cape and Sanananda were nightmares to fight in but the steep, slippery, long zig zag climb, steamy and wet, was terrible,' Private Bruce Martin recalled. 'We used to piss ourselves with effort carrying supplies in.'[40] The 2/9th infantrymen dug into the side of the ridge and set up their two-man tents to keep out the rain. There seemed to be a perpetual mist up on the ridge and the men were able to catch the dew and rain that ran off the tents to fill their water bottles.[41] At one stage the 2/9th went three days without water after it didn't rain for three nights.

Captain Herb Pearson was a Salvation Army chaplain attached to the 18th Brigade at Shaggy Ridge. On his first climb up the ridge he carried two cans of hot coffee and writing material for the men and it left him with shaking knees and needing a dose of salt water from the aid post. Pearson helped to open up the Salvation Army hut halfway up the ridge where a relatively flat area was dug out of the spur and named 'Johnno's Jungle Joint' after Corporal Charles Johnson who had been attached to Pearson. Despite having being twice wounded, Johnson complained about being taken away from the front. As Bill Spencer observed, 'Padre Pearson and his helpers were always where they were most wanted.' At one stage Pearson met General Vasey, a man renowned for his swearing. 'Padre, you'll have to forgive me,' Vasey told him, 'I can't bloody well talk if I can't bloody well swear.' Pearson told him that bloody was a corruption of my blessed lady, a reference to the Virgin Mary. 'You make me feel guilty now,' Vasey replied.[42]

In mid-January, nineteen British officers from Burma arrived for attachment to the 18th Brigade as observers. The idea was for them to gather ideas about jungle fighting from the Australians and then go back and use that knowledge in Burma. The 2/10th had five while the 2/9th had six of them allocated, including Captain Arthur Stanton of the 14/20 King's Hussars. He was the son of a general and the holder of the King's Gold Medal from Sandhurst. 'They became more than observers when the action commenced,' Bill Spencer noted.[43]

•

Sergeant Shawn O'Leary had been a journalist before the war and later wrote of his time on Shaggy Ridge with the 2/9th Battalion for the 1944 army 'Christmas book', *Jungle Warfare*. 'The ridge falls away in sheer declivities and the top is, in places, no more than a few inches wide. The forward platoon holds one sand-bagged sniper's post and beyond that the Japs hold Intermediate Pimple and Green Sniper Pimple. There is no way of advance along the top.'[44] The snipers 'gave them hell,' Lance Corporal Max Smith said, 'you just had to put up a hat on a rifle' and it would be shot. Private Tommy Wilkie was a bit of a wild boy who had changed his name to help dodge some police warrants. He had been recommended for bravery awards on a number of occasions and never had one granted. On 6 January he got hold of a periscope of sorts, actually two mirrors on a hinge, and reckoned 'he'd get the bastard'. But soon after putting the periscope up, there was a shower of glass and Wilkie was badly cut.[45]

On 4 January the forward company of the 2/9th on Shaggy Ridge was shelled from the new Japanese gun position on Prothero, wounding one man that day and another two three days later.[46] Then on 10 January there were five mountain-gun casualties in 8 Platoon and Private Charles Layton died as he was being carried out. Shawn O'Leary captured the feeling: 'You must lie under the drizzling sky and the thin whine of shells, cursing the enemy and finding bitter joy in the dull detonations you can hear.'[47] Despite the shelling, there was a procession of people visiting Shaggy Ridge to have a look and traffic control posts had to be established. Bill Spencer was not impressed with this type of battlefield tourism. 'No 2/9th Buna survivor could possibly picture traffic control posts organising visiting personnel to line up in twos to witness the courage and carnage of 18 December 1942 at Cape Endaiadere,' he wrote.[48]

●

In early January Warrant Officer Colin Halmarick, a 29-year-old photographer with the army history section, flew into Dumpu to help record the upcoming operation. Halmarick had been doing a lot of work around Port Moresby and had endured a period when his value had been questioned. Three months previously when there had been a request to release Norm Stuckey from his work, there had been a suggestion from higher up that 'if a photographer has to be released it might suit us that it should be he',

referring to Halmarick. The letter stated that 'he has not been espe-
cially prolific' and that Halmarick's 'best is very good but he does
not seem to be the most consistent photographer we have'.[49]

On 11 January Halmarick visited Guy's Post and the next day
went forward and worked with the 2/10th Battalion intelligence
officer to get some photos of Japanese territory from the forward
positions on the Faria River. The next day Halmarick's feet had
swollen from the trek up the river and he couldn't get his boots
on so he rested up for three days at Dumpu. During that time
Halmarick met up with Norm Stuckey, who had been in the area
since the start of the campaign. There were now three photographers available for the upcoming operation so it was decided that
one would be attached to each of the three 18th Brigade battalions. Sergeant Darrell 'Joe' Kinna, who was a cinematographer
and who had been in the area as long as Stuckey, had already
joined up with the 2/10th Battalion, leaving Halmarick and
Stuckey to decide which battalion they would cover. Although
Halmarick had seniority, Stuckey had previously worked with the
2/16th Battalion on Shaggy Ridge and 'was anxious to do it again'
with the 2/9th. Halmarick considered that Stuckey 'had a liking
to finish a job that was left unfinished previously' and believed
it only fair that he should do so. Halmarick was also confident
he would get some better pictures while attached to the 2/12th
Battalion. On 17 January he made his way back to Guy's Post
and the next day photographed the air attacks at the head of the
Faria Valley using the long lens of his Graflex camera. 'I exposed
two packs,' he wrote, 'and should have some excellent pictures of
the strike.'[50]

•

The air attacks that Halmarick covered on 18 January started once the morning mist lifted at 9.30 am. 'Men are fighting above the cloud level this morning,' the war correspondent Fred Simpson noted from a circling aircraft, 'since below the peaks there's an unfolding layer of cloud.' The attacks were carried out by B-25 Mitchells and went on for most of the day, the largest such operation in support of ground forces up to that time in New Guinea. They included the dropping of 60 delayed action bombs on the Japanese-occupied head of the Faria River valley as well as concentrated strafing of the area. A number of specially modified Mitchells equipped with a 75-mm cannon mounted under the chin were also used to target the crest of the ridge. The cannon, as used in a Sherman tank, was an extraordinary weapon to be carried by an aircraft. To enable it, the nose on the B-25G model was shortened and the cannon breech positioned behind the pilot from where it could be loaded by the navigator for firing by the pilot who would press a button on his control wheel. The weapon proved inefficient against shipping but it was thought that it may be useful against ground targets.

In the lead up to the use of the 75-mm-equipped B-25Gs at Shaggy Ridge, Alex Miller-Randle was told to accompany one of the aircraft on a test flight to test the gun's range. Miller-Randle was told that the pilot 'would like to do it while having a shot at Shaggy Ridge, he's asking for somebody to show him where to shoot'. 'Cor Blimey,' Miller-Randle exclaimed, 'I don't believe it, the damned thing will recoil out through the arse of the aircraft.' Miller-Randle was told to stand alongside the gun with the gun loader behind it. The barrel of the gun ran along the floor of the aircraft and out the nose in between the two pilots and to the right there was a rack with four extra shells.

Miller-Randle's apprehension grew when he saw that the gun's recoil mechanism had been discarded and the gun was directly attached to the aluminium framework of the aircraft. The aircraft soon reached Shaggy Ridge and Miller-Randle pointed out the target area. The approach would be from the east to allow the fall of shot to be seen on the open side of the ridge and to ensure any missed shots would not threaten the Australian positions. When the gun went off 'my eardrums nearly burst and my head started ringing,' Miller-Randle wrote, and 'the aircraft seemed to stop dead still in the air'. Then the gun loader was pushing by 'in great haste to talk to his Major'. Apparently 'the aircraft frame wasn't as straight as it used to be'.[51]

Fred Simpson was on one of the gunned-up Mitchells on 18 January. As the bomber approached the 'jagged, sharp peaked landmass' of Shaggy Ridge, he saw the smoke rising from the bombers that had gone in before him. 'A swarm of Mitchells had gathered, waiting their turn. A shell has just gone into the cannon below my feet, ready.' Then his plane made its run 'above and across the valley floor, towards the crest of the ridge'. Simpson's plane dived down, 'the bush clad ridge top . . . rushing up to meet us' as the machine guns opened fire, 'then the fire from our cannon and the shells of death and destruction are tearing toward the enemy'. Bombs were also dropped. 'We're over, we're over, we're over and away,' Simpson concluded, 'the broad valley of the Ramu spreads beneath us, we are speeding homewards.'[52]

Simpson's colleague Bill Marien watched the air attacks from down below. 'Flight after flight swept in to the target, guided by perfectly timed smoke-shells laid down by the artillery.' He watched 'the bombs falling, losing themselves in the trees, and then the explosion'. He also felt the blast, as it 'ran across the canyon'. Those bombs that went down the western side of the ridge exploded in 'a flurry of foliage, a snow-storm of falling leaves, and the crash of falling timber'. Other bombs seemed to bury themselves in the open side of the ridge and Marien watched as 'the earth surged up and great fissures and cracks appeared'. He also saw other Mitchells come in lower in groups of three: 'there was the rattle of the forward machine guns, and, in line abreast, a belching sheet of flame, as the big cannon cut loose'.[53] Frank Rolleston watched the gunned-up Mitchells 'diving down and firing what appeared to be rocket-propelled missiles as well as bombs'.[54] Out to the west of Shaggy Ridge on Feature 5500, Allen Osborne had a grandstand view: 'This thing would fly in towards the hill and fire and it'd almost stop and shudder and then go on.'[55]

First Lieutenant Ray Stout was a bombardier with the 405th Bomb Squadron and at around midnight on 18 or 19 January the operations officer and some other officers from 5th USAAF command had paid him a visit. There were concerns about the effectiveness of the bombing on Shaggy Ridge due to the narrowness of the target area along the top and Stout's advice was sought on dropping time-delay bombs to detonate above the Japanese foxholes rather than sliding down the sides of the ridge when they missed the crest. It was decided that the Mitchells needed to maintain a flight level of 11,000 feet and the fuses were set for time-delayed ignition based on that height.[56] Over three successive days from 18 to 20 January the Mitchells flew 180 sorties against Shaggy Ridge, firing 135 rounds of 75 mm at the ridge as well as dropping around 200 tons of bombs. The aircraft also fired about 90,000 rounds of .50 calibre.[57] The machine-gun salvos were particularly effective. From his accompanying Boomerang,

Alex Miller-Randle saw 'Mitchells strip the trees of Shaggy Ridge clean and shatter the limbs and trunks to matchsticks'.[58]

On the receiving end, Kumao Ishikawa watched as dozens of aircraft, 'like falcons aiming at prey', circled with 'composure and in orderly formation' before sweeping down to bomb and strafe then climb back into the sky. The sight was spectacular 'but in reality the ground below was nothing but hell'. Each one of Ishikawa's 32 men 'was exhausted to the extreme' by the uncontested Allied air control over the battlefield.[59]

With a desire for more bombs on the crest of the ridge, Kittyhawk fighter-bombers out of Gusap had a go at it on 20 and 21 January. Captain Joe Stevens was an Australian air-liaison officer in a Mitchell above Shaggy Ridge, directing the Kittyhawks onto the Japanese positions along the crest. The forward Australian lines were marked with white cloth markers while 3-inch mortar smoke rounds dropped on the target, Green Sniper's Pimple. Most bombs missed and went well down the side of the ridge but Lieutenant Louis Iglehart finally hit the target, 'carving out a huge chunk of the ridge top'. On 26 January, after the ridge had fallen, Stevens took a group of 7th Squadron pilots including Iglehart up onto the ridge to observe the bombing.[60] For Kumao Ishikawa at Kankiryo, the switch in bombing and artillery from the Faria Valley to the Japanese positions along the top of Shaggy Ridge came as a relief. However, Ishikawa thought it 'very hard that there would be any survivor in that stronghold'.[61]

The 2/9th watched the air attack from further back on the ridge. One of the bombs hit the side of the ridge and then went over the top of the troops down to a patch of timber where there was a water spring. Gordon Davidson was told by his platoon commander, Lieutenant Hector Potter, to go find out where the bomb had landed. Davidson went down with Private Doug Wade but they soon decided an unexploded bomb was not something you really wanted to look for so they sat on the side of the ridge until the timer ran down and the bomb went off.[62]

•

Although General Blamey had given General Vasey very specific instructions not to get involved in large-scale operations or to advance to the coast, it was decided that all of Shaggy Ridge and not just the key heights needed to be captured. Brigadier Chilton was told it would be a limited operation and if casualties were heavy it was to be called off.[63] The main concern, as Captain Norm Sherwin noted, was that 'it was thought prudent not to leave an estimated seven or eight hundred Japanese on that flank . . . it was decided to clean them out'.[64] On 14 January the operation order for Operation Cutthroat was issued and detailed planning proceeded with D-day scheduled for 20 January. A diversionary attack on Cam's Saddle to the east of Shaggy Ridge would be made on that day with the main attacks starting on 21 January. The 2/12th Battalion would attack Prothero at the northern end of Shaggy Ridge and the 2/9th would then advance along the top of the ridge. There would be 13,000 rounds from eight 25-pounder guns available for support with another four guns soon to join them. On 18 January Vasey wrote to General Morshead to say that the Cutthroat plan was complete. 'I see no reason why the whole operation should not be successful.'[65]

•

The 2/10th Battalion would kick off the Cutthroat operation with a diversionary attack on the Cam's Saddle area to draw Japanese reserves away from the main game on Shaggy Ridge. The attack was delayed by heavy overnight rain, which made the going difficult and also cut the phone lines from the battalion headquarters to the front lines. Nonetheless the men of Captain Wally Gunn's A Company moved forward through thick mud from Sprogg's Ridge to attack Cam's Saddle following a supporting artillery barrage. Gunn had the challenging task of making progress against well-defended enemy positions atop a steep and slippery slope. Corporal Alf Bell was a battalion original and led the way up the slope accompanied by another original, Corporal Tim Hughes, who had been decorated for bravery at Buna. Hughes told Bell not to go to the top but was ignored and moments later Bell slid back down the slope, again alongside Hughes, but now dead. Four other men were wounded before Captain Gunn pulled his men back 200 metres for the night.[66] From up on Shaggy Ridge, Shawn O'Leary listened to the attack out to the east. 'The move along the right flank had begun', he wrote. 'You'd heard the firing thousands of feet below you, and wondered how that battalion was going.'[67] It had not gone well on that first day but hopefully the attacks had the desired diversionary effect.

Although the main attacks on Shaggy Ridge began the next day, the 2/10th kept the pressure on the Japanese left flank. Patrols on 21 January discovered that the defenders had pulled back along Faria Ridge closer to Kankiryo and the 2/10th men were able to occupy Cam's Saddle. On 22 January D Company attacked north along Faria Ridge towards Kankiryo while B Company attacked south in order to open up the supply line

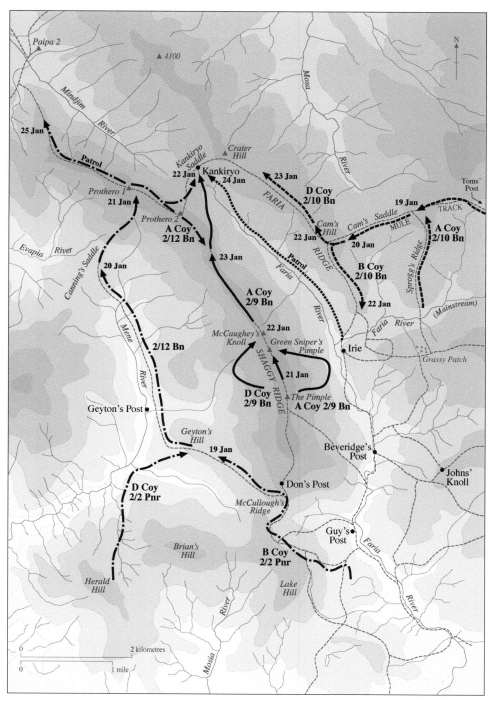

Map 10: Operation Cutthroat (Keith Mitchell)

back from Trevor's Ridge. The Japanese defenders were positioned on a dominant knoll approached along a narrow spur from the north, and the ten-man section that was dug in there had two light machine guns and a grenade discharger.[68] The attack would be made by 11 Platoon with supporting Bren-gun fire from the other two platoons. The only artillery support would be a smoke shell on the target. Corporal Len Bradford was wounded trying to cut the barbed wire across the approach route before Private Harold Thomas and the platoon sergeant Ron O'Grady were also hit. O'Grady would die from his wounds the following day. Lieutenant Roly Wilson was the 2IC (second-in-command) of B Company and the supply officer, a job that did not require him to be in the front line. But Wilson, who had come across from the 11th Motor Regiment, wanted to see action so had swapped his revolver for a rifle and attached himself to 11 Platoon. Seeing the two wounded men in need of help, Wilson went out to help, only to be killed as he reached them. Stoddart Diggles then went out with a Bren gunner providing cover. He reached Corporal Pat Higgins, a mate from Warwick who had a shattered leg. Diggles bandaged a rifle to the leg as a splint but was unable to move the bigger man himself. Private Ron Baggaley later crawled out and stayed with Higgins well into the night until the stretcher bearers were able to get him out.[69]

By now more men had come forward to help with covering fire. Private Charlie Schofield and Corporal Jack Lee, both Bungendore boys from southern New South Wales, kept the enemy bunker busy while the wounded men were brought in. Schofield was like a jack-in-the-box, ducking behind tree trunks after he fired, his aim so accurate that the Japanese were unable to fire a shot. Meanwhile Private Tommy Ryan was firing his Bren at an enemy bunker with camouflaged firing slots covered by a trap door which would open to allow a burst of fire before slamming shut. Ryan fired bursts from his Bren whenever the door opened until his Bren gun was shot out of his hands. The gun fell near a weapon pit where Lance Corporal Jim Mewes picked it up and the next time the trap door swung open he shot the unsuspecting enemy machine gunner.[70]

The attacks by the 2/10th Battalion east of Shaggy Ridge had been carried out with a determined vigour which the Japanese could not ignore, and no doubt limited their freedom to reinforce the positions on Shaggy Ridge, which now came under intense pressure from the rest of 18th Brigade.

Chapter 13

PROTHERO

The success of Operation Cutthroat hinged on the bold 2/12th Battalion attack on Prothero at the northern end of Shaggy Ridge, an attack based on some excellent reconnaissance work carried out over the preceding three months.

On 19 October 1943 a Papuan Infantry Battalion patrol under Lieutenant Doug Stuart left Kumbarum on a seven-day patrol along the Mene River around the south-western side of Shaggy Ridge to the high point at the northern end of the ridge. On his return Stuart discussed a name for the feature with Captain John Chalk and they decided to name it Mount Prothero in honour of Lance Sergeant Ron Protheroe, who had drowned in the Watut River during operations on 4 July 1943.[1] On 15 November Jack Reddin and Bluey Whyte went out on another patrol to the same location, again following the Mene River around the western side of Shaggy Ridge. They spent some time at Canning's Saddle, and found the spur that led up to the top of the ridge at Prothero.[2]

On 18 December a five-day patrol from the 2/2nd Pioneer Battalion followed the same route and was also able to observe the enemy outpost on Prothero. There appeared to be no more than one platoon based there. On 26 December an eight-day patrol led by Captain Allan McInnes and Captain Colin Stirling carried stocks of rations to a cache near Canning's Saddle, named after the pioneer battalion's signals officer, Lieutenant Lindsay Canning. A smaller party set out to scale Shaggy Ridge until the men reached a barbed-wire position on the approach track, which McInnes and Private Bill Barnes crawled under and went up to the crest of the ridge. According to McInnes there was a large group of Japanese troops up there having lunch in a crater-like depression. 'Jap observed but no sign of bunkers or field works,' he reported. The patrol had been 'skillfully manoeuvred inside a wired position on the crest and withdrawn just as adeptly' without any suspicion of their presence.[3] Stirling wanted to shoot up Prothero with the artillery, but after nearly four months of constant use his walkie-talkie was not working.[4]

Following the New Year arrival of 18th Brigade and the evolving Cutthroat plan to move the 2/12th up the Mene River to assault Prothero, more reconnaissance was called for. On 5 January the 2/2nd Pioneers sent out a patrol under Lieutenant Harry Conley to have another look at the approach to Prothero from Canning's Saddle. There was a steep climb up to a false crest where a track led along a razorback ridge and, though the ridge grade was not so steep, it had very precipitous sides. There was good cover against observation from the Mene River to the false crest.[5]

Captain Sherwin from the 2/12th carried out another reconnaissance a week before the attack, reaching the false crest from where he could hear the enemy up on Prothero without seeing them. 'I didn't press it any further,' Sherwin said. 'When I found you could get up I sent a message back to Colonel Bourne. By the time I got back to battalion all the orders had been drawn up.'[6] Bourne had also taken the opportunity to take a flight over Prothero so he could get an idea of where his battalion was heading.

•

On 18 January the advance party under Major Colin Fraser left for Canning's Saddle and the rest of the battalion followed the next day. The men followed the Mene River for six hours and camped overnight by the river as it steadily rose with the falling rain. 'At the first camp there was a heavy storm and the point platoon was nearly washed away,' Lieutenant Brodie Greenup said.[7] The pioneers had spent a number of days carving the track out of the jungle and rigging ropes at the more difficult points. As Captain Trevor James noted, the pioneers 'were spoiling for a fight as since the capture of Lae they had done little except marching'. Following the river, which was 'flowing like a rocket', the pioneers guided the battalion to Canning's Saddle. 'We had to form human chains across these streams and we crisscrossed backwards and forwards, goodness knows how many times,' Sergeant Max Thow remembered. Bill Etchells 'wondered if the Japs were deaf' given that the pioneers had cut down huge trees to form walkways across gullies and creeks. 'The long single file moved silently up the deep ravines, scaling cliff faces with the aid of ropes and lawyer vines,' James wrote of the gruelling day.[8]

'The rain during the night had increased the flow of water,' recalled Corporal Terry Wade, 'we were up to our waists at times'. Wade lightened his load, discarding his tent shelter, mosquito net, half a towel, half a blanket, change of clothes and mess gear. On reaching Canning's Saddle he scraped out a shelf on the side of the hill for the night. Wade and his fellow stretcher bearers sat in the mud with their half blankets and ground sheets wrapped around them.[9] 'It poured all night and the bloody water came down like a bloody waterfall; Jesus Christ it rained,' Etchells said.[10] Private Ted Crawford observed that it was probably nearly as dry in the river as out.[11] Bluey Whyte and Colin Stirling accompanied the 2/12th; their ability to direct supporting artillery fire would be vital to the success of the operation. They 'carted miles of wire' and had signallers lay a phone line all the way up the Mene River valley. As the thunderstorm crashed around them, the two artillery officers tried to get some rest.[12]

•

In the morning Lieutenant Francis's 14 Platoon led the way up the ridge, helped up the cliff from the river by the pioneers. 'Ropes were used, particularly at the start where the cliff went almost straight up,' Francis said. 'We travelled as lightly as we safely could.' Private Denis 'Bluey' Berwick saw it was 'almost straight up and we had to dig steps and cut down sago palms and bamboo to be split and to be used as steps in the bank'.[13] At 9.20 am Francis's men crossed the start line above the cliff after the men were told to ensure there was no clanking equipment and that any talking or smoking was taboo.[14]

Francis let his forward section leader set the pace, wary of any ambush: 'The knowledge of what was actually up on top, the actual strength, was pretty sketchy,.' His own briefing had been straightforward, as he'd just been told 'the Japs are up there somewhere', and they were to do something about it. The higher they got the louder the sound of the mountain gun became, as every 2 or 3 minutes it blasted away at the 2/9th Battalion at the other end of the ridge. At its widest the track 'could only accommodate a couple of scouts forward, a few paces abreast' as the spur fell away precipitously on both sides. It was at its worst only some 200 metres from the top where the sides were almost vertical. There were two trees at this point with about a 1-metre gap between them and 'between these trees in the centre of the track was what appeared to be a land mine'.[15]

Francis knew that with the battalion strung out behind him 'like Brown's cows', he had to keep moving. 'Every second's delay was making us vulnerable to discovery, if our presence had not already been detected.' Francis spotted a possible enemy post higher up and had his Bren gunner fix his sights on it while he directed his men to continue the advance. A man was sent back to bring up some engineers to deal with the mine while Francis pushed on. 'We would either be blown up or we wouldn't,' he said, 'but a whole battalion was waiting on us.' The men then gingerly edged their way between the mine and the tree on the left and continued up the spur past an unmanned post.[16] 'I think that if it had been manned, the position it was in, I think they'd have slaughtered us,' Max Thow said.[17]

Francis's men continued up the spur and soon reached the top where the country began to open out somewhat. Still unchallenged, Francis deployed the platoon in a defensive position around what he called a 'crow's nest' feature and waited for the rest of the company to arrive. There was still no sign of the enemy and they had not heard the sound of the enemy gun for some time. Francis thought they may have been spotted back at the mined position and that an observer had warned the gunners.[18]

Lieutenant Johnny Seear's 13 Platoon was the second platoon up and the men had cut a dog-eared pack of cards to see who would be forward scout. 'Teddy Edwards drew the big black ace,' Ted Crawford said, so his section led the way up.[19] As the platoon approached the top of the ridge, the men came across a small tent with a Japanese soldier lying on a bed inside. 'Watch out!' someone called and an Owen gun opened up and he was shot.[20] 'The stupid thing was we shot him,' Etchells said, as the soldier had obviously been sick. Another bloke 'took off like a rocket' dodging the gunfire. 'This would have alerted the Japs on Prothero,' Etchells reckoned.[21] Francis's platoon had apparently missed this position after it 'got tangled up in the jungle' and 'got out of touch on the right'.[22]

Back down the ridge the pioneers were improving the track along the narrow spur. As Padre Wotton noted, 'One part of the track was so narrow that a rope was necessary to prevent the weary troops from falling into the void below.'[23] Carrying a coil of signals wire across his back, Bluey Whyte came up with the headquarters company, his signallers laying phone line all the way.[24] The other forward observer, Colin Stirling, had gone up with the forward company carrying extra phones and more wire.[25] The mortar section had the toughest job. The bipod weighed 20 kilograms, the base plate 17 kilograms and the barrel 15 kilograms. 'They put it on their back and up they went,' Captain Angus Suthers said. 'That was why a lot of them just dropped dead after the war.' Having reached the top, Suthers told the mortar men to drop their gear, grab a bunch of empty water bottles and head back down to the Mene River to fill them and then bring them back.[26]

•

It was about 1.00 pm when a breathless Japanese messenger reported to Lieutenant Yo Baba at the mountain-gun bunker on Prothero One. The news could not be worse: enemy troops in strength were moving up onto the ridge from the Mene River. Baba's gun had been firing at the 2/9th Battalion attack at the other end of Shaggy Ridge for the last two hours but now he called a halt, not wanting to draw attention to his position. Baba then ordered the gun dismantled, turned around and reassembled to fire out the back door of the bunker.

Alwyn Francis and his men had already moved past the well-hidden gun position. Although he wore no badges of rank, Francis realised that his command actions made him a likely target for enemy snipers. 'No sooner did I move than a bullet cracked past my ear.' However, his men had spotted the sniper and shot him down from the tree soon afterwards. 'But that was the signal for all hell to break loose,' Francis added.[27] He then heard Major Cameron's voice calling out 'Push on Alwyn, push on!'[28] As the men advanced towards higher ground they tended to bunch together and as Lance Sergeant Abraham Beth-Halevy tried to get them to spread out he was shot dead. As a Jew, Beth-Halevy had more reason than most to fight in the war but, after having survived so many battles from the Middle East to the Papuan beachheads, his luck had run out. The former champion foot-baller, 'always reserved and reticent' according to Francis, on that day 'seemed in something of a daze'.[29]

Seear's 13 Platoon was further back when the sound of small-arms fire was heard. Lance Corporal Gordon Marsh looked around for any sign of the enemy and spotted some movement at the gun bunker, which was only about 30 metres away. 'There are the yellow bastards!' he called out, and the moment he did so the gun opened fire. 'About half of 13 Platoon were casualties, mostly bad,' Ted Crawford wrote.[30] Unable to depress sufficiently when firing out the rear door, the mountain gun had opened fire into the thick covering of trees, aiming the gun at the largest trees in its limited field of traverse. There was 'a series of mighty explosions in our midst,' Sergeant Sam Webb recalled, 'the shells bursting in the trees just above our head'.[31] 'It was a big tree they were firing at and the shrapnel size was unbelievable,' said Bill Etchells. 'I never heard such a bloody noise in my bloody life.' At such close range there was no warning gap between the sound of the gun firing and the resultant explosion.[32]

The men in Private Brian McNab's section were sliding down one side of a gully with the bunker on the other side when the gun opened up. Private Robert 'Homey' Connell was killed by the first blast before the men followed their section leader, Gordon Marsh, around to the left. McNab jumped over a body, only to realise it was Marsh; he had suffered a massive head wound, which had killed him instantly.[33] Private 'Pop' Alcorn had lost an arm and had then been hit in the face and killed while another ten men from 13 Platoon were wounded including Lieutenant Seears. 'There was Gordon Marsh, Homey Connell and Pop Alcorn,' Bill Etchells remembered, 'and they were terribly knocked about the face with shrapnel, big bits of shrapnel too, you know.'[34] The big redhead, Private 'Bluey' Rowe, had been mortally wounded by machine-gun fire from the bunker. Private Bob Davis saw the dying Rowe 'sitting against a tree with a stunned look on his face, trying to hold his guts in'.[35]

Bluey Berwick dived behind a big log but it did not protect him from the tree bursts: 'All of a sudden I heard this big bang and felt my legs go numb, no pain, nothing for a moment or so and I looked down, saw all the blood coming from my legs and then the pain started,' he wrote. Berwick's right leg was hanging off and his left leg was damaged at the knee. 'Ed, I think I've been hit!' he called out to Private Teddy Edwards on his right.[36]

Corporal Norm Maxwell was busy digging in, 'in top gear'. At this stage there were only 5 seconds between shells so Maxwell was counting up to four while he dug and then 'would go to ground until the explosion went off and start digging again'. His platoon sergeant Horrie Veivers was wounded and Maxwell took over that role. 'A piece of shell came whizzing through the air like a bull-roarer, and whacked me on the thigh,' Maxwell wrote. 'It was red hot and I soon got rid of it.' Not long afterwards Horrie's brother, Private Ron Veivers, was shot in the groin by a sniper and killed. 'Young Ronnie had been claimed by his brother and had come over to join his unit but didn't survive his first action,' Maxwell noted.[37] Privates Len Drews and Wes Lendrum had just reached the crest when the shelling started and found shelter under a tree. When they realised the shells were hitting the trees they decided to get up and move away. Moments later a tree burst blew them down the slope, wounding Drews.[38]

Private Eric Haynes had been seconded to battalion headquarters as a runner for A Company alongside Private Bernie Nunn, who was the B Company runner. Colonel Bourne had led the headquarters group up onto near-even ground when there was 'this enormous blast out of the silence' and Nunn, who was ahead of Haynes, was mortally wounded after being struck in the groin by a shell fragment. 'I dragged Nunn into a hollow while the shells kept coming,' Haynes wrote. The men from A Company moved swiftly through it all and went to cover out of the blast zone. 'Braithwaite, go around, go around,' Bourne yelled out to the 7 Platoon leader Lieutenant Charlie Braithwaite. 'I can still hear Bourne's voice this day,' noted Haynes. 'It was 3 pm in the afternoon.'[39]

Brodie Greenup was with Bourne when the gun opened fire. 'What do you make of that?' Bourne asked him, and Greenup replied, 'sounds like a demolition to me'. Soon after that one of Greenup's Bren gunners went down after being struck by a shell fragment and Bourne realised they were being shelled. He told Greenup to stay put and hold the track while the headquarters group went further around into dead ground. But that was the

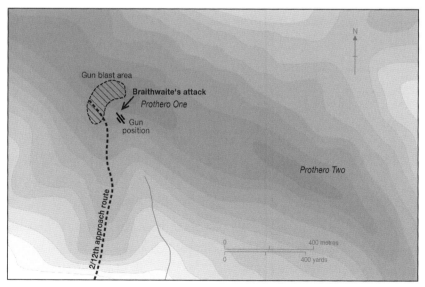

Map 11: 2/12th Battalion on Prothero One, 21 January 1944 (Keith Mitchell)

trap. Although Bourne had gone behind the crest into dead ground, the area was wide open to the tree bursts, resulting in 'shrapnel coming straight down'.[40]

Norm Sherwin, who was with the headquarters group, saw that the gun, which had initially been firing quite rapidly, was now slowing down. He watched as one shell fragment sheared off a small tree at the base. 'Foolishly we weren't dug in, just sitting there.' Suddenly Bourne rolled over, grabbed at his abdomen and called out, 'I'm hit!' Sherwin asked him where he had been struck and Bourne told him 'in the stomach'. He lifted Bourne's shirt and pulled down the trousers to see a red line with a small metal shard poking out but no blood. 'Oh, you're alright Charlie, it's only a little bit of shrapnel I think,' Sherwin said. He grabbed it between his finger and thumb and pulled it out, only to realise it was 15 centimetres long with a serrated edge. Bourne passed out. When he later saw the doctor who treated Bourne, Sherwin was asked, 'Are you the bloody idiot who pulled it out?' The signallers had laid the phone line up to the ridge so Sherwin let brigade headquarters know that Bourne had been badly wounded and was told to get Major Fraser to take over.[41]

Unknown to Sherwin, Fraser was already up there with the headquarters group. 'Strictly speaking it was not the province of the 2IC to be with the CO,' Fraser said, 'I was there to take over, fortuitously.'[42] According to Roy Wotton, Fraser had trouble taking over as Bourne had 'told Fraser practically nothing' about the operation.[43]

Angus Suthers was 'going up this blasted mountain' when he received a message that he was required forward. 'Oh Christ,' he thought, 'I am about the last bloke of seven hundred fellas climbing up the bloody mountain.' He discarded his equipment and headed up, moving past the line of men. 'I'm Suthers, get out of the way,' he told them. 'When I got up there, blow me buttons, here's the commanding officer Charlie Bourne, he's sitting on the side of the track and the doc was with him.' Bourne had 'this great shell dressing stuck in his belly' but was conscious. 'What can I do, what do you want?' Suthers asked him. 'Angus you are to take over from Colin Fraser. You're Battle 2IC.' Suthers knew that Major Cameron was the senior major so said, 'Hang on sir, I'm not arguing but how about Major Cameron, he's senior to me?' 'Let him earn his spurs,' Bourne replied.[44]

Colin Fraser had been very surprised to get onto the ridge unmolested and now tried to sort out where the gunfire was coming from. 'It was very difficult to separate the shot of discharge of the gun from the bursting of the shell because they were so close, and it was equally difficult to locate where it was coming from.' It took a while to identify the source but once the location was clear, 'it gave us something to point at'.[45] At this stage Fraser had Cameron's C Company in the area around the gun with Captain 'Jim' Geason's A Company just arriving on the ridge. Kevin Thomas's D Company had moved further forward along the ridge. 'Kevin Thomas came up and he went right through, as his orders said; he went right through the company that was attacking,' Norm Sherwin noted. Captain Fred Haupt's B Company was out to the west to protect the flank having turned left when it had reached the ridge.[46]

As Kevin Thomas moved his company forward, he also saw Bourne propped against a tree with a stomach wound: 'Norm Sherwin the adjutant was quite excited telling me that the CO had been killed. Cameron did not seem to know what was happening so I passed right through his company.' Thomas's company took at least three casualties as the men moved through the firing arc of the mountain gun. 'No one went near Bourne, they all went rushing past and into fire positions,' Jack Beard recalled. 'The branches off the trees were coming down over them as they moved forward.' Thomas kept his men moving until they reached the end of Prothero One and took up defensive positions to prepare for any counterattack.[47]

•

From up on Prothero One, Alwyn Francis could now see the gun position and how it was firing out of the back door. However, 'their traverse was only as great as the opening was wide' and Francis had his men out of that arc of fire. He also realised that, with the gun position right on the edge of the escarpment, his platoon had moved past it without seeing it.[48] The gun was at the head of a gully, with a steep slope at the embrasure end and machine guns deployed on either side of the gun, parallel with the bunker. 'You wouldn't be able to see. You'd walk right on top of it,' Bill Etchells said.[49] 'It was screened by trees, and well concealed, like a pimple stuck on a hill,' wrote Colin Fraser. The pimple turned out to be a well-constructed gun emplacement, 'a log cabin type pillbox', and the trees around it screened both the noise and the vision. However, once they had the location they could take action.[50] Amid what was controlled confusion, someone yelled, 'Bring up a Vickers gun!'[51]

A Vickers gun was brought around through dead ground to the east flank of the bunker and Sherwin positioned it in the gap between the gun and the forward company at the base of a tree and trained it on the opening at the back of the bunker, about 50 metres away. It was 'straight opposite the bloody thing,' according to Bill Etchells who was alongside. With the Vickers firing in the back door it is likely some of the Japanese gunners were killed and it would certainly have made it more difficult to operate the gun. 'I don't know how many thousands of bullets they must have poured into it,' Etchells said. 'Ah Christ, that went for bloody ages.'[52]

With the Vickers gun in position, Fraser detailed Lieutenant Braithwaite's 8 Platoon to go in and capture the gun position. 'I can still hear him giving orders to our platoon commander to take that mountain gun,' George Schollick wrote.[53] Braithwaite told Kevin Thomas he would take the gun by direct assault across the gully. It could not depress to cover the gully and the assaulting platoon would be fairly well covered once across it. With little room for manoeuvre Braithwaite would use about ten men for the attack while Thomas would have his men take care of anything forward of the gun.[54]

At 4.00 pm the Vickers gun stopped firing and Braithwaite's men attacked across the gully, in defilade from the mountain gun but very vulnerable to small-arms fire, which stopped their attack. The men pulled back under heavy machine-gun fire. 'Braithwaite showed his inexperience,' Bob Davis observed. 'It was his first time in action and he ran in gung ho with his platoon.' Braithwaite wanted to go again but Thomas told him to 'just settle down a bit' while he arranged for all the available Bren guns to target the gun bunker. At 5.00 pm Braithwaite's platoon made another attack, with Corporal 'Nugget' Robinson moving forward with his Bren gun slung from his neck, heading for the door of the gun bunker. But there was a light machine gun covering the bunker from behind which opened up on him and Robinson was hit and killed. 'You could see the back of his shirt popping where the bullets came out,' Bob Davis said. The platoon sergeant Don McCulloch then threw a blast bomb at the bunker and there was an enormous explosion.[55]

This stunned the enemy defenders, giving Private Richard Lugge, who was the number two on the Bren, the chance to go forward and pick up Robinson's gun. 'He jumped over in front of the Jap mountain gun, rolled on his back and fired from side to side and riddled the entrance to the gun pit,' Private Drew Hunter said.[56] He was then able to get to the door of the gun position and finish off the rest of them. Bob Davis recollects Lugge going around to the side of the bunker before other men went forward throwing grenades through the gun embrasure. 'From what I saw I thought the bomb skittled them,' Brodie Greenup recalled, before 'they went in and threw hand grenades.'[57] 'It was a damned brave thing to do,' Colin Fraser said. Fraser inspected the captured bunker and noted it was strongly constructed and well-camouflaged. It had gun ports that allowed fire in several different directions, which had made it difficult to attack. The gun crew were about to fire the next round, Fraser observed, though 'fortunately it was interrupted by Braithwaite'.[58] There were sixteen bodies found in the bunker, 'just piled up in a heap,' Max Thow said.[59]

Colin Stirling had a look and noted that 'they had a narrow firing slit cut and it lined up right on the twin pinnacles of Shaggy Ridge'. Around the bunker there were no signs of any aerial bomb craters or artillery damage; if the gun had not been captured it would have continued to operate against the other end of the ridge.[60] 'Inside it was a proper mess with no shield on the gun,' Bluey Whyte said, and 'there was a shell up the spout'. Another 50 unfired rounds were in the bunker and, although there was not much room to manoeuvre, Whyte was able to remove the gun sight. 'That is something for me to look after,' he observed and had it sent back to the rear.[61]

When asked in later years to comment on the loss of Baba's platoon at the gun position, a pensive Captain Yano recalled, 'I am sorry for what I did to my artillery men, I do not know how it came about.'[62]

•

After the gun was captured Colin Stirling moved forward with Thomas's company. By the time the company was in position, there was only about an hour of daylight left, 'but it was enough time to have some defensive fire ranged,' Stirling said. The signallers had managed to get the phone line forward to Stirling who sent his fire orders back to brigade headquarters for relay to the Australian guns, which were firing along the east side of Shaggy Ridge. 'The guns were firing straight at you,' said Stirling, 'and thus it was necessary to reduce their range as you went forward'. Stirling's biggest problem was the rounds hitting trees and exploding towards the observation officer. Stirling had previously practised directing such fire from a slit trench, 'bringing the artillery close enough for the shrapnel to pass overhead'. The technique was called splinter ranging but it was always done with the guns behind; 'never in training had the guns fired straight at you'. Despite the risk, Stirling was able to register the guns and tightly concentrate their fire before night fell. The fire would only require slight adjustments to allow for the cooler evening air.[63]

During that first night up on the ridge, Stirling brought down six to eight rounds at a time from eight guns, bringing the fire in as close as he could, relying on the accuracy of the guns. Salvo ranging was quite new and not part of the gun drill but on such a narrow front the guns needed to be concentrated. It was hard for Stirling to see the fall of one round, but with a salvo of six to eight it was easier to see the bursts and Stirling did not have to range by sound. The range was approximately 6200 metres with a plunging trajectory using charge three, the most powerful available for that role. Stirling stayed with the forward platoon all night with his first signaller 25 metres further back to relay the message to the phone set, which was 100 metres away.[64] 'The forward observation officers were mad,' Norm Sherwin observed. 'Everyone was dug in but Stirling who sat on an ammo case out in front directing the fire.'[65] On Stirling's recommendation, two of his signallers, Gunner Geoff Walker and Signaller Walter Green, were later awarded Military Medals for their work up on Prothero. Green had brought the signal wire forward under fire, and despite being wounded refused evacuation until he had done his job, including going out three times to fix line breaks.[66] Stirling was awarded a Military Cross. 'The artillery did an extraordinary good job right along the line,' Colin Fraser later said.[67]

•

That night, 'all we could do was dig foxholes and site our guns for all round defence,' Kevin Thomas wrote. It rained heavily and 'the night was cold as Christ with misty rain'. The perimeter was attacked by small groups of infiltrators all night. 'At one stage a single Jap got into my HQ but did not get out.'[68] Most of the stretcher bearers were back at the aid post tending to the wounded but Jack Beard spent the night on Prothero One. Corporal Arthur Prentice dragged

Private Albert Russell back during the night after he had been hit in the head and Beard worked on him at the edge of his weapon pit. Corporal Eric Keam then took Russell back to the aid post, but he died later that night. The men had been told not to go out at night and had orders to do their business in their foxholes, but Private Frank Henderson left his weapon pit, lost his way in the dark and was tragically shot by his good mate as he returned.[69]

Jim Christensen was the sergeant major in Thomas's company. He was praying for dawn so he could see something to shoot at when someone suddenly dropped into his trench right on top of him. 'I felt two-toed boots and knew it was a Jap,' Christensen said. The pressure of the enemy's body meant Christensen was unable to get at his revolver or knife and his opponent was similarly restricted so they wrestled for their lives. Christensen tried to grab his opponent around the throat, 'but he was as slimy as an eel, covered from head to foot in mud made slippery by the teeming rain'. The infiltrator slipped away and Christensen saw him slide head first into another trench. 'I jumped out at him, and, as I thought, on to him,' Christensen recalled. 'But I soon found I was wrestling with my sergeant who in turn was wrestling with the Jap.' Christensen groped around for a weapon and ended up with the enemy helmet. 'I bashed him over the head with it twice,' he said; 'he went limp and the sergeant relaxed his grip.' But as Christensen observed, 'it was a wily oriental trick. He squirmed free, leapt to his feet and ran.' The two men thought he had escaped but next morning in a pile of Japanese bodies Christensen 'recognised one with two gashes on his head where I must have hit him with the steel helmet'.[70] Christensen did not escape unscathed, shot through both wrists. His brother had been wounded a few hours earlier.[71]

As the night went on Colin Stirling realised that he should have dug his weapon pit with the dirt behind so as not to be hit by nervous gunfire from the Australians behind him. His pit was on the forward slope only 10 metres from the perimeter, with Thomas in a nearby pit. Stirling was talking on the phone line with Bluey Whyte to relay orders to the guns when a near-naked infiltrator fell into Stirling's pit. The two men grappled before the enemy soldier literally slipped away. Stirling got on with his job, calling down defensive fire in front of the perimeter about four times that night.[72] 'The anticipation was that we would face a counterattack,' Colin Fraser said, 'but it was a very unimpressive counterattack.'[73]

Further back C Company was in position covering the edge of the ridge. 'It rained like buggery that night,' Bill Etchells recalled. He shared a weapon pit with Brian McNab, 'sitting in water up to our bloody tits all night'. Everyone's nerves were on edge and when one man thought an enemy soldier was in his pit, he 'jammed a .45 into his arse but didn't shoot—it was a signaller'.[74] Norm Sherwin remembered a night of confusion, 'with a hell of a tropical storm lashing the ridge'. The weapon pits filled with water and the men had to sit on the edge wearing their gas capes as raincoats. There was a story that two of the men sitting on the edge of their weapon pit had someone come up and sit between them and it wasn't until there was a flash of lightning that they saw he was an infiltrator. 'They dived one way and he dived another,' said Sherwin.[75]

Brodie Greenup's platoon held the right-hand edge of the sector around the captured gun position. 'It was dark by the time we were given our positions and the night was pretty grim,' Greenup remembered. 'A couple of my fellows were a bit trigger happy.' One of them threw a grenade into a tree 'pretty well straight in front' so it came back right on top of Greenup's position. 'The guys screamed out to run. I just screamed out to duck down.' Fortunately nobody was injured.[76]

In the morning there were nine dead Japanese within Kevin Thomas's company area, one of whom carried a light machine gun. Private 'Kit' Evans, who had been at Buna and Sanananda, later said it was the worst night he had endured in the war.[77]

Chapter 14

LIFE AND DEATH ON SHAGGY RIDGE

The capture of Prothero One was only the end of one battle; another was at hand to save the wounded. At the forefront were the stretcher bearers and medical teams from the 2/5th Field Ambulance. As it would require two days to get any casualties from Prothero back to the main dressing station at Guy's Post, an advanced dressing station was established at about the halfway point to hold those patients unable to be immediately evacuated. On 19 January an advance detachment made the eight-hour trek to Geyton's Post to set up the dressing station on a broad ledge above the eastern bank of the Mene River. The site had a good water supply and was also under tree cover, safe from air observation. The field ambulance commander, Lieutenant Colonel Alex MacIntosh, had asked Sergeant Lloyd Tann that morning if he was feeling fit. 'Fit as a Mallee bull, sir,' Tann replied and he was on his way. On 20 January a surgical ward was built from half tents on a framework erected by native workers. A small medical ward was also built using a half tarpaulin and four more wards were added over the next two days.[1]

There were two surgeons attached to the 2/5th Field Ambulance and one of them, Captain Clarence Leggett, went to Geyton's Post. He was accompanied by his theatre assistants Privates Norm Ely and Joe Hughes while an anaesthetic section under Lieutenant James Rutherford was also attached to the surgical team. The initial assessment was that there would only be a few casualties held at the dressing station and they would only be held overnight.[2] 'They had intended to do not much more than advanced first-aid, just patch them up enough to get back to Guy's Post,' Lloyd Tann said. However, most of the patients treated had severe wounds and were not able to go back to Guy's Post; more beds would have to be built for the wounded as they arrived.[3]

A 24-man bearer section from the field ambulance under Lieutenant Charles Jacobs would also be attached to the 2/12th Battalion for the attack on Prothero. In open country there would be four men to a stretcher but carrying a stretcher down Shaggy Ridge could require up to sixteen men. Normal army stretchers were useless in such steep terrain so the bearers would make their own using half blankets. Colonel Bourne agreed to have 100 half blankets taken forward to Canning's Saddle for that purpose. The bearers would cut saplings for the 4-metre long side rails, which enabled a number of bearers to grab each corner. Each bearer would carry a ball of twine and two bagging needles to attach the half blankets, which were allowed to sag so as to keep the patient in. The patients were also usually tied into the stretcher.[4]

At 8.30 am on 20 January the bearer party left the dressing station at Geyton's Post and headed up the Mene River to

Canning's Saddle where the pioneers had set up a small regimental aid post. Before moving up the ridge from Canning's Saddle, each member of the bearer section picked up a half blanket from the supply dump, but of the 100 half blankets that had been promised there were only 30 available at the dump. As the infantrymen had found, the track up the spur was very bad, being unformed and slippery, and so steep that in places the men had to pull themselves up by means of ropes tied to trees. These ropes later proved very useful when bringing stretcher cases down.

At 2.30 pm a call came down the ridge for all 24 stretcher bearers to immediately head up to the top and it was clear from the sound of the explosions that there would be casualties up there. Once they were up Lieutenant Jacobs formed the men into three squads of eight and three stretchers were constructed. The mountain gun 'was firing point blank into the huge tree trunks around us and shrapnel was flying everywhere,' Terry Wade wrote. Lance Corporal Ernie Waugh, in charge of one of the squads, constructed a stretcher for Bluey Berwick while in the open under mountain-gun fire. It took 15 minutes as other men were being killed and wounded around him while he worked, and Waugh had to attend to one of the other wounded men at the same time. Despite the danger, the first three casualties were on their way down the ridge by 3.30 pm. Colonel Bourne was on the first stretcher taken down and Bluey Berwick the second.[5] It took 19 hours to evacuate Bourne and he was lucky that his wound was manageable for the time it took to get him down the hill.[6]

'We got rid of any surplus gear & equipment we had, for we expected a long hard carry down to the saddle,' Terry Wade wrote. It was extremely difficult getting the stretchers down the slope, although they were pleased to escape the bursting shells and sniper fire that 'whistled all around'. But just after passing the enemy outpost position, 'we met a train of natives and they relieved us of the stretchers'.[7] Three native carrier squads were formed, each of sixteen men, and they carried the wounded down to Canning's Saddle. It was not so much a carry as a passing operation as each stretcher was passed from hand to hand down the slope. On reaching Canning's Saddle the carriers kept going all the way to the dressing station at Geyton's, enabling the three badly wounded men to undergo surgery that night. 'The native carriers never stopped,' Lloyd Tann observed. He watched them cross a fallen tree about 6 metres above a creek when one of them started to slip. 'The boss boy jumped onto the log and grabbed the stretcher to save it from falling while the bearer regained his balance.'[8]

Colonel MacIntosh went to Geyton's to assist with the operation on Bourne.[9] Bourne had severe injuries to his abdomen and Lloyd Tann worked by torchlight to build a backrest as Bourne had to sit up due to the nature of the wound. A lump of shrapnel passed through Bluey Berwick's legs and both his knees had been shattered. 'If you can imagine,' Tann said, 'like if someone hits you with an axe'.[10] Suspended in his Thomas splint, Berwick was moaning with pain and one night said he could feel crawling in his legs from the maggots. Clarence Leggett came over and said to keep him doped with morphine as the maggots only fed on dead or decaying tissue and would clean the wound better than he could, as long as Berwick could endure it. As the war correspondent John Scarlett wrote, 'for this freckled, red-haired lad the war has ended, although he was only 16 when it began'.[11]

•

By the time the bearer section had returned to Prothero the mountain gun had been captured but there were at least another fifteen stretcher casualties and many walking wounded to be treated. No more native carriers were available and insufficient light remained for any more casualties to be carried down to Canning's Saddle that day. The 2/12th Battalion stretcher bearers had also been busy gathering all the wounded at the aid post atop the ridge, and one of those bearers, Private 'Tex' Parnell, had been badly wounded himself. Parnell had the bone in his upper arm completely shattered, the arm just hanging by particles of skin and flesh. 'I was horrified when I saw his arm,' Max Thow said. 'From his shoulder to his elbow . . . I could see daylight straight through.' 'Hey, Doc, look what I have done to my arm! Can you do anything for it?' Parnell asked the dumbfounded medical officer, Captain Jim McDonald. 'I'm afraid it's got to come off, Tex,' McDonald told him and Parnell just said, 'Righto, Doc, whip it off!' Parnell held the arm with his hand 'while the doctor cut the remaining flesh and skin away'. He then spent a night of suffering in the cold and wet on the mountain before being carried back to Geyton's Post the next day. He would die on the way out.[12]

The bearers worked until dusk helping Jim McDonald and his staff make the casualties comfortable for the night, using their own blankets to keep them warm. They spent the night in the open under steady rain with little to eat and only the rainwater to drink.[13] A wounded Ted Crawford had 'very grim memories of us all lying in mud and rain'. It was the 'longest bloody night of my life, memories of men much worse than I was suffering without complaint and of profound gratitude to Bn MO & s/bearers who battled their guts out to try and help and comfort us,' he later wrote. Private Vic Ellem 'carried seven bullets in him' but when informed by McDonald that his balls were still OK he yelled out 'Hooray!'[14] McDonald 'did a fine job with the wounded in very difficult circumstances,' Colin Fraser said.[15]

The next morning 'the drenched wounded were lying on the side of the mountain,' Bill Etchells observed.[16] 'Most of them were in a very bad state of shock,' Terry Wade said, 'accentuated by the terrifically cold night.' One of the wounded with two bullets in the stomach had died during the night and 'a grave was dug on the spot for him,' Wade added. There was 'also a chap with head, neck and chest wounds [who] would not last much longer according to the Doc'. He was one of the wounded men brought in during the night but he 'battled on and the grave did not claim another victim that day'.[17] George Schollick, himself wounded, later wrote, 'I think I grew up that night and the next day when I saw the courage of those severely wounded men making their way down that tortuous track to the dressing station.'[18]

The bearer section got to work in the morning and constructed sixteen stretchers that day, using Japanese signal wire when they ran out of twine. They were also able to get five squads of infantry bearers and two squads from the pioneers to join their three squads to help get all the stretcher cases down the ridge. Jacobs had his three squads carry part of the way down the track, where one infantry and the two pioneer squads took over and carried down to Canning's Saddle. The other four infantry squads carried their wounded all the way down. At 2.00 pm a party of native carriers came up to Prothero and was able to carry out twelve more stretcher cases. All the walking wounded had left earlier with the infantry bearers.[19]

●

At Geyton's Post the field ambulance crew knew that about 40 casualties were expected on 22 January and two extra medical orderlies were sent up from Guy's Post to help the two already there. Twelve stretcher cases and 30 walking wounded arrived that day. 'As patients came in,' Lloyd Tann said, 'we'd go out into the jungle at night with a machete and a torch, cutting saplings to make more beds and extend the wards.'[20] On 23 January another thirteen casualties came in, most also suffering from exposure when admitted, due to the blanket and shelter shortage up on Prothero.[21]

The operating theatre was constructed of six half tents slung over the branch of a tree with an army stretcher sitting on four forked sticks as the operating table. Light came from a Tilly lamp and a torch. All surgical instruments had to be immersed in boiling water and then kept in sterilised jars. With so many casualties the work was constant, with 'one patient lifted off and the next lifted on'. At times Clarence Leggett would be standing in the one place for hours while operating and would 'gradually sink . . . down in the mud almost to his knees'. In order to move, 'he'd have to get the other boys to drag his feet out of the mud'. Leggett worked till five each morning and then rested for two hours. 'Call me at seven,' he told Lloyd Tann before grabbing those two hours of sleep. He would do dressings first thing in the morning and mark those for evacuation by the native carriers before working on fresh casualties until five the following morning.[22]

Tann had also done a mountain of work. From when he got up on the Friday morning he didn't lie down until the following Wednesday night. He had 'not a wink of sleep in that six days', covering both day and night shifts. Colonel MacIntosh, who came up from Guy's Post on the Wednesday with a relief team, looked at Tann and said, 'How much sleep have you had since you've been up here?' Tann told him he had not had any so MacIntosh ordered him straight to bed.[23]

Of the 58 casualties that the dressing post treated, 41 operations were carried out, with four casualties having two operations each. There were 21 re-dressings that could be carried out without an operation, all of whom were mountain-gun casualties. In addition 47 men moved through with serious illness.[24] 'We never lost a patient at Geyton's,' Tann said. 'Everyone who reached us alive left us alive.'[25] On 27 January the last of the casualties treated at Geyton's, including Colonel Bourne, reached Guy's Post.

•

As the wounded men from the first day and night of battle were brought down from the ridge, another grim task remained on Prothero: to bury the dead. This would include the Japanese dead in the mountain-gun bunker. Colin Stirling had inspected the bunker after it was captured, and thought 'it was like a charnel house with legs and bodies everywhere'.[26] Bill 'Tojo' Etchells and Private Dennis Morris got the job of getting the dead bodies out of the bunker. Worried that there may be live grenades beneath the bodies if they lifted them, the two men dragged them out using lawyer vines. The final body was a tallish man lying across the gun, and after they dragged him out, as Morris untied the vine, he turned to Etchells and said, 'Tojo, he's still warm.' Next thing Etchells saw was one of the onlookers come over with a .45 pistol and put a bullet through the soldier's head.[27] Stirling was alongside one of the signallers watching the bodies being dragged when the signaller said, 'That bloke's still alive, can I shoot him?'

'Go for it,' was Stirling's reply and the signaller shot him.[28] Major Cameron came racing over and asked Etchells, 'What did you do that for?' 'I didn't bloody well do it,' Etchells replied. 'He would have been good to interrogate,' Cameron added. Etchells opened up the bloody shirt of the dead soldier, pulled out his wallet and saw a photo of 'a bloke with his wife and two kids'. 'It's the only time I ever felt sorry for a bloody Jap I think,' Etchells said.[29]

That was one version of events. Terry Wade had gone forward early that morning with two teams of stretcher bearers to bring back two casualties from Thomas's company, and on the way up he had passed the smashed bunker. 'Dead Japs lay everywhere, piled on top of each other,' he wrote. Then he saw that the last body hauled out was alive and, knowing that five pounds was being offered for a prisoner, they intended capturing him 'until the Jap started biting and kicking'. Then one of the men 'stepped back a pace' and shot the prisoner dead. 'They threw the Jap into the big hole with his mates, before he had finished kicking,' Wade added.[30]

Bluey Whyte had a similar account and was also aware that the brigade commander wanted a prisoner. The dragged-out soldier had been shot through the neck but was still alive, however, 'when he opened his eyes he saw a gaggle of wild looking men'. One of those men prodded him to lie down at which point he took off his leather belt and began to lash out with it. According to Brodie Greenup, the prisoner was on a stretcher and while Captain McDonald was checking him 'he tried to hit him with a bit of wood he grabbed from a tree'.[31] Norm Sherwin and Lieutenant Hughie Giezendanner were involved. 'He's got a belt in his hand and he's snarling like a dog,' Max Thow said. 'Hughie's got his pistol out and he's calling on him to surrender.'[32] Giezendanner asked Sherwin, 'What will I do . . . this bloke won't be taken prisoner.' Sherwin's idea was that he was not a prisoner, he was an active soldier, so he said, 'Shoot him.' When someone else asked, 'Will I give him a burst?' Giezendanner replied, 'No, it's my job to execute him.'[33] The prisoner kept coming and when he was only a few metres away Giezendanner fired two shots from his revolver but missed, perhaps deliberately.[34] 'Shoot the bastard,' someone else said and an Owen gun burst killed him. 'Who'd want to carry this bastard back?' another added.[35] 'How'd you come to miss him?' Giezendanner was later asked. 'I tried to shoot between the eyes,' was his reply.[36]

•

It was late in the afternoon of 21 January when Colin Halmarick reached Canning's Saddle. He had walked all day 'over a hellish track' from Guy's Post to get there. On the way he had photographed the preparations being made at the Geyton's Post advanced dressing station and at the 2/2nd Pioneers aid post at Canning's Saddle. The 2/12th Battalion was further ahead, forming up for the attack, but 'The country in which they were moving was very thick jungle and the opportunities for photographs were nil.' Halmarick was advised against going forward on his own so it was not until the next morning that he was taken up to Prothero where he took photos of the mountain gun. 'I had to work with time exposures and extremely low exposures,' he wrote. 'The jungle was very thick and picture taking was just about out of the question.' Having shot six film packs despite the conditions and with only one pack remaining, Halmarick returned to Canning's Saddle. It is a tribute to his photographic skill that he managed to get anything on film at all. 'By going like hell' Halmarick made it back to Guy's Post the next day. Another photographer, Frank Bagnall took Halmarick's and Stuckey's photos back to Port Moresby on the day after that, leaving Halmarick 'in need of a few days rest'.[37]

Halmarick had been hampered in his work by not having his Graphic camera available after it had been lent to Lieutenant Bill Sanders. It had been returned to Halmarick at Guy's Post on 19 January, the day before he left for the front line but he found 'the camera was covered with fungus, rusty and badly bent', making it unsuitable for use. Nonetheless, with his spare Graflex camera he had managed to take over 160 photographs of the Prothero operation.[38]

Chapter 15

'YOU'LL NEVER FORGET SHAGGY RIDGE'

With the 2/10th Battalion attacks east of the Faria River and the 2/12th Battalion attack at Prothero, the time had come for the third of Brigadier Chilton's battalions to join Operation Cutthroat. Lieutenant Colonel Clem Cummings' 2/9th Battalion had a daunting task: an attack along the top of Shaggy Ridge. 'The twenty-fives are pounding, and high in the air there's the stutter of strafing planes. Up and up towards the clouds you trudge,' Shawn O'Leary wrote. 'You climb and climb and climb . . . till suddenly, you are at the top and ahead is the jagged finger of The Pimple stabbing the sky. This is the field of battle . . . tonight some of us will be dead.'[1]

From 10.00 am on 21 January US Kittyhawks strafed and dive bombed the Japanese positions along the top of the ridge. 'There's a whine in the sky and the dive bombers, right on time, appear above the river. A Boomerang peels off, and, as though drawn on a string, makes for Green Sniper Pimple, leading the Kittyhawks in,' O'Leary wrote. 'They follow . . . and the ridge rings with the crash of bombs. Gouts of flame and rising smoke mark the fall: distantly you hear a scream as a Jap gets his.'[2] Private Ron McAuley was down the east side of the ridge with 7 Platoon as the Kittyhawks came over and dropped their bombs. Two of the bombs careered down the slope towards the men waiting to climb up. One bomb went straight over the top of McAuley and the accompanying dirt and debris took the skin off the back of his hands. The bomb exploded down in the valley that night.[3]

As the air attack finished, a section from Major Fred Loxton's A Company moved forward to occupy Intermediate Sniper's Pimple against slight opposition. Loxton was the senior company commander and had earlier told the other officers, 'I am the senior officer, I will do the attack.'[4] The next objective was Green Sniper's Pimple but with so little room along the top of the ridge only two sections from Sergeant Ron McDowell's 9 Platoon could make the initial attack. 'You wouldn't expect the Nips to have much fight in them after the pounding they've just received,' O'Leary thought, 'But they've got it, all right. Guns break into red laughter and slugs churn around you.'[5] Kumao Ishikawa watched from down in the Faria Valley as 'enemy planes left and sounds of shelling became sporadic'. Then Ishikawa 'started to hear machine gun and small arms firing at the front of Byobu Yama . . . finally the all-out assault was on the way'.[6]

Gordon Davidson and Doug Wade had patrolled towards Green Sniper's Pimple prior to the attack and noted that a log-reinforced bunker had been constructed in a dip across the ridge before the feature. During the attack Private Tom Childs was in the lead section moving along the ridge when an enemy defender jumped out of a hidden weapon pit and wrestled with him. As they fought, the Japanese machine gunner in the bunker shot the pair of them and they both rolled down the side of the ridge.[7]

While McDowell's platoon moved along the top of the ridge, Lieutenant Hector Potter's 7 Platoon had descended the east side of the ridge from the first Pimple, moved along the side of the ridge and were now climbing up the steep slope towards Green Sniper's Pimple. 'You've got to climb; climb where there are no holds and the slopes fall down like a leaning wall,' O'Leary wrote. 'You're flat—you're upright—you're slipping. Your chest burns with the pain of effort and you fight for gulps of air. The climbing is worse than the firing. You don't care about the bullets much. You only want to reach the peak where you can lie and rest.'[8]

Ron McAuley grabbed the tufts of grass as he climbed to pull himself up the slope. 'The Japs were down the other side in the trees throwing grenades over,' he recalled. The grenades were rolling down the slope but fortunately they didn't get caught up in the grass and most went past the climbing men before exploding. One blast did pepper McAuley's buttocks with some fragments but he kept going. There was so much stuff going on that 'you didn't know where the bangs were coming from and you couldn't see much on the climb up'.[9] O'Leary was more lyrical: 'Below you a man is killed. His hat leaps into the air, he drops his rifle and rolls over and over, down and down towards the river until he comes to rest on a thin track barely visible. Ahead you see another man fall, clutching a shattered arm.'[10]

'You start to scrabble up the cliff. You reach the top . . . and, as you tense yourself for the levering over the rim, a burst of fire chews the earth within inches of your hands. Panic-stricken, you drop,' O'Leary continued. 'You haven't seen a Jap yet, and you haven't fired a shot. There is only the momentary expectation of another grenade or another burst stitching you into oblivion.'[11]

By the middle of the day McAuley was up on Green Sniper's Pimple. The Australians were engaged in a grenade-throwing duel with defenders who were well dug in on the west side of the ridge and the Australians soon used up the grenades they had carried up. 'Thirty feet from the top you lie, and the grenades commence to rain as the Japs, from the shelter of the lip of the hill, hurl them at you,' wrote O'Leary.[12]

McAuley went back down the ridge to get more grenades from a sergeant who had set up an ammunition dump of sorts further down. When he came back he saw Doug Wade in a higher trench about a metre deep, so joined him. There were other platoon members either side of them, close to the peak of the pimple. But soon after getting in the trench an enemy grenade came over and landed in it, forcing McAuley to quickly get out. Then another grenade landed right next to him so he got back into the trench. The first grenade then went off and McAuley was wounded. He headed back down the ridge to Guy's Post with Private Ralph Hughes who had been shot in the arm. When it got dark the two men became lost until they saw a line of native carriers coming up with their lit cigarettes showing as a line in the darkness, giving them the direction to take off the ridge.[13]

'You have a clear view of Intermediate Pimple from where you lie. The head of an Australian appears above it . . . the man throws a grenade . . . and a foxhole explodes in a blur of smoke,' O'Leary remembered. 'He appears again . . . another grenade is thrown . . . Brens chatter . . . and within a moment our guns are holding the position. You feel like cheering. Only Eric and his grenades have made the summit possible.'[14] O'Leary had been watching Private

Eric Knight who had done great work with grenades, knocking out the bunker in front of Green Sniper's Pimple. Gunfire from the bunker had killed Corporal George Behrens and Tom Childs during the initial attack.[15] Knight wriggled along the side of the ridge below the bunker to within 6 metres of it, then threw some grenades up at the position. The defenders responded 'with a shower of grenades that came over like confetti' but fortunately went past right down the side of the ridge. Knight then called for more grenades before climbing up around the back of the bunker where there was a small opening. He threw the grenades in, surprising the defenders 'who were peering out at the other end'. Knight then called up the rest of the section to cover him while he cleared the bunker with his Owen gun, shooting the one surviving defender as he tried to get away down the side of the ridge.[16]

A sandbagged Bren-gun position had been built further back to provide covering fire for the attack. Doug Wade and Gordon Davidson manned one of the Bren guns there before moving further down the slope as the attack progressed.[17] 'With the covering fire from those Brens you commence to climb again. Others are doing the same beside you, and you are able to inch your way up the side of Green Sniper Pimple,' O'Leary wrote. 'You reach the crest and dig in, not showing your head over the top. You hold one side of the Pimple and the Japs the other.'[18]

Kumao Ishikawa watched from down below through his field glasses: 'I saw a belt of flames at the front line still in smouldering smoke from enemy fire.' The battalion commander, Captain Yano, ordered a counterattack backed up by Captain Masahiko Ohata's two mountain guns, one at Prothero and the other east of Kankiryo, and 'At the agreed time, each gun started firing.' Opposing the 2/9th Battalion were about 30 men from

Lieutenant Shinichi Katayama's 6 Company. Katayama led the counterattack and succeeded in retaking the front-line positions on the west side of Green Sniper's Pimple. With great joy he reported his success but the 2/9th kept the pressure on and soon thereafter Katayama, who was still forward with his men, was killed in action. Lieutenant Takerou Urayama, the commander of the 37 mm rapid-fire gun detachment, took over the company and backed by Ohata's artillery secured the Japanese position.[19]

After midday the 2/9th's D Company moved forward along the side of the ridge to take over the former A Company positions. Frank Rolleston observed that enemy shells were coming over every 20 seconds. At this stage the 2/12th Battalion had not reached Prothero and the Japanese observer for the 75 mm mountain gun had an unobstructed view along the south-west side of the ridge to the positions now being occupied by the 2/9th Battalion. There was no cover on the north-east side of the ridge from the shells bursting along the ridge top. 'It was as if we were standing against a wall,' Rolleston wrote. He watched as two men ran past along the crest carrying ammunition forward. After a shell burst, Private Stephen Sheen staggered back with a knee wound, saying 'Johnno's copped it, I think he's dead.' Private Colin Johnston had been hit in the head by a shell fragment that had penetrated his helmet and killed him. Rolleston and Corporal Bob Booth took over the former forward observation post only to have a sniper put a bullet between their heads as they peered out.[20]

Meanwhile the shellfire had claimed another victim. 'Back on Intermediate Pimple the company commander is killed,' O'Leary noted.[21] Major Loxton was standing up using his binoculars when he was hit.[22] 'A field-telephone line has been laid and while he is talking to an officer at the rear a shell bursts on the tree beside him,' O'Leary wrote. Loxton was killed and his body rolled away down the side of the ridge. The Japanese mountain-gun fire was telling. 'The mountain-guns open a barrage against which Brens can do nothing,' reflected O'Leary. 'This is hell . . . Shrapnel is whining around you and there is nowhere you can go for cover. Go over the ridge and you're a sitting shot for snipers in the trees.' The 2/9th men had to just sit tight and take it. 'You must lie . . . and lie and wait . . . and wait. Wait for the caress of agony from flying steel. One by one men are being wounded around you.'[23]

Doug Wade and Gordon Davidson moved forward, passing captured weapon pits dug in under the crest of the ridge. A large dugout had been built behind the ridge on the western side about 3 metres square with a mortar in it. Not far back was a 37 mm gun on rail lines so that it could be wheeled in and out of its shelter to fire. The Japanese had tried to push it over the bank as they withdrew but it got hung up on the edge of the position. Wade and Davidson were right on top of Green Sniper's Pimple shooting down into a little gully on the other side where there was a fortified position with empty sacks covering the entrance. As Wade stood up to bring the Bren gun to bear and fire a burst into the position, Davidson told him, 'God, be careful.' Then a single rifle shot rang out and Wade was hit in the face, killing him. He fell back into his mate's arms.[24]

Another shot was fired at Private Jim Pacey, who was close by. The bullet hit the buckle of his helmet which pushed the helmet up over his head and the next shot went straight through the raised helmet without hitting the fortunate Pacey. Behind Davidson, Corporal Joe Anderson was also targeted by an enemy sniper, the bullet grazing his skull and exiting near his ear, but he survived. Meanwhile Davidson had taken over the Bren gun with

Private Murray Appledore sent up to him as the new number two. It was now late in the afternoon and the job was to hold Green Sniper's Pimple through the night. Those few men holding the narrow front line were sweating on an enemy counterattack, the normal response after a position had fallen.[25] Further back along the ridge Lance Corporal Jim Fountain was part of a Vickers-gun crew covering the left flank of the attack. At one stage, after a message came through from battalion headquarters that there was an enemy counterattack, he fired the Vickers gun for 4 minutes, putting six belts each of 250 rounds through the gun, a tribute to the reliability of the gun and the efficiency of the gun crew.[26]

As night approached, Private Aubrey Abbott brought tea up to the men at the front. 'There are some things you don't forget on days like this,' O'Leary wrote. 'Such things as Aubrey struggling forward to the advanced sections from the cookhouse at the rear with a four-gallon dixie of hot black tea in each hand.' A number of casualties were dragged up the side of the ridge by ropes that night. 'You watch stretcher-bearers hauling wounded up the cliffs in strait-jackets along the terrain you have passed. There never was country such as this.'[27]

During the night there were hand grenades thrown and mortar fire directed onto Green Sniper's Pimple but there were no further casualties. 'That night you sleep where the Japs have slept, and the hours of dark are quiet,' O'Leary recalled. With the threat of being cut off by the 2/12th Battalion at Prothero, most of the remaining Japanese had pulled out that night. Twenty Japanese defenders lay dead including Lieutenant Katayama.[28] The 37-mm gun had been captured along with three light machine guns.[29] 'There are men lying dead on the slopes,' observed O'Leary. 'They were your mates; men who had lived and laughed by you; and men who had died by you.' Major Loxton and six other men had been killed on 21 January and another sixteen were wounded, twelve by mountain-gun fire. 'You'll remember them; you'll remember everything that happened this day. You'll never forget Shaggy Ridge.'[30]

Norm Stuckey had been up there that day ensuring Shaggy Ridge would not be forgotten. On 19 January Stuckey had been told that the photographs he had taken during the earlier 2/16th attack on Shaggy Ridge had been well received. 'I think they are quite the best photographs you've taken in NG,' his commanding officer wrote.[31] On 21 January Stuckey was back on the ridge recording the 2/9th Battalion attack, this time accompanied by the cine-cameraman Frank Bagnall. Both men were covered with a shower of dirt when one of the aerial bombs crashed down only 50 metres away and a shell from the mountain gun landed close enough to shatter the glass in Stuckey's camera.[32]

•

'In the morning the hill is clear,' wrote O'Leary. 'The enemy have left the scene in panic. The day is bright and although you can hear the sound of another battalion assaulting Prothero, there are only occasional snipers to bother you.'[33] However, that morning a reconnaissance patrol came across a bunker 20 metres ahead with several machine guns preventing an advance along the ridge. At 1.15 pm a message came through that the 2/12th Battalion had captured Prothero Two and units from the battalion were advancing south along Shaggy Ridge. Clem Cummings therefore cancelled artillery support for an attack by D Company.

The defenders who remained expected the attack to continue along the top of the ridge but the plan was for D Company to attack up the south-western face of the ridge. At 5.30 pm artillery and mortars opened up on McCaughey's Knoll as D Company waited at the forming-up point down the side of ridge. Half an hour later 17 Platoon reached McCaughey's Knoll. 'We carefully worked our way up the ridge as silently as possible,' Frank Rolleston recalled.[34] After two men were wounded by grenades, Private Lawrence Kelleher went forward with his Bren gun and grenades and silenced the two forward enemy positions, enabling the platoon to get onto the knoll.[35] A black signal flare went up from the Japanese on the knoll, likely indicating it had fallen and the 2/9th lead section pushed along the ridge hoping to meet the 2/12th coming the other way. 'Are you there, 12th?' was the call. However, an enemy machine gun stopped the advance before any link up. Although the gun opened up from only 50 metres away, no one was hit. 'We threw ourselves flat and slithered back over the rise,' Rolleston wrote. It was now getting quite dark so a halt was called to the advance.[36]

On the morning of 23 January a dawn patrol found the enemy had pulled out in front and only empty cartridges remained where the machine gun had been. Further ahead was a wounded Japanese soldier but he soon exploded a grenade to take his own life. Soon after midday the lead section of the 2/9th Battalion finally met up with the 2/12th.[37]

Chapter 16

TO KANKIRYO

Just before dawn on 22 January Kevin Thomas and Colin Stirling went back to battalion headquarters and worked out the attack plan for the day. Stirling arranged with Bluey Whyte to have a good supply of shells available for the guns and to be ready to fire when called upon.[1] Thomas's main concern was that the guns were only available for a limited time before they were to be switched to other tasks.[2] At 8.00 am the 25-pounders opened fire and, as Colin Fraser observed, 'after about 10 to 15 minutes of artillery bombardment, the first Japs began to run. Once they got the idea of running to safety, they simply vacated their foremost positions.' It was the first time Fraser had seen the Japanese on the run, 'an encouraging sight at that time'.[3]

Kevin Thomas, known to all as KB, had a unique style of command. 'Cane in one hand, revolver in the other and a whistle in the corner of his mouth' was how Sergeant George Dawson remembered him. 'When I blow the whistle, you go,' Thomas would tell his men, 'when you run out of Japs, you stop.'[4] 'He didn't stick to the military book at all,' Norm Sherwin added. Thomas preferred platoon commanders who were in their early 20s, single and who had seen no action so they were more likely to not question his orders. He also didn't mind new troops as they would also do as they were told. 'If you lined them up and told them which way to go, they'd go,' was his idea. 'If you've got a mob of old hands they'd start looking around for ways to get around it.'[5] They were the sort of tactics that had seen so many killed in the First World War but may have worked in the confines of the jungle and terrain in New Guinea.

At 8.30 am KB Thomas blew his whistle for the attack to start. 'I had exposure to the whistle blowing tactics, but they were very effective,' Fraser said. Not everyone agreed. On hearing the whistle blow, Private Len Bugg sung out, 'Shove that fucking whistle up your arse.' 'By Christ it was funny,' Bill Etchells said, 'he'd blow this bloody whistle and away they went . . . they all said this bastard's gone mad.' Bluey Whyte was alongside Thomas, and observed: 'He had a bloody big whistle like a referee's whistle and when he blew it all the troops got up and charged while firing, then drop down 100 yards further on. Then he would blow again and up they would get again.' The leading troops struck strong opposition, including snipers in the trees, and Thomas decided that his men should 'rush the position firing with every weapon that we had'. They charged in cheering madly, 'firing everything at anything'.[6]

After taking the forward positions the lead platoon moved south along the ridge until the ground to the right levelled out and Thomas was able to bring another platoon alongside. The

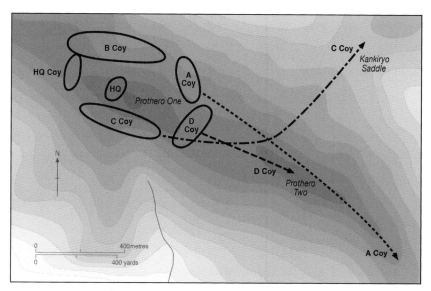

Map 12: 2/12th Battalion, 22 January 1944 (Keith Mitchell)

reserve platoon followed behind the other two. 'All platoons were in the fire fight,' Thomas wrote. Colin Stirling and his signaller 'Bluey' Green moved forward close to the front, ready to bring down artillery support. Stirling had grabbed himself a rifle and was busy using it. 'I had a couple of rifle shots just for the hell of it,' he said. When Thomas asked him 'What are you shooting at?' Stirling told him 'There may be something in the trees.' Thomas watched Len Bugg and Private Joe Alexander firing rapidly from behind a tree when he saw Bugg's Bren-gun pouches catch fire. Bugg threw them off from around his shoulders and kept firing his gun. When Thomas asked why they weren't moving, Alexander yelled back that 'there was a bloody sniper right on to them'. After Alexander pointed his arm towards the sniper's position up a tree, someone called back that he could see him so Alexander yelled out, 'Then get rid of the bastard!' and that was soon done.[7]

As the company approached the top of Prothero Two the ridge steepened and the withdrawing Japanese were now in a dominating position and able to hold up the attack. Thomas managed to get a section around to the right where the going was easier, and as he followed he could see and hear an enemy light machine gun. That side of the ridge had been cleared of vegetation by the intense gunfire of the battle and Thomas thought that it would be possible for a couple of men to climb up through the cleared area and lob grenades into the enemy position. If the defenders tried to fire down while the men climbed up, 'they would have to expose themselves clearly and thus could be attended to by the remainder of the section'. Lance Corporal Frank George and Joe Alexander offered to make the attempt and Thomas went with them while the rest of the section watched for any enemy reaction. When the three men got within grenade throwing distance they could see an enemy light machine gunner firing down the ridge unaware of the threat to his flank. Thomas threw a grenade 'but it hit the only stump in the area and began to roll down towards us' so they slid back down the incline again to avoid the blast. Thomas then returned to the other platoons to be told that the artillery support was soon to be withdrawn.[8]

Bluey Whyte had come forward to confer with Thomas, who asked for artillery fire onto the top of the ridge. Whyte was able to get extra time from the guns and helped direct the fire. This was very tricky as the guns were firing directly at the Australian positions so any over-shooting would impact them. 'There was unlimited ammunition and eight guns to fire it,' Colin Stirling said. He was up front with Bob Davis who told him that there were enemy snipers in the trees. 'Where do you reckon they are?' Stirling asked him. When Davis pointed out a position just in front, Stirling called back to one of his signallers to order a smoke round fired onto that grid reference. The guns dropped it spot on, only some 30 metres in front. 'Up 25, 100 rounds high explosive, fire!' Stirling called out to his signaller.[9] Stirling had four signallers strung out behind him at about 25-metre intervals and they played a key role. The telephone was about 100 metres back and from there the fire directions were sent down the phone line which ran all the way back along the Mene Valley to brigade headquarters at Guy's Post. They didn't lose the line at any stage, a credit to the earlier work of those same signallers.[10]

Thomas positioned his men to take advantage of the barrage, and as it finished the attacking platoon quickly advanced up onto Prothero Two and drove the defenders from the position. 'Bayonets were fixed and the attack went in with much yelling and screaming,' recalled Bob Davis. 'They moved so fast they even left three Jap snipers behind who they cleared up later.' Some other defenders just ran in terror, dropping straight over the side of the ridge. The effect of the artillery fire on Prothero Two was obvious: 'the trees had been flattened and there were lots of Japs still in their dug outs,' Stirling noted.[11] At 12.15 pm Thomas reported that his company had captured Prothero Two and there were 45 enemy dead on the position.[12] Three of Thomas's men had been killed and seven wounded in the action.

While the 2/5th Field Ambulance stretcher bearers had their work cut out treating and evacuating the wounded from the previous day and night, the battalion bearers had their own challenges. Jacky Beard had watched the initial attack go in 'in a mad dash' and soon heard the 'stretcher bearer' call. Private Vic Ellem and Lance Corporal Keith Clarke were the first two wounded men and Beard had to treat both. Clarke had been hit in the ear while Ellem had the top of his thumb blown off by a machine-gun burst, which had also struck his Owen gun. A bullet had glanced off the gun into Ellem's groin while the gun's trigger had been sheared off and embedded in his stomach. Beard quickly assessed the most critical wound to treat and that was the groin wound; he stopped the bleeding and saved Ellem's life. Ellem was a much-admired member of the company, having served in the Malayan campaign before escaping from Singapore in a small boat with another soldier and reaching Western Australia.[13]

Private 'Skinny' Jones was Bob Davis's number two on the Bren gun. The men knew that when moving around it was important to run from tree to tree for cover but Jones was shot and killed by a sniper when he ran across open ground. From the nature of the wound it appeared that a dum-dum bullet had been used, but it is more likely that the Japanese round had been moved off centre when it had hit Jones's ammunition pouches and this had caused the more serious wound. Private 'Slim' Irwin was wounded only moments after Jones was hit, shot in the thigh but smart enough to drop his rifle and drag himself into cover behind a tree.[14] Private George McGinty was also shot in the leg but when Private Kevin Fitzgerald stood up to grab him Fitzgerald was shot in the head and killed. Private Les Davies was Fitzgerald's mate, 'together from the time we went into the army till the day Kev was killed and he fell dead beside me,' Davies wrote in 1987. 'He's been dead for 43 years and I have never forgot him.'[15]

The Japanese defenders had been in poor shape, 'but we weren't to know that and when the withdrawal took place off Shaggy Ridge it took us a little by surprise,' Colin Fraser said. 'When they began to filter out of their foremost Shaggy Ridge position, the one closest to the 18th Brigade, the battle was over,' he added. 'We didn't realise that the withdrawal had taken such a decisive form.' Fraser had had good support from Brigadier Chilton who had provided him 'with some sort of reassurance that a Japanese counterattack from the direction of the coast was not a real choice open to the Japanese'.[16]

At the southern end of the ridge Clem Cummings was not at all pleased at having his own artillery support delayed while Prothero Two was captured, but was even angrier that the 2/12th had made no further advance towards him to clear the ridge. Norm Sherwin took the phone call from Cummings who let Sherwin know that his men had done their bit and were awaiting the 2/12th attack. 'He tore a strip off me that we hadn't mounted this attack,' Sherwin said. He told Cummings that 'it'll be mounted immediately, sir'. Orders were then issued for A Company to move through D Company and continue the attack south-west along Shaggy Ridge. The company pushed along the ridge but at 3.30 pm was held up by machine-gun fire, still well short of any link up with the 2/9th.[17]

During the afternoon a line of native carriers brought up ammunition and rations to Prothero and then took sixteen stretcher cases back down the ridge. Another 30 walking wounded also descended the ridge that day heading back to Geyton's Post. The remainder had to spend another night in the rain. As drinking water was scarce the rain was welcome to some degree as the men could gather some to drink. Nonetheless, another miserable night followed.[18]

Max Thow was one of those walking off the ridge that day after falling ill with a high temperature. He was helped down by Privates Tommy Stott and Rus Brown and when they got to

Geyton's Post the doctor said to stay the night, but Stott thought they needed to get Thow to a field hospital. Thow had scrub typhus and would spend eight months in hospital depots. Of the eighteen men in his ward at Nadzab tent hospital, ten died. Thow overheard an orderly say that he hadn't any chance of surviving, but he pulled through.[19]

•

At 2.40 am on 23 January the forward troops of A Company on the ridge were attacked from the south but the attack was repulsed with no casualties. Once daylight came, the company pushed further along the ridge but it was not until 1.30 pm that the forward elements of the 2/9th Battalion were contacted. The Japanese mountain-gun crew, positioned midway between McCaughey's Knoll and Prothero Two, destroyed their 70-mm gun and then slid down the side of the ridge to the Faria River to live to fight another day. When they reported to Kumao Ishikawa at Kankiryo, he was overcome with relief. These men 'never left my mind even a second while I viewed Byobu Yama lying in devastation in the distance,' he wrote. 'I had an urge to embrace them one by one.'[20]

That day the three bearer squads of the field ambulance plus one pioneer and one 2/12th squad carried the remaining casualties down to Canning's Saddle accompanied by more walking wounded.[21] 'The track was getting worse than ever and we finally made the saddle after carrying for 5 or 6 hours,' Terry Wade wrote. After handing over the wounded to the aid post, the bearers had a much-needed feed. 'A kitchen had been set up there and we tore into it!!' Wade wrote. 'Hot M&V [tinned meat and vegetables] tasted like roast chicken. I had 3 jam tins full of tea—straight—the first for days!'[22]

On Prothero Two, KB Thomas ordered his men to take off their boots and change socks. 'An extraordinary thing occurred when we removed our boots,' Thomas wrote. 'We all started crying with the quite excruciating pain caused by the blood going back into our toes.'[23] Every day that went by brought more evacuations, and not just battle casualties. Four men from Thomas's company suffering from dysentery were among the evacuated. Brodie Greenup was also on his way out after his minor wound turned septic in the damp conditions.[24]

One of the attached British officers took over from Greenup. Although they were supposed to be kept out of action, two of them would be wounded during the fighting around Prothero and Kankiryo. 'We got a message to keep them out of the firing because so many were getting knocked,' Norm Sherwin recalled, but 'they were very keen sorts of fellows'. They were certainly absorbing some interesting lessons. One of them had been attached to D Company and had watched KB Thomas's whistle-blowing techinique in action. Some days later the British officer asked Norm Sherwin how he was to return to Burma and tell his men that an Australian company commander did this.[25] Another British captain attached to C Company was not at all impressed at being called 'Bluey' until the men explained that if they called him captain then any enemy troops who heard it would target him.[26]

•

On 24 January the 2/9th Battalion took over the responsibility for Shaggy Ridge up to Prothero Two. The 2/12th could now concentrate on moving down off the ridge to Kankiryo and patrols were sent out to look for suitable ways off the ridge. That morning one of the patrols found the wreckage of Norm Trumper's crashed Boomerang. Trumper's remains, which were still with the aircraft, were buried at Prothero alongside the fallen 2/12th men.[27]

Fred Haupt's B Company moved down to Kankiryo Saddle to attack Feature 4100, a prominent position some 2 kilometres to the north. Norm Maxwell spotted an enemy soldier 'galloping through the scrub and they let him have it'. Haupt then told Maxwell to 'Go out and get him, we need to interrogate him.' Maxwell answered that 'I never heard anyone here speaking Japanese' but knew he had to check if the soldier was still alive. He found the soldier lying face down, dead, and bayoneted the body to make sure he had no grenade. Maxwell took the soldier's sniper rifle and also a thousand-stitch belt, sewn by family members and friends and worn for good luck. 'It was pretty stinking too—he must have worn it since he left Japan.'[28]

Thomas's company was then sent down to assist. The big issue for Thomas was water for his men; their water bottles were empty. He had earlier discussed the problem with Norm Sherwin: 'Norm, we want water and don't go telling me to get groundsheets out to collect the dew.' Sherwin contacted Clem Cummings whose comment was, 'Marshall [the captain of the 2/9th Battalion's lead company] found water alright, why can't you blokes?'[29]

Thomas had his company take up a position to the right of B Company and a section patrol was sent out to find water. Instead, the section contacted the enemy at the head of the Faria Valley and the section leader, the big redhead Corporal Alan Mogg, was hit by fire from an enemy bunker.[30] Bob Davis, who was about 100 metres back up the track having a break with a few other men, 'grabbed a set of Bren magazine pouches and the Bren gun and got to the spot where they were pinned down'. On arrival he found that the section Bren gunner, Private Les 'Gummy' Fuller, was sheltering behind a tree, out of ammunition. 'I threw him two full magazines,' Davis said before the two Bren gunners opened up on the bunkers to give the stretcher bearers a chance to get Mogg out. Privates Len Beal and Kevin Smith managed to drag him back to cover but he died from his wounds soon after. Meanwhile KB Thomas had gone down to see what was going on, only to be met by one of his men who very excitedly sang out 'Come down and organise this bloody war, KB!' Thomas watched as one of his men tried to land a grenade in the bunker by firing his discharger-cup-equipped rifle from the shoulder. Although the range was short, the muzzle velocity of the discharger cup did not lend itself to flat trajectory firing. Someone finally managed to throw a grenade into the bunker and the position was cleared with six dead defenders found. To the left of the bunker the men found a little stream of clear water and the water supply issue was solved.[31]

In July 1943, six months before he was killed, Alan Mogg had been in hospital with his mate Corporal Geoff 'Mick' Fletcher; both men down with malaria. 'He is just as silly as he always was,' Mogg had written to his mother back in Toowoomba about his good mate who was also from that neck of the woods. After his mate's death Fletcher wrote a letter to Mogg's mother and his fiancée saying that 'neither of you could miss him more than I do, he was my only and best pal I am shore [*sic*] he will never be out of my mind'.[32]

Towards evening Fred Haupt sent a patrol up Feature 4100, thinking the Japanese may have withdrawn. The patrol returned at dusk and reported that the enemy positions up on the feature had been vacated and Haupt was not impressed that the patrol had all returned rather than taking over the positions. It was now a dangerous task to send troops up in the dark so the men formed a perimeter for the night.[33]

After helping take the wounded out the previous day, Terry Wade and the other field ambulance stretcher bearers headed back up to Prothero with rations and water. One of the bearers wasn't well enough to go back while another was kept at Geyton's Post as a medical orderly so two other men replaced them.[34] At one point they crossed a patch of kunai grass where some supplies had been dropped by parachute, so the section had a good feed of tinned peas and pineapple. Some passing native carriers were impressed at seeing food coming down from the sky, which seemed a lot easier than carrying it. As Wade observed, 'The poor beggars have been working all the time, except Christmas Day, since the push in the Markham Valley started in September and so their expressions of joy and wonder were understandable.' The section reached Prothero about midday but unfortunately all the bearer section's personal gear, which had been left on Prothero, 'had been ratted by somebody' and there was nothing of any value left.[35]

•

By the time Fred Haupt's company headed back up Feature 4100 on the morning of 25 January, the Japanese had reoccupied their positions. 'The Japs were waiting for us and we got a flogging,' Norm Maxwell wrote. 'The grenades coming down on us from the 4100 feature, they were coming so thick and fast they almost blotted out the sun.' Fortunately the hill was so steep that most rolled past before exploding and 'the trees gave us a fair bit of protection from the blast'. One of the grenades that had rolled past Maxwell exploded next to Lance Corporal Tom Gillieatt, who was badly wounded in the stomach while Maxwell was hit in the back of the neck. 'I was hoping for a Blighty [a minor wound that could send him home],' he wrote, 'but no such luck. Later the 2/9th used the whole battalion to take it,' Maxwell added. 'I reckon we were cheeky trying to take it with a platoon.'[36]

Down at Kankiryo Saddle Clem Cummings was upset that Feature 4100 hadn't been secured on the previous night. To KB Thomas, Cummings 'did not seem to realise the almost certain probability that the Japs would have been back in position, as they certainly were this morning'. Thomas was concerned at the lack of information on the 2/10th Battalion 'who are supposed to be attacking up the Faria Valley'. Colin Fraser noted that 'There was a problem of coordination of the three battalions in which Kankiryo was involved.' Thomas's company was now relieved and his men headed back up to Prothero. 'The climb up from the Saddle was dreadful,' Thomas wrote. 'We seemed to move up four paces and back three, mud quite up to our knees.'[37]

Early on the morning of 25 January the 24 men of the field ambulance bearer section had been sent down to Kankiryo with the 2/12th medical officer, Jim McDonald, to deal with the casualties from the latest fighting. As the section moved along Prothero Two, 'we passed many foxholes and defence systems and there were dead Japs everywhere'. The three casualties 'were at the bottom of a steep hill, up which not even native bearers could have carried,' Charles Jacobs observed. The area was still under fire so the men quickly got to work making up two stretchers. Colin Fraser then offered a platoon of infantry as an escort to carry the two stretcher cases down to the Faria River and out that way but the sound of firing from that direction meant it was still unsafe. There would be no link up with the 2/10th Battalion in the valley until later that afternoon when a 2/10th patrol following the Japanese supply track reached Kankiryo Saddle.[38]

In the end about 70 men from B Company were used to get the stretchers up the slope from Kankiryo Saddle, which was knee-deep in mud. 'We formed two long lines, one each side of the track and sent the stretchers up escalator fashion,' Terry Wade wrote. The 24 stretcher bearers then faced 'a long carry along the treacherous razorbacks of Shaggy Ridge' until they reached the 2/9th Battalion aid post at 4.30 pm from where native carriers took over.[39] Despite his wound, Tom Gillieatt decided he could do without a stretcher and had walked back along Shaggy Ridge. When he told the doctor at the aid post he had done so, the doctor said he was a liar because nobody could do that with half his stomach hanging out.[40] The bearer section then returned to Prothero. 'We moved flat out along the ridge!' Terry Wade wrote. 'We had to get back before dark because moving objects after dark got shot at! And so we fairly flew back!'[41]

•

On 26 January C Company relieved B and immediately mounted another attack on Feature 4100. After John Seears had been wounded at Prothero, one of the British officers attached to the battalion, Lieutenant Marlow, had taken over as the commander of a much weakened 13 Platoon and the men had only met him on the day before the attack.[42] That night the members of the platoon listened to the shells passing over on the way to the enemy positions and were relieved that none dropped short. As the men climbed up in an extended line across the precipitous slope, Private Fred Watling, who was out on the right, said, 'Mister Marlow, I think I heard someone crank a machine gun over there.' When Marlow said to 'go have a look, Fred', Watling told him 'Go have a look yourself.' Then as the men neared the top of the slope the Japanese 'opened up with everything' and threw grenades down the slope. 'We heard the grenades first, they tapped them on their bloody skull,' Bill Etchells said. The Japanese grenade had to be struck against something hard to charge it and a helmet was always handy. Marlow, who was a tall man, 'was hit from his bloody ankle to his hip' by machine-gun fire. He was that close that the bullets had seared his flesh. Marlow yelled out 'Get out of here!' as Watling and Etchells grabbed the badly wounded officer. 'We took him at his word and got down the mountain,' Etchells wrote. 'Take this,' Marlow told George Dawson and handed over his Owen gun.[43]

It was tough even out of the fighting. 'We never had a hot drink or a hot feed up there,' Etchells recalled, 'I don't think for about six days or some bloody thing.' It was also very cold and wet. 'We were freezing . . . we only had the jungle greens on and a gas cape.' Unsurprisingly there was little sleep. 'I reckon I went four nights without any sleep,' Etchells added, 'You start to get a real dull sort of accepted feeling . . . you get past tiredness I think.'[44]

Meanwhile C and D Companies of the 2/9th Battalion had made a wide outflanking move down off the northern end of Shaggy Ridge across the head of the Mindjim River valley and around to the north of Feature 4100. The companies then moved up onto the top of the hill from the north around the flank of the defenders holding the southern approach against the 2/12th

Battalion attacks and captured the summit late in the afternoon. C Company then moved south-east towards Crater Hill before encountering strong opposition along the razorback approach. Lieutenant Eric White was killed in this clash.[45]

All three battalions from the 18th Brigade were now closing in on Crater Hill, with each approaching the enemy redoubt along a different razorback spur. Controlling artillery support fire was particularly difficult given the inaccuracies of the maps being used to plot fire orders. It took time to establish the front-line positions using aircraft to spot 2-inch mortar flares fired from the forward positions. Australian Survey Corps personnel were also on the job and a second edition of the relevant map was published on 26 January.[46]

That day brought good news to the 24 weary men of Charles Jacobs' field ambulance section as it was to be relieved and was to return to Guy's Post. 'We were very pleased at this news,' Terry Wade wrote. 'Our beards fairly bristled with joy!' Making his way back along the ridge Wade observed how 'The arty & dive bombers had wrought terrific damage in the area.' The section reached Guy's Post at 4.30 pm from where there was a jeep ride to the field ambulance base at Dumpu. 'Had a whacking great feed,' Wade wrote, 'then without troubling to wash or shower tumbled into the old bunk in my birthday suit and slept for 16 hours . . . that was the end of our saga in the mountains!'[47]

•

Once Shaggy Ridge had been lost, Kumao Ishikawa had been ordered to move his men and his remaining gun to Kankiryo to help defend the final redoubt on Crater Hill. When Ishikawa reported to Captain Kakuji Yano he was told he was now second in command of the battalion after the incumbent had been killed by the shelling. Yano, who had about 300 men remaining, stressed the importance of holding this final position to keep the Australians from advancing to Madang and cutting off the Huon Peninsula. 'We were convinced beyond any doubt that as long as we occupied even a corner of Kankiryo, the enemy would not advance,' Ishikawa wrote.[48]

Any attack on Crater Hill was going to be costly so Briga-dier Chilton decided to adopt a siege warfare mentality and, in the days that followed, Crater Hill was subjected to consider-able softening up by both artillery and from the air. 'The enemy, by offensive scouting, grasped the outline of the deployment of our position very soon, commencing ferocious artillery fire and bombardment,' Ishikawa wrote. 'The shelling was repeated day in day out, well in excess of 10,000 over one day.' The thick jungle was blasted away, the biggest trees 'left standing stripped of barks'. It was those largest trees that saved many of the Japanese defend-ers as, although the shells would explode in the tree branches, the men sheltering in their well-covered dugouts down below were safe from the flying shell fragments. 'Thus as long as we hid in dugouts avoiding direct hits, casualties were few. We keenly felt the benefit of the trees.'[49]

One morning Ishikawa noticed many unexploded shells lying about near his gun position. Investigating further he 'found the gun destroyed and the pit of the gunners had received a direct hit spreading cartridges in all directions'. It was the fourth gun he had lost over the four months of the battle. Ishikawa knew the men could not survive in such a small area of only 700 by 200 metres when thousands of shells were targeting the area every day. 'The density of landing fire was thick, and the damage to our men continued to increase,' he wrote.[50]

On the afternoon of 29 January the 2/9th Battalion put in another attack on the hill, but after three men were killed and eleven wounded it was called off. One of the attached British officers, Captain Arthur Stanton, was one of those killed. Stanton was serving with B Company but wanted to go in with A Company in the attack. He was wounded in the head and died as he was being carried out.[51]

The bombardments resumed and the defenders endured but there were other considerations. Communications had been cut and 'we relied only on the legs of soldiers,' recalled Ishikawa. However, every messenger that had been sent out to regimental headquarters had not returned. Now the defenders had run out of food and 'many soldiers who had gone down the valley for water did not return', either killed on the way out or the way back in by the Australian outposts. Yano and Ishikawa discussed their position and whether they should attack the Australians in a final show of defiance. 'Two hundred soldiers have reached the limit of extreme exhaustion after four months of fighting,' Ishikawa told Yano, and now there was no food or water. The men were too weak to make any attack. 'Now we should hold back shame,' Ishikawa wrote, 'abandon this position, feed our men, and occupy a new position and launch an attack.'[52]

Yano 'scolded me', Ishikawa wrote. 'The way of the Samurai is to be found in death,' Yano told him. When a messenger finally got through from regimental headquarters, the order from General Nakai was the same: 'Persevere and refrain from reckless actions. Fight bravely.' The next day some supplies finally got through as well as another message from Nakai: 'Evacuate the position, redeploy near Yokopi.' On the night of 31 January the remaining defenders left Crater Hill, withdrawing down the Mindjim Valley. The next day, 1 February, the 2/9th and 2/10th battalions finally occupied Crater Hill. 'Almost every tree had been blasted or shattered,' Frank Rolleston saw. 'Some of the craters from bombs were ten feet deep and thirty feet across, while fragments of human remains could be seen plastered high up on the battered trees still standing.'[53]

•

With the loss of Shaggy Ridge what Japanese forces remained in the Finisterres withdrew towards Madang. The Australian 15th Brigade took over the difficult advance across the ranges and down the Japanese road to the coast, delayed by small enemy rearguards but more so by the limitations imposed by the terrain and the rainfall. Madang was finally captured on 24 April 1944.

Two days earlier, on 22 April, the Americans had made a great leap forward and had landed at Aitape, 450 kilometres north-west of Madang, and at Hollandia, another 250 kilometres further west. The battle for Shaggy Ridge had helped draw most of the Japanese army in New Guinea from these locations, while the capture of the Ramu Valley had enabled Allied airpower to destroy the Japanese air assets at Wewak and Hollandia prior to the landings. Allied forces were fighting a three-dimensional war using naval forces to move their army along the New Guinea coast under the cover of superior air power made possible by the captured airfield sites. The Japanese armed forces in New Guinea were essentially reduced to fighting in only one dimension—the ground—and now those forces had been isolated.

EPILOGUE

Following the fighting at Shaggy Ridge, the Japanese 78th Regiment marched west along the coast to Wewak and fought a brutal battle against the Americans at Aitape in July 1944. Of the 5925 men of the regiment who served in New Guinea, only 112, just 2 per cent, survived the war to return to Japan. Kenji Ueda and Kumao Ishikawa were two of those men. General Masutaro Nakai also returned. Of the 2492 men who served with the 26th Artillery Regiment, 106 or 4.2 per cent returned to Japan including Masahiko Ohata. In 2003 I met Lieutenant Colonel Kazumi Kuzuhara who told Ohata of my research on the fate of the detachment that had manned the mountain gun at Prothero, an issue that had plagued Ohata since the war. For Ohata, 'A headache that had lasted for many years vanished as if it was all a joke,' Kuzuhara observed. Masahiko Ohata died in April 2004 before my first book on this battle, *On Shaggy Ridge,* was published but Kazumi Kuzuhara later presented a copy at his memorial altar.

Most of the Australians who fought at Shaggy Ridge survived the war. George Vasey did not, killed in an aircraft crash off Cairns as he headed back to New Guinea on 5 March 1945. Jack Bishop and Colin Fraser both ended up as generals, Fraser going on to command the Australian forces in Vietnam. Of the battle at Prothero he concluded, 'It was a remarkable operation. Whatever strategic importance you put on this or not, it was a tactical operation of its kind and fortunately it turned out successfully.'

'It's hard to tell you what you see,' Noel Pallier told me. 'It's in your mind.' After he had read *On Shaggy Ridge*, he rang me up and told me, 'Phillip, you were there.' In 2005 I took Noel Bear and two of his sisters to Pallier's Hill to see where their father had fought. Alf Edwards told me about how proud he had felt when Pallier had told him he had done a good job: 'I'll never forget it.' Edwards went on to make a career in the army.

After Shaggy Ridge, Pinky McMahon was classified B2 as a POW guard but knew the old colonel at the camp and was reclassified A1 to return to the 2/16th. When I rang him in 2000 he was in hospital in Perth and spoke to me as if he was alone and fighting for his life on the Pimple at that very moment.

In 1956 Australia's Official Historian of the Second World War, Gavin Long, received a letter from an Australian officer who had had considerable front-line service in New Guinea. He apologised to Long for the delay in replying to a query regarding his service as he had been in hospital to have 'a course of treatment for the nerves'. The 'bad aspects' of the war preyed on his mind. 'Fighting Japs, crocodiles and other worse parasites in my sleep,' he wrote.

After I spoke to Jack Beard he told me he would not sleep that night so I told him I was sorry to have had him talk so openly.

Then he thanked me and said he had been waiting nearly 60 years to talk to someone about it. Ray Nielson had a different outlook, telling me, 'The things that are the toughest, I don't remember, I don't want to remember.'

In 1970 Eric Haynes wrote two angry letters to the Australian War Memorial about the text on the then displayed Shaggy Ridge diorama, which made no mention of the 18th Brigade's role in the ridge's capture. He wrote of those men honoured on the walls of the memorial, 'one of whom died in my arms, a few yards distant from the muzzle of a 75 mm artillery piece on Prothero'. After reading *On Shaggy Ridge* Eric also wrote me two letters, both centred around the loss of his mate. Some men could never forget.

ACKNOWLEDGEMENTS

Thanks to Sebu Kosi, Baggi and the other Agana, Romu, Kaiapit and Kesawai villagers who showed me the way around their lands, and to Vic Lemon and Steve Darmody who accompanied me on two of those journeys. To Grant Jephcott, Bill Clift and Dave Thorald for their hospitality at Dumpu Station. To Ian Priestley for his hospitality in Lae and his help at Kesawai and Kaiapit. To John Douglas for his hospitality in Port Moresby.

Thanks to all the veterans of Shaggy Ridge who helped me piece together this story using their stories. Thanks to Trevor Ball for access to his archives and Margot Wade for access to Terry Wade's photos and diary. Thanks to Keith Mitchell for his fine cartography. Thanks to Roger Lee and David Horner for their support.

Thanks to Peter Williams for making available his interview with Kenji Ueda, and to Harumi Sakaguchi for translating Kumao Ishikawa's and parts of Masahiko Ohata's memoirs. Also thanks to Lieutenant Colonel Kazumi Kuzuhara for interviewing Masahiko Ohata for me.

A big thanks to Rebecca Kaiser at Allen & Unwin for her support for what turned out to be my lockdown project. Thanks to Angela Handley for her astute control of the editing and design process, John Mahony and Michelle Manly for their editing work, and Luke Causby for his outstanding design work.

2/16th Battalion troops arriving at Kaiapit airfield on 22 September 1943.

(PHOTO BY NORM STUCKEY, AWM 057499)

2/6th Independent Company and PIB soldiers celebrating victory on Mission Hill, Kaiapit.

(PHOTO BY NORM STUCKEY, AWM 057500)

2/14th Battalion troops crossing the Gusap River during the advance along the Markham and Ramu valleys. (PHOTO BY NORM STUCKEY, AWM 058642)

Norm Stuckey (LEFT) and Lance Corporal Bill 'Rusty' Cullen stand either side of Masao Takayama, a Korean private captured on 5 October 1943. 'What an innocent little fellow, he looked very shame-faced,' Bob Johns observed. 'He didn't look the mighty enemy that we had been fighting at all.' (AWM 058653)

2/16th Battalion men with Japanese dead around a Juki machine gun east of Johns' Knoll following the failed attack. (PHOTO BY NORM STUCKEY, AWM 059020)

Paddy Carey (LEFT) and Ray Fisher look over a captured Nambu pistol after the 2/27th Battalion action at Johns' Knoll. (PHOTO BY NORM STUCKEY, AWM 059002)

Les Thredgold and George Vandeleur on the southern shoulder of Shaggy Ridge, October 1943. (LES THREDGOLD COLLECTION)

Fred Barker, Harrie Fanning and Arthur Brown enjoy a break at the Halfway Stagger Inn on the track up to Shaggy Ridge, 7 November 1943. (PHOTO BY NORM STUCKEY, AWM 060262)

A wounded Merv
Hall helped back
from the front line by
Private Ron Rowe,
27 December 1943.
(PHOTO BY NORM
STUCKEY, AWM 062294)

Privates Jim Knight and Jim Mortimer waiting to go forward at Shaggy Ridge,
27 December 1943. (PHOTO BY NORM STUCKEY, AWM 062325)

Australian troops from the 2/9th Battalion on Intermediate Sniper's Pimple, 23 January 1944. (PHOTO BY NORM STUCKEY, AWM 064255)

Private James Byrne treating Eric Knight (LEFT) and Private Alf Labudda, both wounded during the 2/9th Battalion attack, 21 January 1944. 'You've seen your cobbers take bad wounds with a wry grin,' Shawn O'Leary wrote. (PHOTO BY NORM STUCKEY, AWM 064235)

A stretcher case on Prothero waiting to be carried off the ridge, 22 January 1944.
(PHOTO BY COLIN HALMARICK, AWM 064219)

Prothero, 22 January 1944. Privates Allan Macqueen, Albert Lord, Ansom Willey and Alan Hackett, 2/12th Battalion. (PHOTO BY COLIN HALMARICK, AWM 064220)

Men from A Company, 2/9th Battalion on Green Sniper's Pimple, 21 January 1944.

Looking east up the Uria River with the King's Hill to Pallier's Hill ridge on the left and Three Pimples Hill to the right. (PHOTO BY JAMES ELING)

The southern shoulder of Shaggy Ridge. Note how the ridge turns sharply to the right (east) at Green Pinnacle. (PHOTO BY JAMES ELING)

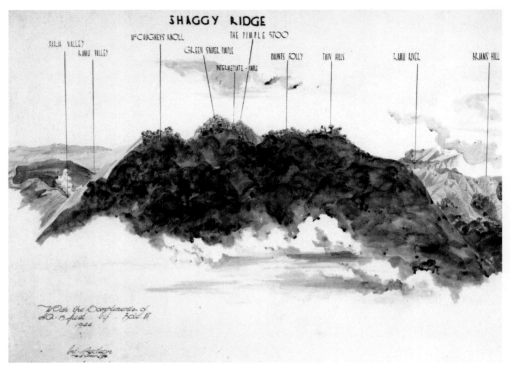

SHAGGY RIDGE

FARIA VALLEY — FARIA VALLEY — McCAUGHEYS KNOLL — GREEN SNIPER PIMPLE — THE PIMPLE 5700 — INTERMEDIATE PIMPLE — MUNTS FOLLY — TWIN HILLS — FARIA RIVER — BRIANS HILL

MT HELWIG 9230 — 5500 EAST — 5500 WEST

Panoramic sketch of Shaggy Ridge and the surrounding features drawn from Prothero Two. The sketch was made by William Green from the intelligence section of the 15th Brigade and presented to General Vasey. (RAY HELLIER COLLECTION)

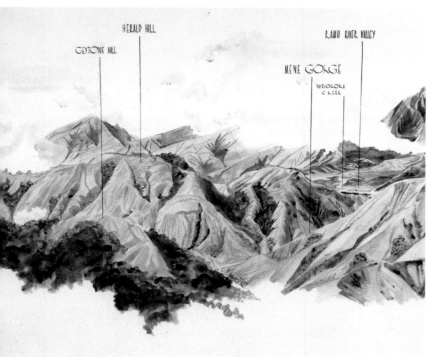

GEYTONS HILL   HERALD HILL   MENE GORGE   RAMU RIVER VALLEY   IUSIOLORE CREEK

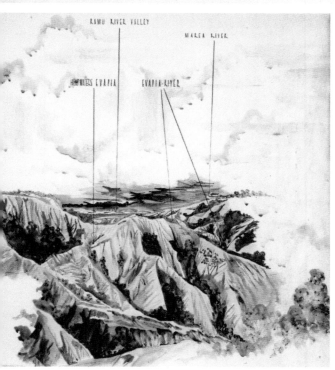

RAMU RIVER VALLEY   MAREA RIVER   HEADWATERS EVAPIA   EVAPIA RIVER

Gordon King, 2/6th Independent Company.
(AUTHOR'S PHOTO)

Bob Johns, 2/27th Battalion.
(AUTHOR'S PHOTO)

Author with Shaggy Bob Clampett,
2/27th Battalion. (AUTHOR'S PHOTO)

Les Thredgold, 2/27th Battalion.
(AUTHOR'S PHOTO)

Noel Pallier and Lindsay Bear, 2/14th Battalion.
(BEAR FAMILY PHOTO)

Monty Stewart, 2/16th Battalion.
(AUTHOR'S PHOTO)

The remains of Norm Trumper's Boomerang at the northern end of Shaggy Ridge.
(PHOTO BY LAWRENCE VAKI)

Looking south-east along Shaggy Ridge towards the Ramu Valley, 19 January 1944. (USAAF HISTORICAL COLLECTION)

View looking north-east from the Ramu Valley road towards Shaggy Ridge, partially covered in cloud in the background. (AUTHOR'S PHOTO)

2/9th Battalion troops dig in along the side of Shaggy Ridge with Green Sniper's Pimple beyond. (PHOTO BY NORM STUCKEY, AWM 064256)

The same location, 1996. (AUTHOR'S PHOTO)

21st Brigade troops marching out of the foothills of the Finisterre Range into the Ramu Valley, 9 November 1943. The Bismarck Range rises like a wall on the other side of the valley. (PHOTO BY NORM STUCKEY, AWM 060483)

The same location, 1996. (AUTHOR'S PHOTO)

NOTES

CHAPTER 1: KAIAPIT

1 AWM52, 25/3/6/9, p. 65. All Japanese names in this book are written with the surname last.
2 See Bradley, *D-Day New Guinea.*
3 AWM55, 3/13, ATIS 1176. See Map 4 for these locations.
4 AWM54, 423/4/16, AE357.
5 AWM55, 3/13, ATIS 1176.
6 Ueda interview.
7 AWM54, 423/4/33.
8 AWM52, 25/3/6/9, p. 31.
9 AWM55, 6/4, IR189. AWM54, 779/3/21, AE73.
10 AWM52, 25/3/6/9, p. 31.
11 King interviews.
12 Horner, *General Vasey's War,* pp. 269–70.
13 Vasey letter, 20 September 1943, NLA, MS3782.
14 Kenney, *General Kenney Reports,* p. 300.
15 AWM52, 25/3/6/9, p. 5.
16 King interviews.
17 Dulhunty, *Our Blood Stained Past,* p. 98.
18 Frazier, *Tsili Tsili Sting, Vol. 2,* p. 131.
19 Ibid.
20 King interviews.
21 Bill Klotz notes. There were fewer than 20 men to a plane.
22 Ashford interviews.
23 Hagan, *1942–1945 Memories,* p. 2.
24 Dulhunty, p. 105.
25 King interviews.
26 Hagan interview.
27 King interviews.
28 AWM52, 25/3/6/9, p. 8.
29 Ibid., p. 30.
30 Mackay interview.
31 King interviews.
32 Ibid.
33 Ryan, *Fear Drive My Feet,* p. 298.
34 King interviews.
35 Ibid.
36 Ibid.
37 Ibid.
38 AWM93, 50/2/23/622.
39 King interviews.
40 Hagan, p. 3.

41 King interviews.
42 Hagan, p. 3. Only A Platoon was involved in the initial attack.
43 Banks interviews.
44 King interviews.
45 Ibid.
46 Ibid.
47 US Army, *Monograph 38*, p. 150.
48 AWM226/7.
49 NAA SP300/3/659. King interviews.
50 AWM254, 266.
51 King interviews.
52 Ibid.
53 Banks interviews.
54 Dulhunty, p. 99.
55 Clews interview.
56 King interviews.
57 Ibid. Dulhunty, p. 99.
58 NAA, SP300/3/638.
59 Dulhunty, p. 99.
60 AWM54, 423/4/16, AE627.
61 King interviews.
62 Ibid.
63 Ibid.
64 Ibid.
65 Ibid.
66 Tozer notes.
67 Weston, 'Bayonets routed Japs at Kaiapit'.
68 Vawdon interviews.
69 Clews interview.
70 King interviews.
71 Ibid.
72 Tozer notes.
73 Clews interview.
74 King interviews.
75 Hagan interview.
76 Banks interviews.
77 Weston, 'Bayonets routed Japs at Kaiapit'.
78 Williams, 'Manes of grass worn by Japanese'.
79 King interviews.
80 Balderstone letters.
81 King interviews.
82 Strika interview.
83 King interviews.
84 Dulhunty, pp. 102–3.
85 King interviews.
86 Ibid.
87 Ibid.
88 King interviews. Frazier, pp. 137–8.
89 King interviews.
90 Dulhunty, p. 104.
91 Frazier, pp. 137–8.
92 NAA, SP300/3/659. Taubada means 'master', as in his officer.
93 Frazier, pp. 137–8.
94 King interviews.
95 AWM52, 25/3/6/9, pp. 10–11.
96 Tozer notes.
97 Hagan interview.
98 King interviews.
99 Vasey letter, 22 September 1943, NLA MS3782.
100 King interviews.
101 Ibid.
102 AWM93, 50/2/23/622.
103 King interviews.
104 Strika interview.
105 Alf Edwards interviews.
106 AWM52, 25/3/6/9, p. 47.
107 US Army, *Monograph 38*, p. 153.
108 AWM52, 25/3/6/9.
109 AWM55, 6/4, IR189. AWM54, 779/3/21, AE73.
110 AWM315, 695/001/009.
111 Ibid.
112 Weston, 'Bayonets routed Japs at Kaiapit'.
113 Tozer notes.
114 Dulhunty, pp. 102–3.
115 King interviews.
116 Ibid.

CHAPTER 2: TO THE END OF THE EARTH

1 AWM55, 6/4, IR189. AWM54, 779/3/21, AE73.
2 AWM55, 6/4, IR187. AWM54, 779/3/22, AE85.
3 AWM55, 3/12, ATIS 1145.
4 AWM55, 3/16, ATIS 1354.
5 AWM55, 3/12, ATIS 1145.
6 AWM55, 3/16, ATIS 1354.
7 AWM55, 3/13, ATIS 1167.
8 Ueda interview.
9 AWM55, 6/6, IR267.
10 AWM55, 3/16, ATIS 1354.
11 AWM55, 3/13, ATIS 1180.
12 Yoshihara, *Southern Cross*, Chapter 12.
13 AWM55, 3/13, ATIS 1167.
14 Ueda interview.
15 Yoshihara, *Southern Cross*, Chapter 12.
16 AWM55, 3/13, ATIS 1180.
17 Yoshihara, *Southern Cross*, Chapter 12. Dennis & Grey, *The Foundations of Victory*, pp. 124. AWM54, 779/3/22, AE94.
18 AWM54, 423/4/33.
19 Ueda interview.
20 AWM54, 423/4/16, AE357. AWM55, 3–13, ATIS 1176.
21 Dennis & Grey, p. 124.
22 Ishikawa, *Nakai Shitai's Battle of Kankerei*.
23 AWM54, 779/3/22, AE89 and AE94.
24 AWM54, 831/3/83.
25 AWM55, 3/11, ATIS 1032.
26 AWM52, 1/2/2/019, pp. 133–5.
27 AWM52, 8/3/27/058, p. 143.
28 Maxwell notes, AWM PR00570.
29 Vasey to Morshead, 18 January 1944, NLA, MS3782.
30 Vasey notes, 22 September 1943, NLA, MS3782.
31 Vasey letter, 24 September 1943, NLA, MS3782.
32 Vasey letter, 26 September 1943, NLA, MS3782.
33 Pearce interviews.
34 Cook interview.
35 Vasey letter, 26 September 1943, NLA, MS3782.
36 Berryman diary, 23 September 1943, AWM, PR84/370.
37 Vasey letter, 27 September 1943, NLA, MS3782.
38 AWM172, 13.
39 Horner, *General Vasey's War*, p. 273.
40 Vasey letter, 30 September 1943, NLA, MS3782.
41 AWM172, 13.
42 AWM93, 50/2/23/357.
43 J. & R. Ackland (eds), *Word from John*, pp. 185 and 215.
44 Ibid., p. 215.
45 Dexter, *New Guinea Offensives*, p. 433.
46 AWM52, 8/3/27/56, p. 2.
47 AWM67, 3/366.
48 Vasey to Robertson, 12 January 1944, NLA, MS3782.
49 AWM67, 3/366. AWM S00790.
50 Clive Edwards diary.
51 AWM52, 2/2/58, October 1943.
52 King interviews. Ashford interview.
53 Dexter, p. 434.
54 Dexter, pp. 434–5. AWM PR00249.
55 Ibid.
56 Ibid. Ian Priestley notes.

CHAPTER 3: 'HOP IN FOR YOUR BLOODY CHOP'

1 J. & R. Ackland (eds), *Word from John*, p. 216.
2 AWM52, 8/3/27/58, p. 2.
3 Clive Edwards diary.
4 AAWFA 1195. Johns interview, AWM S01844.

5   AWM55, 6/4, IR187. AWM54, 779/3/22, AE85.
6   Reddin interview. AWM52, 8/3/27/058, p. 135.
7   US Army, *Monograph 38*, pp. 163–4.
8   AWM52, 8/3/27/58, p. 86.
9   Reddin interview.
10 Fawcett interview.
11 Clive Edwards diary. Burns, *The Brown and Blue Diamond at War*, p. 172.
12 AAWFA 1195. Johns interview, AWM S01844.
13 Johns, 'Ron'. AWM52, 8/3/27/58, pp. 88–9.
14 AWM52, 8/3/27/58, pp. 88–9. Johns interview, AWM S01844. AAWFA 1195.
15 Balderstone interview.
16 King interviews.
17 AWM52, 2/2/58, October 1943
18 AWM52, 2/2/58, October 1943.
19 AWM52, 8/2/21/22, p. 9.
20 AWM, PR84/370, 22 September 1943.
21 Clive Edwards diary. Deering interview.
22 Clive Edwards diary. Thredgold interview. This action took place at Point A on Map 6.
23 AWM S00904. Fawcett interview.
24 AWM S00904.
25 Clive Edwards diary.
26 Zander interview.
27 Clive Edwards interview. Zander interview. This action took place at Point B on Map 6.
28 AWM S00904. Zander interview.
29 Clive Edwards interview. Zander interview.
30 Clive Edwards diary.
31 Reddin interview.
32 AWM52, 8/3/27/58, p. 135.
33 AWM52, 8/3/27/58, p. 93. Burns, p. 176. Weston, 'SA men in daring actions'.
34 NAA, SP300/3/572.
35 Lundie, *Reveille*, p. 16.
36 AWM119/036. Addison interview.
37 J. & R. Ackland (eds), *Word from John*, p. 227.
38 Weston, 'SA men in daring actions'.
39 AWM52, 8/3/27/58, p. 93.
40 Weston, 'SA men in daring actions'.
41 AWM54, 779/3/22, AE89. AWM52, 8/3/27/58, p. 33.
42 Castle interview.
43 AWM S00790. Reddin interview.
44 AWM52, 8/3/27/58, pp. 33 and 93.
45 AWM52, 4/2/4, October 1943.
46 Bullock interviews.
47 Burns, p. 175.
48 Bullock interviews. Weston, 'SA men in daring actions'. AWM119/036.
49 Reddin interview. AWM52, 8/3/27/58, p. 136.
50 Zander interview.
51 Clive Edwards diary. Whyte interview.

CHAPTER 4: 'DO OR DIE'

1   Slim Davidson interview.
2   Moriaty interview.
3   Alf Edwards interviews.
4   Pallier interviews.
5   Ibid.
6   Bear interviews.
7   Moriaty interview.
8   Russell, *The Second Fourteenth Battalion*, p. 220.
9   Alf Edwards interviews.
10 AWM PR87/221, p. 36.
11 Pallier interviews.

12 Dandy, *The Kookaburra's Cut-throats Vol. 1*, p. 115.
13 Harry Norton interview. Brune, *We Band of Brothers*, p. 245.
14 Bisset interviews.
15 Russell, pp. 227–8.
16 Moriaty interview.
17 Dandy, p. 116.
18 Ibid.
19 Russell, pp. 227–8. Dandy, p. 117.
20 Pallier interviews.
21 Moriaty interview. Cooke interview.
22 AWM54, 779/3/22, AE92 and AE85.
23 O'Day interview.
24 Russell, p. 231. Alf Edwards interviews. Pallier interviews.
25 Pallier interviews.
26 Ibid.
27 Ibid.
28 Russell, p. 232. AWM52, 8/3/14/69, pp. 33–4.
29 Pallier interviews.
30 Russell, pp. 233–4.
31 Alf Edwards interviews.
32 AWM52, 8/3/14/69, pp. 8–9.
33 AWM172, 13.
34 AWM52, 8/2/21/022, p. 10.
35 Ibid.
36 AWM172, 13.
37 Pallier interviews.
38 Alf Edwards interviews.
39 O'Day interview. Pallier interviews.
40 Alf Edwards interviews.
41 Malcolm interview.
42 Pallier interviews.
43 Ibid.
44 Ibid.
45 Malcolm interview.
46 Russell, pp. 234–5.
47 NAA, NA9720B.
48 Pallier interviews.
49 Ibid. Alf Edwards interviews.
50 Stirling interviews.
51 Cooke interview.
52 AWM52, 8/3/14/69, pp. 33–4.
53 O'Day interview.
54 Alf Edwards interviews.
55 Alf Edwards interviews. Pallier interviews.
56 Malcolm interview.
57 O'Day interview. Moriaty interview.
58 NAA, NA9720B.
59 Pallier interviews.
60 Alf Edwards interviews.
61 NAA, NA9720B.
62 Alf Edwards interviews. Pallier interviews
63 Ibid.
64 Russell, pp. 235–6.
65 Pallier interviews.
66 NAA, NA9720B.
67 Alf Edwards interviews.
68 Pallier interviews.
69 Ibid.
70 Twine interview.
71 Alf Edwards interviews.
72 Harry Norton interview.
73 O'Day interview. Moriaty interview.
74 Stirling interviews.
75 Pallier interviews.
76 Bear interviews.
77 Russell, pp. 237–8.
78 Pallier interviews.
79 Butcher, 'Digger braves the bullets'.
80 Pallier interviews.
81 Twine interview.
82 Alf Edwards interviews.
83 Russell, p. 236.
84 NAA, NA9720B. NAA, NA9720B.
85 Alf Edwards interviews.
86 Pallier interviews.

87 Pallier interviews. NAA, NA9720B.
88 Pallier interviews.
89 Alf Edwards interviews.
90 O'Day interview.
91 Alf Edwards interviews.
92 Pallier interviews.
93 Ibid.
94 Alf Edwards interviews.
95 Ibid.
96 Pallier to Bear letter, 24 December 1943, Bear family records.

CHAPTER 5: 'WE'D OUTFOUGHT THEM THERE'
1 Ranger interview. Lofberg interview.
2 AAWFA 1195.
3 Johns, 'Johns' Knoll'. Johns letters. Fisher interview.
4 Reddin interview, AWM S01844.
5 Johns, 'Johns' Knoll'. Johns letters.
6 Johns, 'Ron'. Fisher interview.
7 Clive Edwards diary.
8 AAWFA 1195.
9 Johns, 'Ron'.
10 Johns, 'Johns' Knoll'. AAWFA 1195.
11 Johns interview, AWM S01844.
12 Johns, 'Johns' Knoll'. Fisher interview.
13 AWM52, 8/3/27/58, p. 102. Addison interview.
14 Addison interview.
15 Ibid.
16 Johns interview, AWM S01844.
17 Reddin and Clampett interviews, AWM S01844.
18 Johns and Clampett interviews, AWM S01844.
19 AWM52, 8/3/27/58, pp. 106–7.
20 Ibid., p. 104. Zander interview. Thredgold interview.
21 AWM52, 8/3/27/058, p. 102.

22 Reddin interview, AWM S01844.
23 Fisher interview.
24 Addison interview.
25 AWM52, 8/3/27/58, pp. 104–7.
26 Ibid., p. 103.
27 Ibid., pp. 105 and 137. NAA, SP300/3, 572.
28 NAA, SP300/3, 572. Ashton interview.
29 AWM52, 8/3/27/58, p. 105.
30 AWM S00902.
31 Fisher interview. Weston, 'SA men in daring actions'.
32 Ranger interview.
33 Clive Edwards diary.
34 Weston, 'SA men in daring actions'.
35 Reddin interview, AWM S01844.
36 Addison interview and letter.
37 AAWFA 1195. Addison interview.
38 AWM54, 779/3/22, AE94.
39 AWM52, 8/3/27/58, pp. 41 and 58. Johns interview, AWM S01844.
40 AWM52, 8/3/27/58, p. 137.
41 Reddin interview.
42 AAWFA 1195. Johns interview, AWM S01844.

CHAPTER 6: 'THE BRIG WANTS THAT HILL TONIGHT, MAC'
1 See Bradley, *D-Day New Guinea*, pp. 172–8.
2 Crooks, *The Footsoldiers*, p. 326. MacDougal interview.
3 Ibid. MacDougal notes.
4 AAWFA 0135.
5 Ibid.
6 AAWFA 0135. MacDougal interview. Crooks, pp. 328–9.
7 MacDougal interview. Crooks, pp. 328–9.
8 Crooks, pp. 329–30. AAWFA 0135.

9   Crooks, pp. 330–1. MacDougal interview. Nielson interview.
10 Crooks, pp. 330–1. AAWFA 0135. MacDougal interview.
11 AWM52, 8/3/33/12, p. 6.
12 AAWFA 0135.
13 MacDougal interview. MacDougal never received a DSO.
14 Crooks, pp. 338–40.
15 AAWFA 0135.
16 MacDougal interview.
17 Balfour-Ogilvy notes.
18 Crooks, p. 341.
19 Crooks, pp. 342–4.
20 Crooks, p. 341.
21 Crooks, pp. 344–6. AAWFA 0135.
22 NAA SP300/572.
23 Crooks, pp. 347–9.
24 Nielson interview. MacDougal notes. AAWFA 0135.
25 AWM52, 8/3/33/12, p. 8.
26 Nielson interview.
27 AAWFA 0135.
28 Morshead to Vasey, 18 October 1943, NLA MS3782.
29 Vasey to Morshead, 20 October 1943, NLA MS3782.
30 Ibid.
31 Ibid. Morshead to Vasey, 14 November 1943, NLA MS3782.

CHAPTER 7: ONTO SHAGGY RIDGE

1   AWM52, 8/3/27/58, p. 44.
2   Clive Edwards diary.
3   Reddin interview, AWM S01844.
4   Ibid. AWM PR00876, 25 December 1943.
5   Clampett interview. Clampett interview, AWM S01844.
6   Clampett interview. Reddin interview, AWM S01844.
7   J. & R. Ackland (eds), *Word from John*, p. 219.

8   AWM52, 8/3/27/58, p. 27. Clampett interview, AWM S01844.
9   Reddin interview, AWM S01844.
10 Clampett interview, AWM S01844. Thredgold interview.
11 J. & R. Ackland (eds), *Word from John*, p. 217.
12 Reddin interview, AWM S01844.
13 Ibid.
14 AWM52, 8/3/27/58, p. 60.
15 Reddin interview, AWM S01844. Whyte interview.
16 AWM52, 8/3/27/58, p. 121.
17 Thredgold interview.
18 Ibid. AWM52, 8/3/27/58, p. 65.
19 Duffell interviews.
20 Ibid. AWM S00928.
21 Duffell interviews.
22 Ibid.
23 Ueda interview.
24 Dickson, 'Flying for the Army', p. 69.
25 Ibid.
26 Dickson, pp. 71–2.
27 Dickson, pp. 73–5.
28 Dickson, pp. 78–9.
29 Ibid.
30 Ishikawa, *Nakai Shitai's Battle of Kankerei*.
31 Clive Edwards diary.
32 Clive Edwards diary. Thredgold interview.
33 AWM52, 8/3/27/59, p. 30.
34 Ibid.
35 Ueda interview.
36 AWM52, 8/3/27/59, p. 33.
37 Clive Edwards diary.
38 Bullock interview.
39 Ueda interview.
40 AWM52, 8/3/27/59, p. 34.
41 Ueda interview.
42 Ibid.
43 Duffell interviews.

44 Crooks, *The Footsoldiers*, p. 360.
45 J. & R. Ackland (eds), *Word from John*, p. 222.
46 Ibid., pp. 226–8.
47 Vasey to Morshead, 5 December 1943, NLA MS3782.

CHAPTER 8: KESAWAI
1 King interviews. AWM93, 50/2/23/622.
2 Mackay interview.
3 Banks interviews.
4 Bottrell, *Cameos of Commandos*, p. 57.
5 King interviews.
6 Hagan, '1942–1945 Memories', p. 6.
7 Ibid.
8 King interviews.
9 Mackay interview.
10 Henry, *The Story of the 2/4th Field Regiment*, p. 282.
11 King interviews.
12 US Army, *Monograph 38*, pp. 158–60.
13 AWM254, 266.
14 AWM52, 2/2/58, December 1943.
15 US Army, *Monograph 38*, pp. 166–8. HQ V Fighter Command, A2 Report 267.
16 Bottrell, pp. 64–5. AWM52, 2/2/58, December 1943.
17 Ralston letter.
18 Henry, pp. 281–3.
19 King interviews.
20 Balderstone interview.
21 AWM52, 2/2/58.
22 Ball notes.
23 Morshead to Vasey, 10 December 43, NLA MS3782.
24 AWM54, 595/7/26.
25 Ibid.
26 Carpendale interview.

27 AWM54, 595/7/26. AWM52, 8/3/25/25, p. 84.
28 Henry, p. 287.
29 AWM54, 595/7/26. AWM52, 8/3/25/25, pp. 79–80.
30 Ibid., pp. 86–7. Carpendale interview.
31 US Army, *Monograph 38*, p. 174.
32 AWM54, 595/7/26. AWM52, 8/3/25/25, p. 81.
33 Vasey to Morshead, 13 December 1943, NLA MS3782.
34 Dexter, *The New Guinea Offensives*, p. 697.
35 AWM52, 8/3/16/29, p. 12.
36 Ishikawa, *Nakai Shitai's Battle of Kankerei*.
37 Ibid.
38 Ibid.
39 Stewart interview. Jack Smith diary.

CHAPTER 9: MISSING
1 Reddin notes.
2 Ibid.
3 Reddin notes. AWM52, 8/3/27/59, p. 136.
4 Reddin notes.
5 Reddin notes. Fawcett notebook.
6 Reddin notes.
7 Reddin notes. Fawcett notebook.
8 Reddin notes. Reddin refers to Perkins as Evans but the battalion war diary, Fawcett's notebook and another member of 16 Platoon confirm it was Perkins.
9 Reddin notes. Fawcett notebook.
10 Ibid.
11 Reddin notes.
12 Ibid.
13 Ibid.
14 Thredgold interview.
15 Ibid.
16 Ibid.

17 AWM52, 8/3/25/25, pp. 102–3.
18 Ibid.
19 Ibid.
20 Morel Service Record, NAA B883.
21 AWM52, 8/2/18/51, p. 97. AWM54, 595/7/17.
22 Bullock interviews. Thredgold interview.
23 NAA, B3856, 145/4/21.

CHAPTER 10: THE ONE-MAN FRONT

1 Bidner interview.
2 Mantle interview.
3 Murphy interview.
4 Pearce interview.
5 Ishikawa, *Nakai Shitai's Battle of Kankerei.*
6 AWM52, 8/3/16/27, p. 73.
7 Ishikawa, *Nakai Shitai's Battle of Kankerei.*
8 Ibid.
9 Kyro emails.
10 AWM52, 8/2/21/23, pp. 2–3.
11 Murphy interview. AWM52, 8/3/25/25, p. 32.
12 Jack Smith diary.
13 Harley interview.
14 AWM52, 8/3/16/28, pp. 24–5.
15 Murphy interview.
16 Leicester interviews.
17 Jack Smith diary.
18 Harley interview. AWM52, 8/3/16/029, p. 64.
19 Ibid.
20 Trunk interviews. Cook interview. Pearce interviews.
21 Ueda interview.
22 Ibid.
23 US Army, *Monograph 38*, p. 158.
24 Ishikawa, *Nakai Shitai's Battle of Kankerei.*
25 Ueda interview.
26 Ibid.

27 US Army, *Monograph 38*, pp. 165–6.
28 AWM52, 1/2/2/19, p. 56.
29 AWM52, 8/3/16/25, p. 21.
30 Christian notes.
31 Murphy interview.
32 Symington interview.
33 Ibid. AWM54, 595/7/11.
34 Webber interview. AWM54, 595/7/11.
35 Christian notes.
36 Ibid.
37 Murphy interview.
38 Roberts interview.
39 *The West Australian*, 'Yank in the AIF'.
40 Roberts papers. Stewart interviews.
41 AWM315, 695.
42 www.awm.gov.au/collection/ C169356.

CHAPTER 11: THE PIMPLE

1 Tommy Roberts letter. Jackstraws were small sticks.
2 49th Fighter Group record, p. 98. AWM52, 8/3/16/29, p. 22. McInnes interview.
3 AWM52, 4/2/4, December 1943.
4 Stirling interviews.
5 Tommy Roberts letter.
6 49th Fighter Group record, p. 98. Slessor, 'How Australians took Shaggy Ridge'.
7 Murphy interviews.
8 AWM52, 2/2/58, December 1943.
9 Ishikawa, *Nakai Shitai's Battle of Kankerei.*
10 Collingwood, 'The Pimple'.
11 Stewart interviews.
12 Symington interview.
13 Magick interview.
14 McMahon interview.
15 McMahon interview. Magick interview. McMahon told me his hand 'was buggered and still is'.

16 Stewart interviews.
17 Stewart interviews. Magick interview. McMahon interview.
18 Jack Smith diary.
19 Stewart interviews.
20 Stewart interview. Bidner interview. Murphy interview.
21 AWM315, 695/001/009.
22 Murphy interviews.
23 Cook interview.
24 Butler interview.
25 Murphy interviews.
26 Stewart interviews. Pearce interviews. Cook interview.
27 Murphy interviews.
28 Ibid.
29 AWM52, 4/2/4, December 1943.
30 AWM52, 8/3/16/29, p. 24.
31 Mantle interview.
32 Ibid.
33 Peck, *Sappers of the Silent Seventh*, pp. 328–9.
34 Hoskin interviews and notes.
35 Ibid.
36 Scott interview.
37 *Pigeon Post*, March 1997. Hoskin notes. Pearce interviews.
38 Mantle interview. Trunk interview, Webber interview.
39 Ibid.
40 *Pigeon Post*, March and June 1997.
41 *Pigeon Post*, June 1997.
42 Trunk interview. *Pigeon Post*, March 1997.
43 Hoskin notes.
44 *Pigeon Post*, March 1997.
45 *Pigeon Post*, June 1997. Scott interview. Farley interview. Waldon interview.
46 Hoskin notes.
47 *Pigeon Post*, September 1997.
48 Ibid.
49 *Pigeon Post*, June 1997.
50 McCulloch interviews. Bidner interview.
51 Bidner interview.
52 Mantle interview.
53 Bidner interview.
54 *Pigeon Post*, June 1997.
55 Bidner interview.
56 Ishikawa, *Nakai Shitai's Battle of Kankerei*. AWM52, 4/2/4/22, p. 96. AWM54, 595/7/4.
57 McCulloch interviews.
58 Mantle interview.
59 Waldon interview.
60 Bidner interview.
61 Harley interview.
62 Ibid.
63 Symington interview.
64 AWM52, 8/2/18/51, p. 97.

CHAPTER 12: 18TH BRIGADE
1 Miller-Randle, 'Invictus Asbestos', pp. 121–2.
2 Ibid., p. 123.
3 Ibid., pp. 123–4.
4 Osborne interview. Osborne notes.
5 Osborne interview.
6 AWM52, 8/2/18/51, p. 98.
7 AWM54, 171/2/9.
8 Leicester interviews.
9 Vasey to Robertson, 12 January 1944, NLA MS3782.
10 McAuley interview.
11 Rolleston letters.
12 AWM52, 8/3/12/10, pp. 38, 83–4.
13 Graeme-Evans, *Of Storms and Rainbows*, p. 337.
14 AAWFA 0399.
15 Wotton interview.
16 Francis interview.
17 Graeme-Evans, p. 338. Atebrin was a malaria suppressant.
18 Fraser interview.
19 Beard interview.
20 Davis interview.

21 Etchells interviews.
22 Davis interview.
23 AWM52, 8/3/10/26, p. 2.
24 Foster interview. Diggles interview. NAA SP300/3, 670.
25 AWM55, 6/6, IR267.
26 Kitamoto, *A Record of Marathon Adventures*, pp. 92–3.
27 US Army, *Monograph 38*, pp. 174–5.
28 AWM52, 8/2/18/51, p. 97.
29 AWM54, 423/4/16, AE 1272.
30 US Army, *Monograph 38*, p. 176.
31 Dennis & Grey, *The Foundations of Victory*, pp. 126–7. AWM54, 595/7/4.
32 AWM54, 423/4/16, AE1263.
33 AWM52, 8/2/18/51, p. 98.
34 Ishikawa, *Nakai Shitai's Battle of Kankerei*.
35 Spencer, *In the Footsteps of Ghosts*, p. 171.
36 Francis interview.
37 Spencer, p. 174.
38 Rolleston, *Not a Conquering Hero*, p. 157.
39 Gordon Davidson interview.
40 Martin letter.
41 Stack interview.
42 Pearson interview. Spencer, pp. 175–6.
43 Spencer, p. 176.
44 AMF, *Jungle Warfare*, pp. 147–9.
45 Max Smith interview. AWM52, 8/3/9/32, p. 4.
46 AWM52, 8/3/9/32, p. 4.
47 AMF, *Jungle Warfare*, pp. 147–9.
48 Spencer, pp. 178–9.
49 AWM315, 695/001/009.
50 AWM315, 695/001/001.
51 Miller-Randle, *Invictus Asbestos*, pp. 131–3.
52 NAA, SP300/3, 820.
53 NAA, SP300/3, 671.

54 Rolleston, p. 158.
55 Osborne notes.
56 Stout emails.
57 AWM54, 595/4/6.
58 Miller-Randle, *Invictus Asbestos*, p. 133.
59 Ishikawa, *Nakai Shitai's Battle of Kankerei*.
60 Stevens interview. De Haven emails.
61 Ishikawa, *Nakai Shitai's Battle of Kankerei*.
62 Gordon Davidson interview,
63 AWM93, 322.
64 Sherwin interviews.
65 Vasey to Morshead, 18 January 1944, NLA MS3782.
66 Allchin, *Purple and Blue*, p. 346. Foster interview.
67 AMF, *Jungle Warfare*, pp. 147–9.
68 AWM54, 595/7/4.
69 AWM54, 391/11/26. Diggles interview.
70 SP300/3, 670. Diggles interview.

CHAPTER 13: PROTHERO

1 AWM254, 266. Originally named Mount Protheroe, but the e was soon dropped.
2 Whyte interview.
3 McInnes interview. Aitken, *The Story of the 2/2nd Pioneer Battalion*, p. 222.
4 Stirling interviews.
5 AWM52, 8/6/2, January 1944.
6 Sherwin interviews.
7 Greenup interviews.
8 Aitken, p. 229. Etchells interviews. AWM S00574.
9 Wade diary.
10 Etchells interviews.
11 Crawford notes, AWM PR00570.
12 Stirling interviews.
13 AWM PR01593.

14 Francis interview. Sherwin interviews.
15 Francis interview.
16 Ibid.
17 AWM S00574.
18 Francis interview. Dyne letter, AWM PR00570.
19 Crawford notes, AWM PR00570.
20 Dawson interview.
21 Etchells interviews.
22 Greenup interviews.
23 Wotton letter, AWM PR00570.
24 Whyte interview.
25 Stirling interviews.
26 AAWFA 0399.
27 Francis, 'Before the Battle Clears', p. 25.
28 Etchells interviews.
29 Francis, p. 26.
30 Crawford notes, AWM PR00570.
31 Webb letters, AWM PR00570.
32 Etchells interviews.
33 McNab interview.
34 Etchells interviews.
35 Davis interview.
36 AWM PR01593. Berwick interview.
37 Maxwell notes, AWM PR00570. Maxwell interview.
38 Dempster interview.
39 Haynes letters.
40 Greenup interviews.
41 Sherwin interviews.
42 Fraser interview.
43 Wotton interview.
44 AAWFA 0399.
45 Fraser interview.
46 Sherwin interviews.
47 Thomas diary. Beard interview.
48 Francis, p. 26.
49 Etchells interviews.
50 Fraser interview. Davis interview.
51 Whyte interview.
52 Etchells interviews.
53 Schollick letter, AWM PR00570.
54 Beard interview. Thomas diary. Greenup interviews.
55 Davis interview.
56 Hunter letter, AWM PR00570.
57 Greenup interviews.
58 Fraser interview.
59 AWM S00574.
60 Stirling interviews.
61 Whyte interview.
62 Ishikawa, *Nakai Shitai's Battle of Kankerei*.
63 Stirling interviews.
64 Ibid.
65 Sherwin interviews.
66 AWM119, 049.
67 Fraser interview.
68 Thomas diary. Maxwell interview. AWM52, 8/3/12/14, p. 9.
69 Beard interview. Davis interview.
70 NAA, SP300/3, 670.
71 Thow interview.
72 Stirling interviews.
73 Fraser interview.
74 Etchells interviews.
75 Sherwin interviews.
76 Greenup interviews.
77 Beard interview.

CHAPTER 14: LIFE AND DEATH ON SHAGGY RIDGE

1 AWM54, 19/7/7. Tann, *2/5th Australian Field Ambulance*, p. 81.
2 AWM54, 19/7/7.
3 AWM54, 19/7/7. AAWFA 0063.
4 Tann interview. Wade diary.
5 Wade diary. Wade photo caption.
6 Fraser interview.
7 Wade diary.
8 Dickins, *Ordinary Heroes*, p. 62.
9 AWM54, 19/7/7.
10 Dickins, p. 64.
11 Tann interview. Weston, 'War ends for youthful soldier'.
12 AWM S00574. Wade diary.

13 AWM54, 19/7/7.
14 Crawford notes, AWM PR00570.
15 Fraser interview.
16 Etchells interviews.
17 Wade diary.
18 Schollick letter, AWM PR00570.
19 AWM54, 19/7/7.
20 Dickins, pp. 63–4.
21 AWM54, 19/7/7.
22 Tann, pp. 83–8. Tann interview. Dickins, p. 63. AAWFA 0063.
23 AAWFA 0063.
24 Tann, pp. 85–7.
25 AAWFA 0063.
26 Stirling interviews.
27 Etchells interviews.
28 Stirling interviews.
29 Etchells interviews.
30 Wade diary.
31 Greenup interviews.
32 AWM S00574.
33 Giezendanner interview.
34 Sherwin interviews.
35 Whyte interview.
36 Thow interview.
37 AWM315, 695/001/001.
38 Ibid.

CHAPTER 15: 'YOU'LL NEVER FORGET SHAGGY RIDGE'

1 AMF, *Jungle Warfare*, pp. 147–9.
2 Ibid.
3 McAuley interview.
4 Stack interview.
5 AMF, *Jungle Warfare*, pp. 147–9.
6 Ishikawa, *Nakai Shitai's Battle of Kankerei*.
7 Gordon Davidson interview.
8 AMF, *Jungle Warfare*, pp. 147–9.
9 McAuley interview.
10 AMF, *Jungle Warfare*, pp. 147–9.
11 Ibid.
12 McAuley interview. AMF, *Jungle Warfare*, pp. 147–9.

13 McAuley interview.
14 AMF, *Jungle Warfare*, pp. 147–9.
15 McAuley interview.
16 *Kalgoorlie Miner*, 'On Shaggy Ridge'.
17 Gordon Davidson interview.
18 AMF, *Jungle Warfare*, pp. 147–9.
19 Ishikawa, *Nakai Shitai's Battle of Kankerei*. AWM52, 1/2/2/019, p. 131.
20 Rolleston, *Not a Conquering Hero*, p. 159. McAuley interview.
21 AMF, *Jungle Warfare*, pp. 147–9.
22 McAuley interview. Stack interview.
23 AMF, *Jungle Warfare*, pp. 147–9.
24 Gordon Davidson interview.
25 Ibid.
26 Fountain interview.
27 AMF, *Jungle Warfare*, pp. 147–9.
28 AWM52, 1/2/2/019, p. 131.
29 AWM52, 8/3/9/22, pp. 12–13.
30 AMF, *Jungle Warfare*, pp. 147–9.
31 AWM315, 695.
32 Peterson, 'Cameraman in thick of fight'.
33 AMF, *Jungle Warfare*, pp. 147–9.
34 Rolleston interview.
35 AWM 119, 049.
36 Rolleston, pp. 161–2.
37 Rolleston, p. 162.

CHAPTER 16: TO KANKIRYO

1 Stirling interviews.
2 Thomas diary.
3 Fraser interview.
4 Dawson interview.
5 Sherwin interviews.
6 Thomas diary. Fraser interview. Davis interview. Etchells interviews. Whyte interview.
7 Thomas diary.
8 Ibid.
9 Ibid. Davis interview.

10 Stirling interviews.
11 Ibid.
12 Thomas diary. Davis interview.
13 Beard interview.
14 Davis interview.
15 Davies letter, AWM PR00570.
16 Fraser interview.
17 Sherwin interviews.
18 Wade diary.
19 Thow interview.
20 Ishikawa, *Nakai Shitai's Battle of Kankerei.*
21 AWM54, 19/7/7.
22 Wade diary.
23 Thomas diary.
24 Greenup interviews.
25 Sherwin interviews.
26 Dawson interview.
27 Maxwell notes, AWM PR00570.
28 Maxwell interview. Maxwell notes, AWM PR00570.
29 Sherwin interview.
30 Thomas diary.
31 Davis interview, 5 March 2000. Thomas diary. Maxwell notes, AWM PR00570.
32 AWM PR84/189.
33 Thomas diary.
34 AWM54, 19/7/7.
35 Wade diary.
36 Maxwell interview. Maxwell notes, AWM PR00570.
37 Thomas diary. Fraser interview.
38 AWM54, 19/7/7. Wade diary. AWM54, 595/6/3.
39 AWM54, 19/7/7. Wade diary.
40 Maxwell notes, AWM PR00570.
41 Wade diary.
42 Webb letter, AWM PR00570.
43 Etchells interviews. Etchell notes, AWM PR00570. Dawson interview.
44 Etchells interviews.
45 AWM54, 595/6/3.
46 Ibid.
47 Wade diary.
48 Ishikawa, *Nakai Shitai's Battle of Kankerei.*
49 Ibid.
50 Ibid.
51 Max Smith interview.
52 Ishikawa, *Nakai Shitai's Battle of Kankerei.*
53 Rolleston, *Not a Conquering Hero,* p. 164.

BIBLIOGRAPHY

Interviews and Private Communication

Addison, Keith, 2/27th Battalion, interview: 3 April 2003; letter: 28 July 2005

Ashford, Fred, 2/6th Independent Company, interviews: August 2000, April 2002

Ashton, Harry, 2/27th Battalion, interview: 1 August 2002

Balderstone, Bob, 2/6th Independent Company, interview: 28 July 2002; letters: September, December 2002

Banks, Charlie, 2/6th Independent Company, interviews: 4 March & 24 March 2002

Bear, Lindsay, 2/14th Battalion, interviews with Martha Bear and Bruce McIntyre: 21 May 2000 & 20 April 2005

Beard, Jack, 2/12th Battalion, interview: 4 April 2000; letter: 19 March 2005

Berwick, Dennis, 2/12th Battalion, interview: 7 January 2003

Bidner, John, 2/16th Battalion, interviews: 28 June, 16 September 2000

Bisset, Stan, 2/14th Battalion, interviews: 8 July 2000, 6 June 2002, 25 April 2003; letters: July 2000, June 2002

Bullock, Alan, 2/27th Battalion, interviews: 16 April & 24 April 2000; letters: 1996–2000

Butler, Rolfe, 2/16th Battalion, interview: 30 April 2000

Carpendale, Roy, 2/25th Battalion, interview: 14 December 2001

Castle, Brian, 2/27th Battalion, interview: July 2000

Chilton, Fred, 18th Brigade, letter: 26 April 2000

Clampett, Bob, 2/27th Battalion, interview: September 1997; letter: 25 April 2001

Clews, Jim, 2/6th Independent Company, interview: 13 May 2002; letter: June 2000

Cook, Allan, 2/16th Battalion, interview: 22 May 2000

Cooke, Brian, 2/14th Battalion, interview: 25 April 2000

Davidson, Gordon, 2/9th Battalion, interview: March 2000

Davidson, Slim, 2/14th Battalion, interview with Steve Darmody, 12 August 2008

Davis, Bob, 2/12th Battalion, interview: 5 March 2000

Dawson, George, 2/12th Battalion, interview: January 1998

De Haven, Robert, 7th Fighter Squadron USAAF, emails: 2002; letter: June 2002

Deering, Bruce, 2/27th Battalion, interview: 16 September 1997

Dempster, Vic, 2/12th Battalion, interview: November 2000

Dexter, David, 2/2nd Independent Company, interview with Ian Priestley: 1990

Diggles, Stoddart, 2/10th Battalion, interview: 7 April 2003

Duffell, Don, 2/27th Battalion, interview: 5 July, 1 August 2002

Edwards, Alf, 2/14th Battalion, interviews: 9 September 2000, 11 November 2001

Edwards, Clive, 2/27th Battalion, interview: 19 December 2000; letters: 15 April 1996, 29 November 2000

Etchells, Bill, 2/12th Battalion, interviews: 30 July, 24 December 2000; letter: 12 August 2000

Farley, Ron, 2/16th Battalion, interview: 8 January 2001

Fawcett, Guy, 2/27th Battalion, interview: 14 February 2003

Fisher, Ray, 2/27th Battalion, interview: 29 June 2000; letter: July 2000

Foster, Don, 2/10th Battalion, interview: 4 July 2002

Fountain, Jim, 2/9th Battalion, interview: January 1998

Francis, Alwyn, 2/12th Battalion, interview: 6 March 2001; letter: 16 December 1999

Fraser, Colin, 2/12th Battalion, interview: 4 March 2001

Giezendanner, Hugh, 2/12th Battalion, interview: 26 September 2000

Greenup, Brodie, 2/12th Battalion, interviews: 12 September 2000, 19 May 2002

Hagan, Wally, 2/6th Independent Company, interview: 11 September 2000

Harley, Bud, 2/16th Battalion, interview: 4 June 2000

Haynes, Eric, 2/12th Battalion, letters: 27 March, 17 April 2007

Hoskin, Len, 2/5th Field Company, interviews: 2000–2003

Johns, Bob, 2/27th Battalion, interviews: 16 September 1997, 12 March 2000; letters: 1996–1999

King, Gordon, 2/6th Independent Company, interviews: 13 April, 21 July 2002

Kyro, Erick, 41st Fighter Squadron USAAF, emails: 2001–2002

Leicester, Vic, 2/16th Battalion, interviews: 13 April, 6 October 1999

Lofberg, Charlie, 2/27th Battalion, interview: May 2000

McAuley, Ron, 2/9th Battalion, interview: January 1998

McCulloch, Jim, 2/16th Battalion, interviews: 30 July, 10 September 2000

MacDougal, Dave, 2/33rd Battalion, interview: 4 October 2002; letter: 8 July 2003

McInnes, Allan, 2/2nd Pioneer Battalion, interview: 29 September 2001

Mackay, Alex, 2/6th Independent Company, interview: 23 May 2002

McMahon, Tom, 2/16th Battalion, interview: 18 May 2000

McNab, Brian, 2/12th Battalion, interview: November 2000

Magick, Jim, 2/16th Battalion, interview: 25 July 2000

Malcolm, Bob, 2/14th Battalion, interview: 3 August 2000

Mantle, Ray, 2/16th Battalion, interview: June 2000; letter: May 2001

Martin, Bruce, 2/9th Battalion, interview: January 1998; letter: January 1998

Maxwell, Norm, 2/12th Battalion, interview: 25 August 2000

BIBLIOGRAPHY

Miller-Randle, Alex, RAAF No. 4 Squadron, interview: 11 February 2003; letter: 7 March 2003

Moriarty, Tim, 2/14th Battalion, interview: 16 August 2002

Murphy, Frank, 2/16th Battalion, interviews: 9 May & 27 December 2000, November 2002

Nielson, Ray, 2/33rd Battalion, interview: 9 October 2002

Norton, Harry, 2/14th Battalion, interview: July 2000

O'Day, Gerry, 2/14th Battalion, interview: 11 July 2000

Ohata, Masahiko, 78th Regiment IJA, interviews with Kazumi Kuzuhara: 2003

Osborne, Allen, 2/6th Independent Company, interview: 3 February 2001; letters: 2000–2002

Pallier, Nolan, 2/14th Battalion, interviews: 24 June 2000, 24 December 2000 & 8 May 2002

Pearce, Tich, 2/16th Battalion, interviews: May & June 2000, 28 May 2003

Pearson, Herb, Salvation Army, interview: 27 April 2010

Ranger, Frank, 2/27th Battalion, interview: 16 May 2000; letter: April 2000

Reddin, Jack, 2/27th Battalion, interview: 7 March 2001

Roberts, Ted (brother of Tommy Roberts) interview: 22 August 2003; emails: 1999–2003

Rolleston, Frank, 2/9th Battalion, interview: January 1998; letters: 13 February & April 2000

Scott, Jack, 2/16th Battalion, interview: April 1999

Sherwin, Norm, 2/12th Battalion, interviews: 4 October 2000, 2 April 2001

Smith, Max, 2/9th Battalion, interview: November 2001

Stack, Austin 2/9th Battalion, interview: January 1998; letter: 3 March 2000

Stevens, Joe, Army Air Liaison, interview: July 2001; letters: 2001–2002

Stewart, Monty, 2/16th Battalion, interviews: 2000–2003; letters: 1999–2000

Stirling, Colin, 2/4th Field Regiment, interviews: 16 April, 11 May & 14 May 2000

Stout, Ray, 405th Bomb Squadron USAAF, emails: June 2002

Strika, Tom, 2/6th Independent Company, interview: 4 December 2000

Symington, Garth, 2/16th Battalion, interview: 21 May 2000

Tann, Lloyd, 2/5th Field Ambulance, interview: 15 February 2001; letter: 6 March 2001

Thow, Max, 2/12th Battalion, interview: 13 April 2000

Thredgold, Les, 2/27th Battalion, interview: 15 September 1997

Trunk, Clarrie, 2/16th Battalion, interviews: 6 June & 27 September 2000

Twine, John, 2/14th Battalion, interview: July 2000

Ueda, Kenji, 78th Regiment IJA, interview with Peter Williams: 1 October 2011

Vawdon, Lorie, 2/6th Independent Company, interviews: September & 4 December 2002; letter: 13 January 2003

Waldon, Bill, 2/16th Battalion, interview: 23 June 2000; letter: April 1999

Webber, Vic, 2/5th Field Ambulance, interview: 10 January 2003

Whyte, Bill, 2/4th Field Regiment, interview: 11 March 2000

Wotton, Roy, 2/12th Battalion, interview: 14 April 2000; letter: 6 June 2000

Zander, Edgar, 2/27th Battalion, interview: 12 January 2001

Published References

Ackland, J. & R. (eds), *Word from John*, Cassell and Company Ltd, Sydney, 1944

Aitken, Edward, *The Story of the 2/2nd Pioneer Battalion*, 2/2nd Pioneer Battalion Association, Melbourne, 1953

Allchin, Frank, *Purple and Blue*, Griffin Press, Adelaide, 1958

Australian Military Forces, *Jungle Warfare*, Australian War Memorial, Canberra, 1944

Bottrell, Arthur, *Cameos of Commandos*, self-published, 1971

Bradley, Phillip, *On Shaggy Ridge*, Oxford University Press, Melbourne, 2004

——, *Hell's Battlefield*, Allen & Unwin, Sydney, 2012

——, *D-Day New Guinea*, Allen & Unwin, Sydney, 2019

Brune, Peter, *We Band of Brothers*, Allen & Unwin, Sydney, 2000

Burns, John, *The Brown and Blue Diamond at War*, 2/27th Battalion Ex-Servicemen's Association, Adelaide, 1960

Crooks, Bill, *The Footsoldiers*, 2/33rd Battalion Association, Brookvale, 1971

Dandy, Philip, *The Kookaburra's Cut-throats, Volume 1*, self-published, 1995

Dean, Peter (ed.), *Australia 1943*, Cambridge University Press, Melbourne, 2014

Dennis, Peter & Grey, Jeffrey (eds), *The Foundations of Victory*, Army History Unit, Canberra, 2004

Dexter, David, *Australia in the War of 1939–1945, Series 1, Vol. VI, The New Guinea Offensives*, Australian War Memorial, Canberra, 1961

Dickins, Barry, *Ordinary Heroes*, Hardie Grant, Melbourne, 1999

Dulhunty, Larry, *Our Blood Stained Past*, Aurora Publications, 1984

Frazier, Everette, *Tsili Tsili Sting*, Vol. 2, Desk Top Production, San Antonio, TX, 1992

Graeme-Evans, Alex, *Of Storms and Rainbows,* Vol. 2, 12th Battalion Association, Hobart, 1991

Henry, Russell, *The Story of the 2/4th Field Regiment*, Merrion Press, Melbourne, 1950

Horner, David, *General Vasey's War*, Melbourne University Press, Carlton, 1992

Ishikawa, Kumao, *Nakai Shitai's Battle of Kankirei*, Maru supplement no. 2, Ushio Shobō, Tokyo, 1986

Kenney, George, *General Kenney Reports*, Duell, Sloan & Pearce, New York, 1949

Kitamoto, Masamichi, *A Record of Marathon Adventures in the New Guinea War*, Australian War Memorial, Canberra, 1968

Lundie, Frank, *Reveille*, Hassell Press, Adelaide, 1946

Odgers, George, *Australia in the War of 1939–1945, Series 3, Vol. II, Air War against Japan 1943–1945*, Australian War Memorial, Canberra, 1957

Ohata, Masahiko, *A War Diary of New Guinea Field Artillery Unit*, Kojinsha, Tokyo, 2008 (reprinted 2017)

Peck, Lindsay, *Sappers of the Silent Seventh*, 7th Division Engineers Association, Sydney, c. 1989

Rolleston, Frank, *Not a Conquering Hero*, self-published, Eton, 1984

Russell, Bill, *The Second Fourteenth Battalion*, Angus & Robertson, Sydney, 1948

Ryan, Peter, *Fear Drive My Feet*, Angus & Robertson, Sydney, 1959

Spencer, Bill, *In the Footsteps of Ghosts*, Allen & Unwin, Sydney, 1999

Tann, Lloyd, *2/5th Australian Field Ambulance,* self-published, 1987

United States Army, *Japanese Monograph 38—18th Army Operations Vol. II*, Department of the Army, 1958

Williams, Peter, *Japan's Pacific War*, Pen & Sword Books, Barnsley UK, 2021

Yoshihara, Kane, *Southern Cross*, Doris Heath translation, Australian War Memorial, Canberra, 1977

NEWSLETTERS

2/16th Battalion Association, *Pigeon Post*, March 1997, June 1997, September 1997

NEWSPAPER, JOURNAL AND MAGAZINE ARTICLES

The Advertiser
> 21 October 1943, Mervyn Weston, 'SA men in daring actions'

The Herald
> 8 February 1944, Frank Peterson, 'Cameraman in thick of fight'

Kalgoorlie Miner
> 25 January 1944, 'On Shaggy Ridge'

Melbourne Sun
> Undated, Andrew Butcher, 'Digger braves the bullets'

Sydney Morning Herald
> 28 September 1943, Harry Williams, 'Manes of grass worn by Japanese'
> 26 April 1944, John Scarlett, 'War ends for youthful soldier'

Tweed Daily
> 3 January 1944, Kenneth Slessor, 'How Australians took Shaggy Ridge'

West Australian
> 24 September 1943, Mervyn Weston, 'Bayonets routed Japs at Kaiapit'
> 1 April 1944, 'Yank in the AIF'

Western Mail
> 30 March 1944, H.E. Collingwood, 'The Pimple'

INTERNET

Australian War Memorial, www.awm.gov.au

Australians at War Film Archive, http://australiansatwarfilmarchive.unsw.edu.au/
> 0063   Lloyd Tann
> 0135   Dave MacDougal
> 0399   Angus Suthers
> 1195   Bob Johns

Department of Veterans' Affairs, www.ww2roll.gov.au

Hell's Battlefield, www.facebook.com

Hyperwar archive, www.ibiblio.org/hyperwar

National Archives of Australia, www.naa.gov.au

National Library of Australia, www.trove.nla.gov.au

Pacific Wreck Database, www.pacificwrecks.com

Unpublished References

Balfour-Ogilvy, Jack, 2/33rd Battalion, notes (via Matt Sloan)

Ball, Charlie, 2/6th Commando Squadron, notes (via Trevor Ball)

Bear, Lindsay, 2/14th Battalion, family records

Bellairs, Morrie, 2/4th Field Regiment, notes

Christian, Ron, 2/16th Battalion, notes (via Andrew Pittaway)

Dickson, Ron, No. 4 Squadron RAAF, 'Flying for the Army'

Edwards, Clive, 2/27th Battalion, diary

Fawcett, Guy, 2/27th Battalion, commander's notebook

Francis, Alwyn, 2/12th Battalion, 'Before the Battle Clears'

Hagan, Wally, 2/6th Independent Company, '1942–1945 Memories'

Hoskin, Len, 2/5th Field Company, notes

Johns, Bob, 2/27th Battalion, 'Johns' Knoll' and 'Ron'

Klotz, Bill, 2/6th Independent Company, notes (via Trevor Ball)

MacDougal, Dave, 2/33rd Battalion, notes

Miller-Randle, Alex, No. 4 Squadron RAAF, 'Invictus Asbestos'

Osborne, Allen, 2/6th Independent Company, notes

Ralston, Jack, 2/6th Commando Squadron, letter (via Trevor Ball)

Reddin, Jack, 2/27th Battalion, notes

Roberts, Tommy, 25th Photo Recon Squadron, papers (via Ted Roberts)

Seale, Walter, US 871st Engineer Aviation Battalion, memoirs

Smith, Jack, 2/16th Battalion, diary (via Elaine Earthroll)

Thomas, Kevin, 2/12th Battalion, diary (via Paul Hope)

Tozer, John, 2/6th Independent Company, notes (via Trevor Ball)

Wade, Terry, 2/5th Field Ambulance, diary and photographs (via Margot Wade)

Unpublished Records

NATIONAL ARCHIVES OF AUSTRALIA

A9186, RAAF Squadron Operational Records

B3856, 145/4/21, Correspondence concerning Corporal Morel

B883, Second Australian Imperial Forces Personnel Dossiers, 1939–1947

NA9720B, Hugh Norton, 2/14th Battalion, interview with Bill Marien

SP300/3, ABC Radio Transcripts, 1939–1945

    572   Dudley Leggett, 'There's no holding these fellows'

    659   Bill Marien, 'Australian courage'

    670   Bill Marien, 'Fighting against shadows'

    671   Bill Marien, 'Air support in New Guinea'

    820   Fred Simpson, 'American Mitchells bomb Shaggy Ridge'

AUSTRALIAN WAR MEMORIAL, CANBERRA

AWM52, 2nd AIF and CMF unit war diaries, 1939–45 War

AWM54, Written records, 1939–45 War

AWM55, Allied Translator and Interpretive Section (ATIS) publications

BIBLIOGRAPHY

AWM67, Official History, 1939–45 War: Records of Gavin Long, General Editor
    3/131   Tom Foster, 2/2nd Independent Company, notes
    3/167   Edmund Herring, New Guinea Force, records
    3/366   Charlie Sims, 2/27th Battalion, diary
    10/12   Takushiro Hattori, IJA, notes
    10/12   Masutaro Nakai, IJA 78th Regiment, interview notes
AWM93, Australian War Memorial registry files—First series
    50/2/23/269   Ken Eather, 25th Brigade, notes
    50/2/23/322   Fred Chilton, 18th Brigade, notes
    50/2/23/357   Ivan Dougherty, 21st Brigade, notes
    50/2/23/358   Bill Robertson, 7th Division, letter
    50/2/23/393   Jack Bishop, 2/27th Battalion, letter
    50/2/23/622   Gordon King, 2/6th Independent Company, notes
AWM119, Office of Military Secretary, Army honours and awards confidential working files
AWM226, Records of war crimes enquiries and trials, 1939–45 War
AWM172, Official History, 1939–45 War, Series 1 (Army), Volume VI: Records of David Dexter
    06   Edmund Herring, New Guinea Force, interview: 6/4/51
    13   Ivan Dougherty, 21st Brigade, interview
AWM254, Written records, 1939–45 War, second series
    266   John Chalk, Papuan Infantry Battalion, diary
AWM315, Australian War Memorial registry files—Second series
    695/001/001   Colin Halmarick
    695/001/009   Norm Stuckey

Sound Archive:
S00574 Max Thow, 2/12th Battalion, 17 April 1989
S00790 Jack Reddin, 2/27th Battalion, 31 January 1990
S00799 Bob Johns, 2/27th Battalion, 22 February 1990
S00902 Bob Innes, 2/27th Battalion, 2 March 1990
S00904 Guy Fawcett, 2/27th Battalion, 9 March 1990
S00928 Bruce Deering, 2/27th Battalion, 22 March 1990
S01844 Jack Reddin, Bob Clampett, Bob Johns, 2/27th Battalion, 24 June 1997

Private Records:
PR00249   David Dexter papers
PR00570   2/12th Battalion history collection
PR00876   Bob Clampett letters
PR01593   Denis Berwick memoir
PR84/189   Alan Mogg letters
PR84/370   Frank Berryman diary and papers
PR87/221   James Milbourne memoirs

NATIONAL LIBRARY OF AUSTRALIA, CANBERRA
MS3782 George Vasey papers

MACARTHUR MEMORIAL LIBRARY AND ARCHIVES, NORFOLK, VIRGINIA, USA
RG54   George C Kenney diary and papers

USAAF RECORDS
49th Fighter Group records
HQ V Fighter Command, A2 Report 267

INDEX

Printed in Great Britain
by Amazon

43635023R00199